STEPHEN R. JUNEAU

THE ALPHA THROUGH OMEGA PROJECT

I-A
AGAPE:
The Unfailing Love of God

vs.

The Unconditional Love of Satan

A Tribute to God

For many are called, but few are chosen.
(KJ Mt 22:14)

- - - - - - -

Jesus said: *If ye continue in my word, then are ye my disciples indeed; and ye shall know the truth, and the truth shall make you free.*
(KJ Jn 8:31–32)

Author and Designer: *Stephen R. Juneau*
Publisher: THE ALPHA THROUGH OMEGA PROJECT
Email: TheAlphaThroughOmegaProject@gmail.com
Original Date of Publication: March 30, 2018 / **Updated: March 25, 2024**
Copyright by *Stephen R. Juneau*
Library of Congress Registration Number: TXu 1-374-030
All rights reserved. No part of this publication may be reproduced or altered in any form, or by any means, electronic or mechanical, including photocopying, recording, or any information browsing, storage, or retrieval system, without permission in writing from the publisher.

Title: AGAPE: *The Unfailing Love of God vs.*
The Unconditional Love of Satan [Vol. I - A]
Series: THE ALPHA THROUGH OMEGA PROJECT

ISBN 978 0 998961408 Hard Cover: *Signature Edition* [standard full color–large print]
ISBN 978 0 998961415 Hard Cover: *Kingsman's Edition* [premium full color–large print]
ISBN 978 0 998961422 Paperback: *Illuminate Edition* [black & white – large print]

Edited with the help of Grammarly

CB—Scripture taken from the Chronological Life Application Study Bible.® © Tyndale House Publishers, Inc., Carol Stream, Illinois, © 2012.

KJ—Scripture taken from THE HOLY BIBLE, Authorized King James Version, 1611.® Regency, P.O. Box 141000, Nashville, Tennessee, © (updated) 1992 ; and also from The (Authorized) King James Bible @ www.KingJamesBibleOnline.Org., © 2018.

NIV—Scripture taken from THE HOLY BIBLE, NEW INTERNATIONAL VERSION,® ©1984, and the NIV LIFE APPLICATION STUDY BIBLE, ©2005. Used by permission of Zondervan. All rights reserved. P. O. Box 62970, Colorado Springs, Colorado 80962-2970 U.S.A.

NCV—Scripture taken from THE NEW TESTAMENT NEW CATHOLIC VERSION, Catholic Book Publishing Corporation, New Jersey, © 2016.

Acknowledgment of Artist and Photographers:
Front Cover: RED ROSE — © *Pears*
Front Cover: SWORD — © *Lugo*
Back Cover: GOLD CROWN EMBLEM — © *Bobey*
Back Cover: PLANET EARTH — © *M-Gucci*
Back Cover: AUTHOR [*Stephen R. Juneau*] — © *The Picture People*
Welcome: ALPHA AND OMEGA EMBLEM - p. i — © *Alek Koltukov & S. R. Juneau*
Stairway to Heaven - p. ii — © *Yuri Arcurs*
CROSS-DOVE-THORNS-WREATHE - p. iv — © *Alek Koltukov & S. R. Juneau*
Table of Contents: WHITE HORSES - p. vi & vii — © *Zaricm*
Old Testament: PROPHET MOSES - p. viii — © *Liron Peer*
New Testament: CRUCIFIX - p. ix — © *Mbolina*
The Ten Commandments: GAVELS - p. x & xi — © *Allex*
THE ALPHA THROUGH OMEGA PROJECT: BIBLE WITH AMERICAN FLAG - p. xii — © *Kledge*
Introduction: LIFE'S JOURNEY [ROAD SIGNS] - p.2 — © *3D-Generator*
[All remaining artists are credited with their work throughout the book.]

THE ALPHA THROUGH OMEGA PROJECT
I-B

*It is the glory of God to conceal a thing:
but the honour of kings is to search out a matter.*
(KJ Pr 25:2)

Illuminate Edition
The Alpha through Omega Project: 1-A
Agape:
The Unfailing Love of God
Vs.
The Unconditional Love of Satan

It is written: And this I pray, that your love may abound yet more and more in knowledge and in all judgment; that you may approve things that are excellent; that ye may be sincere and without offence till the day of Christ; being filled with the fruits of righteousness, which are by Jesus Christ, unto the glory and praise of God. (KJ Php 1:9–11)

Supplemental Reading and Study Guide for Decoding the Bible: Genesis through Revelation

DEDICATION

This book is devoted to making known the Bible's hidden and spiritually coded historical and literal aspects, in conjunction with its allegory and symbolic interpretations concerning God's unfailing love.

Dedicated it is to the following: Almighty God of Abraham, Isaac, and Jacob (KJ Ex 3:15), Creator of the Ends of the Earth (Isa 40:28); Jesus Christ, the Author and Finisher of our Faith (Heb 12:2); and the Holy Spirit, the Counselor of Truth (Jn 14:26, 15:26). Inspired by all, I gained tremendous insight and inspiration for this work and four others.

Also, I dedicate this project to all men, women, and children—past, present, and future—who gave their lives for their Biblical values. Finally, I dedicate this work to all readers, hopeful you will be among the elect chosen for God's kingdoms (Mt 22:14).

[The meaning of the Bible is *"Books"* (66 total): 39 in the KJ Old Testament, 27 in the KJ New Testament.]

TABLE OF CONTENTS
A ✝ Ω

Old Testament..viii

New Testament..ix

The Ten Commandments...x

The Alpha through Omega Project..........................xii

God's Names and Titles..xviii

References...xx

Kingsmen...1

Introduction..2

I. Actions: *Humanity's Identifiable Traits*.................6

II. The Creation Decoded.......................................14

III. The World Loved by God
    vs. The World Loved by Satan...............................30

Descendants of Noah's Sons:..................................64

Adam to Abram Genealogy....................................66

IV. Abominations that cause Desolation.................68

TABLE OF CONTENTS
A † Ω

V. Destructive Forces of Satan..................96

VI. Destructive Forces of God..................135

VII. The Favored by God..................164

VIII. Unfailing Love vs. Unconditional Love........174

IX. Charity..................188

X. Tithing: *Appreciation vs. Bartering*..................194

XI. Parental Love: *The Essence of Agape*..................208

XII. Trustworthy Friends: *A Reflection of Agape*......236

XIII. Persecution: *The Effect of Agape*..................252

XIV. The Magnitude of Repentance..................282

XV. Misleading through Snippets..................285

Theme Song..................304

Moving Forward..................306

Introduction to Agape I-B..................308

The Old Testament
Scripture references and their abbreviations

Genesis / Ge

Exodus / Ex

Leviticus / Lev

Numbers / Nu

Deuteronomy / Dt

Joshua / Jos

Judges / Jdg

Ruth / Ru

1 Samuel / 1Sa

2 Samuel / 2Sa

1 Kings / 1Ki

2 Kings / 2Ki

1 Chronicles / 1Ch

2 Chronicles / 2Ch

Ezra / Ezr

Nehemiah / Ne

Ester / Est

Job / Job

Psalms / Ps

Proverbs / Pr

Ecclesiastes / Ecc

Song of Solomon / SS

Isaiah / Isa

Jeremiah / Jer

Lamentations / La

Ezekiel / Eze

Daniel / Da

Hosea / Hos

Joel / Joel

Amos / Am

Obadiah / Ob

Jonah / Jnh

Micah / Mic

Nahum / Na

Habakkuk / Hab

Zephaniah / Zep

Haggai / Hag

Zechariah / Zec

Malachi / Mal

The New Testament
Scripture references and their abbreviations

Matthew / Mt

Mark / Mk

Luke / Lk

John / Jn

Acts / Ac

Romans / Ro

1 Corinthians / 1Co

2 Corinthians / 2Co

Galatians / Gal

Ephesians / Eph

Philippians / Php

Colossians / Col

1 Thessalonians / 1Th

2 Thessalonians / 2Th

1 Timothy / 1Ti

2 Timothy / 2Ti

Titus / Tit

Philemon / Phm

Hebrews / Heb

James / Jas

1 Peter / 1Pe

2 Peter / 2Pe

1 John / 1Jn

2 John / 2Jn

3 John / 3Jn

Jude / Jude

Revelation / Rev

The Ten Commandments

[*God's Expression of Love for His Elect*]
(KJ Jn 14:21 & 23, 1Jn 5:3)

And God spake {& wrote} all these words (KJ Ex 20:1) and hast founded them forever (KJ Ps 119:152) saying,

I am the Lord thy God, which have brought thee out of the land of Egypt, out of the house of bondage.

I. Thou shalt have no other gods before me.

II. Thou shalt not make unto thee any graven image, or any likeness of any thing that is in heaven above, or that is in the earth beneath, or that is in the water under the earth. Thou shalt not bow down thyself to them, nor serve them. For I the Lord thy God am a jealous God, visiting the iniquity of the fathers upon the children unto the third and fourth generation of them that hate me, and shewing mercy unto thousands of them that love me, and keep my commandments.

III. Thou shalt not take the name of the Lord thy God in vain; for the Lord will not hold him guiltless that taketh his name in vain.

IV. Remember the sabbath day, to keep it holy. Six days shalt thou labour, and do all thy work; but the seventh day is the sabbath of the Lord thy God. In it thou shalt not do any work, thou, nor thy son, nor thy daughter, thy manservant, nor thy maidservant, nor thy cattle, nor thy stranger that is within thy gates. For in six {allegorical} days the Lord made heaven and earth, the sea, and all that in them is, and rested the seventh day (2Pe 3:8). Wherefore, the Lord blessed the sabbath day, and hallowed it.

The Ten Commandments

[God's Expression of Love for His Elect]
(KJ Jn 14:21 & 23, 1Jn 5:3)

V. Honour thy father and thy mother: that thy days may be long {filled with peace and happiness, prosperity and success, safety and well-being} *upon the land which the* Lord *thy God giveth thee.*

VI. Thou shalt not murder (NIV Ex 20:13); {but} *A time to* {legally} *kill* (KJ Ecc 3:3) {to defend against the wicked, serve justice, and uphold righteousness}.

VII. Thou shalt not commit adultery (Lev 18:1–30).

VIII. Thou shalt not steal (Lev 19:11–13).

IX. Thou shalt not bear false witness against thy neighbour {or anyone else}.

X. Thou shalt not covet thy neighbour's house {or land}. *Thou shalt not covet thy neighbour's wife, nor his manservant, nor his maidservant, nor his ox, nor his ass, nor anything that is thy neighbour's* {or belonging to anyone else}.

(KJ Ex 20:1–17, Dt 5:6–21, Mt 5:17–20)
[Numbers added by author]

And it shall come to pass, if thou shalt hearken diligently unto the <u>voice</u> of the Lord *thy God, to observe and to do all his commandments which I command thee this day, that the* Lord *thy God will set thee on high above all nations of the earth. And all these blessings shall come on thee, and overtake thee, if thou shalt hearken unto the <u>voice</u> of the* Lord *thy God . . .* (KJ Dt 28:1–14)

THE ALPHA THROUGH OMEGA PROJECT

Where there is no vision {God or justice}, the people perish: but he that keepeth the law, happy is he.

(KJ Pr 29:18)

With great honor and respect, I welcome you to the messages put in my heart by the Bible and its *Spirit of Truth*. They are written for all people, regardless of background, searching for the hidden truths about God. Due to the magnitude of these messages, I collectively entitled them THE ALPHA THROUGH OMEGA PROJECT.

THE ALPHA THROUGH OMEGA PROJECT separates reality from deception as a decisive life-saving ark of Bible truth that decodes *Genesis through Revelation*. Furthermore, what may be considered unpopular or outright wrong in societies may be life-saving in the Kingdoms of God. Although contradictory with a clear majority of worldly beliefs and religious teachings about God, known as a paradox, these messages are a vital supplement for the correct and intended interpretation of the Bible. That correct interpretation—*the mystery of God* (Rev 10:7)—is essential for understanding all aspects of God in overcoming adversities in the world in which we live. Through divine order, the correct interpretation has forever been to reveal *the mystery of God* at its appointed time.

> It is written: *But in the days of the voice of the seventh angel, when he shall begin to sound, the mystery of God should be finished, as he hath declared to his servants the prophets.* (KJ Rev 10:7)

Since *there is a mystery to be accomplished in the days of the seventh angel's voice when he shall begin to sound,* that mystery remains unknown among many in today's world. THE ALPHA THROUGH OMEGA PROJECT sets out to make it known in *Faith, Hope, and Love.*

The Bible is transparent about God's expectations for His people. They could free many from deception if discovered, understood, and lived. They could catapult believers who become doers into the Kingdoms of God and Heaven: the few committed to *righteousness, truth, and every word of God.* Scriptures by which the Bible points this out are as follows:

> It is written: *...For he cometh, for he cometh to judge the earth. He shall judge the world with righteousness, and the people with his truth.* (KJ Ps 96:13)

> It is written: *Man shall not live by bread alone, but by every word that proceedeth out of the mouth of*

God. (KJ Dt 8:3, Mt 4:4)

It is written: *For many are called, but few are chosen.* (KJ Mt 22:14)

Since *God will judge the peoples in His truth,* along with *man shall not live by bread only, but by every word that proceedeth out of the mouth of God,* whereby **called are many but chosen are few**, I sincerely believe answered are all questions about human spirituality throughout God's intended interpretation of His authorized Bible. That accurate account may be shocking to most since it does not conform to mainstream beliefs about Him. Discovered it is through the Bible's full context written in many allegories. It incorporates *God and His Glory, Jesus Christ and His Apostles, the Holy Spirit, angels, and Prophets of Old.* Encounters with them also reveal that *mystery.* Bible references to those encounters include the following:

1) **God Personally**—both seen and unseen (KJ Ge 18:1, Ex 24:9–18 and 33:17–23, Jos 5:13–6:5, 1Ki 3:5 and 9:1–9, 2Ch 7:12–22, Job 42:1–5)

2) **The Glory of the Lord** (KJ Ex 16:10–11, 24:15–18, 33:17–23, 40:34–38; Dt 4:32–40; 1Ki 8:10–11; 2Ch 7:1–3; Isa 40:5; Eze 8:1–4, 10:3–4, 10:18–19, and 43:1–5)

3) Both the living and resurrected *Jesus Christ* (KJ Mt, Mk, Lk, and Jn, Ac 9:1–20; Rev 1:8, 11, 18–20, and Chapters 2–4)

4) **The Holy Spirit** or **Counselor,** also referred to in the Bible as **The Spirit of Truth** (KJ Jn 14:16–17) and **His visible hands** (KJ 2Ki 3:15, Eze 8:1–3, Da 5, Ac 2:1–21, Ro 8, Eph 4:30)

5) *Angels* including *Michael and Gabriel* fulfilling divine duties for God (KJ Ge 19; Jdg 2:1-5 and Chpt 6; 2Sa 24:15-17; Lk 2:9; Jn 20:10-13; Acts 12:22-23; Heb 13:2; Rev 2, 3, 5, 7, 8, 9, 10, 14, 15, 16, 17, 18, and 21)

6) **Old Testament Prophets**, including **Moses** and **Elias** (*Elijah*), reappearing hundreds of years after having been taken up and out of our dimension, found standing with **Jesus** at **His transfiguration** (KJ Dt 34:5-7, 2Ki 2:1-11, and Mk 9:1-7).

These supernatural phenomena occurred because God intended that a *few* (KJ Mt 22:14)—regarded by Him as *Kings* (KJ Pr 25:2), while considered as *aliens and strangers in the world* (KJ Job 19:15)—would be inspired to research, discover, and act upon His *mystery* (KJ Rev 10:7). Destined were they to find the hidden truth through His allegorical, historical, and literal word in His appointed time. Doing so enables them and their under-aged children, should they have any, to metaphorically travel through the well-hidden portals leading to His kingdoms (KJ Mt 7:13-14).

Having chosen to read and study the entire Bible a little at a time, daily or nightly, for forty years, I discovered that hidden and coded life-saving mystery. It is shocking but inspiring. Hence, *the mystery of God* is not mainstream propaganda about Him. Mainstream beliefs about God—being highly ominous—opened the floodgates to the *spirit of evil*: that which led to abominations on a grand scale by all indications (KJ Ge 4:7, 1Pe 5:8, Eph 6:12). And so, I now offer what I learned through reading and studying the Bible, along with the

Spirit of Truth and personal life-changing experiences.

AGAPE: ***The Unfailing Love of God vs. The Unconditional Love of Satan*** is the first in THE ALPHA THROUGH OMEGA PROJECT series. It is available in two parts: **A** and **B**. Although both embrace *Genesis through Revelation* regarding **AGAPE, Part A**—recommended as the first reading—relies primarily on the mysteries of the Old Testament. **Part B** relies mainly on the secrets of the New Testament. United in full context, both deliver what God destined concerning His love and relationship with humanity.

I now wish you the very best in your journey through the pages of this surprising and inspiring message, sure to stir your beliefs and spirit, designed to foster living per God's intended truths. However, before getting started, let Webster distinguish four words of confusion by which this book series is to be clearly and undeniably understood.

> **Agape:** *1. the love of God or Christ for humankind. 2. the love of Christians for other persons corresponding to the love of God for humanity. 3. unselfish love for one person to another without sexual implications; brotherly love.*[1]

> **Allegory:** *1. a representation of an abstract or spiritual meaning through concrete or material forms; figurative treatment of one subject under the guise of*

---

[1] *Agape*, Webster's Encyclopedic Unabridged Dictionary of the English Language: New Rev. Ed. (New York, NY: Random House Value Publishing, Inc., Gramercy Books, 1996).

another. 2. *A symbolical narrative.*[2] [Example: The Parables of Jesus Christ as recorded in the synoptic Gospels of Matthew, Mark, and Luke.]

Metaphor: *a figure of speech in which a term or phrase is applied to something to which it is not literally applicable to suggest a resemblance as in, A Mighty Fortress is our God.*[3]

Simile: *a figure of speech in which two, unlike things, are explicitly compared, as in, She is like a rose.*[4] [All similes are metaphors and referred to as such.]

Additionally, this work will refer to individuals—past, present, and future—who act(ed) upon the Bible's undeniable truths as *Kingsmen*. Doing so serves a dual purpose: (1) aligns them with Proverb 25:2 and (2) distinguishes them from government officials. That Scripture once again is:

It is the glory of God to conceal a thing:
but the honour of kings is to search out a matter.
(KJ Pr 25:2)

A ✝ Ω

---

[2] *Allegory,* Ibid.

[3] *Metaphor,* Ibid.

[4] *Simile,* Ibid.

GOD'S NAMES AND TITLES

God identifies Himself as having names and titles corresponding to His nature. Found in the King James Bible, they are:

I. *ELOHIM: Ubiquitous and Omnipresent is He.* (NIV Ge 1:2, 2Ch 16:9, Ps 139, Jer 16:17). He was to whom Christ cried out, *Eloi, Eloi — My God, My God.* (KJ Mt 27:46-*Eli*, Mk 15:34). [Familiar name of God among Orthodox (Traditional) Jews]

II. *EL SHADDAI–Almighty God: Creator of the Universe; The One Who is More Than Enough* (KJ Ge Chpt 1 and 2:1-2, 17:1, CB Ge 35:11} Kenneth E. Hagin explains:

> *"El Shaddai is one of six covenant names through which God revealed Himself to Israel. In Hebrew, El Shaddai means 'the All-Sufficient One' or 'the God who is more than enough.' The translators of the King James Version translated* El Shaddai *as 'Almighty God.'"*[5]

III. *I AM THAT I AM {YAHWEH (CB)}: THE GOD OF ABRAHAM, THE GOD OF ISAAC, AND THE GOD OF JACOB: this is my name forever, and this is my memorial unto all generations* (KJ Ex 3:14-15).

IV. *JAH: He rides upon the heavens: A father of the fatherless and a judge of the widows.* All-knowing and compassionate Father to those enduring longsuffering who are among *His elect.* (KJ Ps 68:4-5)

V. *JEALOUS—is He for His elect* (KJ Ex 34:14). *Evil will slay the wicked; the foes of the righteous will*

---

[5] Kenneth E. Hagin, EL SHADDAI: The God Who Is More Than Enough. The God Who Satisfies With Long Life (RHEMA BIBLE CHURCH-Kenneth Hagin Ministries, P.O. Box 50126, Tulsa, OK, 1980), p.1.

be condemned. The Lord redeems His servants; condemned will be no one who takes refuge in Him {*Genesis—Revelation*}. (NIV Ps 34:21-22)

VI. JEHOVAH: *The Most High over all the earth* (KJ Ps 83:18); *The strength, song, and salvation* (KJ Isa 12:2) *of His repentant people chosen out from Satan's world* (KJ Ps 37:40, Isa 12:2); *Judge, lawgiver, king, and protector* (KJ Isa 33:22) *for His chosen few persecuted for righteousness* (KJ Mt 5:10).

VII. JEHOVAH-JIREH (KJ Ge 22:14): *Provider and Redeemer for His elect who hear and obey His voice and commandments* (KJ Ge 22).

VIII. JEHOVAH-NISSI (Ex 17:15): *Provider and protector committed to annihilating the wicked* (KJ Ex 17).

IX. JEHOVAH-RAPHA: *Hebrew for, I am the LORD that healeth thee* (KJ Ex 15:26).

X. JEHOVAH-SHALOM (KJ Jdg 6:24): *God of vengeance, annihilates the wicked, merciful to repentant individuals, defender of His saints* (KJ Jdg 6,7,8: The Life of Gideon).

XI. KING OF GLORY: *The LORD strong and mighty, the LORD mighty in battle* (KJ Ps 24:7-8)

XI. LORD OF HOSTS: *Sovereign God of Heaven's Armies and Israel* (appears 284 times throughout the KJ Bible as in Ps 24: 10 and Zec 1:3, 7:12, and 8:14).

XII. OUR FATHER, which art in heaven: *Caring Father—Shepherd for all who obey Him* (KJ Mt 6:9, Lk 11:2)

XIII. THE LORD OUR RIGHTEOUSNESS: *The Role Model for Holiness, Righteousness, Truthfulness, and Integrity—The Only True God, Watchman* (KJ Jer 23:6)

REFERENCES

The absence of quotation marks in Scripture follows the protocol of the original Bible manuscripts, as does the LORD in the Old Testament and the Lord in the New Testament. Therefore, the author took the liberty of italicizing *Scripture* rather than using quotation marks like the NIV. Also, the text within {these brackets} clarifies Scripture.

The Old Testament was first written in Hebrew, while written originally in Greek was the New Testament. In 1611, translated into English, they were both under the authorization of James Charles Stuart. At the time, Stuart was King James IV of Scotland while serving as King James I of England, France, and Ireland. The King James Bible is the only authorized English version of the Holy Bible with royal sponsorship.

In 1978, published was the New International Version (**NIV**). It was a 12-year undertaking (1966-1978) for a straightforward Bible involving scholars across the globe. Its revisions are ongoing on behalf of accuracy.

[The Standard King James is the primary source for THE ALPHA THROUGH OMEGA PROJECT. Identified with KJ is Scripture pulled from it. Scriptures quoted from the CB (Chronological Life Application Study Bible), the NIV (New International Version), and NCV (New Catholic Version of the New Testament) are to provide better comprehension and ease of reading.]

KINGSMEN

Biblically, *Kingsmen* are sincere *truth seekers*. *Pure in heart*, God is attracted to them. Acquiring a *Kingsman's status* is God's will. About them,

> It is written: *Blessed are they which do hunger and thirst after righteousness; for they shall be filled.* [and] *Blessed are the pure in heart; for they shall see God.* (KJ Mt 5:6 & 8)

It is among *Kingsmen* with whom God works miracles and wonders. The Bible is a living testimony to that impressive fact. For example, God hand-picked *Kingsmen* throughout the Old Testament as *prophets* and *seers*. He did mighty works through these individuals, passionate about truth and doing right in His sight. Likewise, in the New Testament, John, the baptizer—a *Kingsman*—pointed the way of righteousness to Christ. Like the *Prophets of the Old Testament*, his priority was to serve God in truth.

A desire for truth is the first condition required by God to qualify for *Agape*. Hence, becoming a *Kingsman* or *truth seeker* is God's will for a *chosen few* because *truth* leads to *righteousness*, and *righteousness* leads to the *Kingdoms of God*.

THE ALPHA THROUGH OMEGA PROJECT reveals the truths of *God's Spoken Word* to *Kingsmen: truth seekers*. Two revealed truths are: (1) God identifies Himself according to His actions. (2) He recognizes and judges all according to our actions.

INTRODUCTION

No matter how thin you slice anything, it always has two sides. For example, the Bible offers a mainstream and worldly interpretation of Scripture known to most who regard themselves as Christians. However, it also provides a hidden and spiritually coded argument discovered in its full context: that which undeniably conflicts with mainstream and worldly beliefs about God. Found by looking at the Bible as having united two different aspects is this two-fold secluded and coded interpretation:

- A historical and literal document, such as the *Ten Commandments* found in its Book of Exodus, Chapter 20, verses 1–17, —AND—

- A spiritually allegorical and symbolic work, such as *The Seven Woes* in the Gospel of Matthew, Chapter 23.

This PART A of VOLUME I in THE ALPHA THROUGH OMEGA PROJECT sets out to reveal that hidden and spiritually coded interpretation regarding the magnitude of *God's unfailing love* (NIV Ex 15:13, Ps 6:4, Isa 54:10). Additionally, it contrasts the importance of **His unfailing love** against the illusions of Satan's *unconditional love*.

Thus, regardless of your past, current situation, or beliefs concerning God loving you and your love for God, I challenge you to be open about what you read and encourage you to note what stands out in your mind throughout this profound message. Although this book—a paradox—addresses many contradictions and false beliefs in how God relates to humanity, you will discover that all topics are associated with *agape* facts. Spiritually written were they to make known His factual interpretation through the full context of Scripture.

Therefore, to get the most out of your reading and understanding, consider this work as books within a book, necessary to explore all aspects of the Almighty's *unfailing love,* as discovered throughout the *Books* within the Bible (ex: NIV Ps 13:5, 18:50, and 21:7). Hence, I am confident that you will not be the least bit disappointed by what you will read and come to know. Jesus Christ addressed this phenomenon by saying how it would come to be.

> It is written: *But the hour cometh, and now is, when the true worshipers shall worship the Father in spirit and in truth; for the Father seeketh such to*

worship him. God is a Spirit: and they that worship him must worship him in spirit and in truth. (KJ Jn 4:23-24)

It is written: *No man, when he hath lighted a candle, covereth it with a vessel, or putteth it under a bed; but setteth it on a candlestick, that they which enter in may see the light. For nothing is secret, that shall not be made manifest; neither anything hid, that shall not be known and come abroad.* (KJ Lk 8:16-17)

Hence, the primary question in beginning any endeavor is:

Where do I start?

The most reliable place is with **your Owner's Manual: the Bible.** That road less traveled tested me in patience through many failures and rejections. It required repentance and self-determination. Greeted with insult, slander, and other life-changing experiences is how it was and continues to be. And finally, it needed a sincere dedication to the full context of the Bible and its *Spirit of Truth*. Without all, there would have been no way for me to reveal what you will come to know. Therefore, should you genuinely desire absolute honesty concerning God loving you and your love for God, know that you will discover what you have been searching for through an *honest and good heart.*

It is written: *But that* {Word of God sown in sincerity} *on the good ground are they, which in **an honest and good heart**, having heard the word, keep it, and bring forth fruit with patience.* (KJ Lk 8:15)

With an honest and good heart through patience in trials and tribulations, promised by God, one *brings forth truthful returns* worthy of His kingdoms. In other words, what is required by God—in this day and age and throughout eternity—is to be sincere about wanting the truth. There alone is how to discover the real God and the truthful Christ. From there, what is needed is to act upon those discoveries. Doing so pleases where the prize is the Kingdom of Heaven.

Therefore, as you journey down this less traveled road, remember that doing so *patiently with a good and honest heart* fulfills Scripture. Fulfilling Scripture by setting aside all nonsense leads to significant and beautiful blessings from God. It begins by developing a passion for *every Word of His* (KJ Mt 4:4), that is, being *poor in spirit* (KJ Mt 5:3). Also,

> It is written: *Study to shew thyself approved unto God, a workman that needeth not be ashamed, rightly dividing the word of truth.* (KJ 2Ti 2:15).

THE ALPHA THROUGH OMEGA PROJECT is dedicated to teaching to *rightly divide the word of truth*. So advance with that eye-opening mission.

I. ACTIONS:
Humanity's Identifiable Traits

It is written: *I the* L*ord* *search the heart and examine the mind, to reward a* **man** *{or woman} according to his {or her} conduct, according to what his {or her} deeds deserve.* (NIV Jer 17:10)

[NOTE: Throughout the Scriptures, often understood that *"a man"* also implies *"a woman."* Likewise, *"men"* sometimes include *"women."* These understandings will apply from here forward without the notations.]

It is written: *And I saw the dead, small and great, stand before God; and the books were opened: and another book was opened, which is the book of life:* **and the dead were judged** *out of those things which were written in the books,* **according to their works.**

And the sea gave up the dead which were in it; and death and hell delivered up the dead which were in them: **and they were judged every man according to their works.**

And death and hell were cast into the lake of fire. **This is the second death.** *And whosoever was* **not** *found written in the book of life was cast into the lake of fire.* (KJ Rev 20:12–15)

Since men and women presiding over people regarding themselves as Christians began preaching and teaching that God's love is unconditional, I thought, "WOW! *That sounds very accommodating to a growing evil world."* Then I thought: *"If God's love is unconditional, it makes Him out as a lover of liars, thieves, murderers, and destroyers."* Fortunately, I took the time to read and study the entire Bible carefully—ongoing for decades—and found where, on the contrary, Jesus Christ said:

> *The thief comes only to steal and kill and destroy. I have come that they {who repent—forsake evil} may have life and have it to the full.* (NIV Jn 10:10)

Since Jesus distinguished himself from the wicked, I could not understand why so many men and women of today, presiding over people considered Christians throughout various religious and nondenominational churches, were so adamant about preaching and teaching that God's love was and is unconditional. The full context of the Bible and Scripture proves otherwise. So vital is this that Jesus issued a warning to all regarding lying.

> It is written: *But I say unto you, that every idle word that men shall speak, they shall give account thereof in the day of judgment. For by thy {honest and truthful} words thou shalt be justified, and by thy {lying and fraudulent} words thou shalt be condemned.* (KJ Mt 12:36-37)

Hence, due to a determination to manipulate Scripture and mislead the *many called* by God, on the part of many residing over God's people, there was desperation in the name of accurate facts to reveal the *accomplished mystery* of God regarding *agape* and other Bible topics. For example,

> It is written: *For it is God's will that by doing good you should silence the ignorant talk of foolish {devious, lying} men. Live as free men, but do not use your freedom as a cover-up for evil; live as {righteous} servants of God.* (NIV 1Pe 2:15–16)

A † Ω

Precisely Who and What God Hates

The Bible clearly defines who and what God hates, and if God hates, then God's love is conditional.

> It is written: *There are six things the* Lord *hates, seven that are detestable to him: 1. haughty eyes, 2. a lying tongue, 3. hands that shed innocent blood, 4. a heart that devises wicked schemes, 5. feet that are quick to rush into evil, 6. a false witness who pours out lies, 7. and, a man who stirs up dissension among brothers {of truth}.* (NIV Pr 6:16–19 / numbers added by author)

Note that the first five of the seven are each an allegory. *Haughty eyes, lying tongues, hands that shed innocent blood, hearts that devise wicked schemes, and feet that are quick to rush into evil* cannot, do not, and never will act apart from people possessing those identifiable traits. That clarifies that God does not separate one's actions apart from who a person is. Numbers six and seven personify that undeniable truth. Jeremiah 17:10 and Revelation 20:12-13, which you read at the beginning of this chapter, also exemplify that truth. God hates people who are any of those seven. Hence, one's actions determine whether one is loved or hated by God.

> It is written: *I the LORD have spoken it. It shall come to pass, and I will do it. I will not go back, neither will I spare, neither will I repent {be merciful}. According to thy {evil} ways, and according to thy {devious} doings, shall they judge thee, saith the LORD God.* (KJ Eze 24:14)

I could now rest my case against every claim that God's love is unconditional, and a just and well-informed jury would have to agree. However, there is much more to learn regarding *God's complete mystery* concerning His unfailing love and other spiritually inspiring divine topics. Introduced are upcoming subjects at the end of each book in the series.

A † Ω

In summarizing this first chapter, **ACTIONS: *Man's Identifiable Traits*,** it all comes down to God loving or hating people per their actions. God does not separate a person from their behaviors.

> It is written: *Behold I am coming soon! My reward is with me, and I will give to everyone according to what he has done.* (NIV Rev 22:12).

God identifies all per their deeds, whereby being righteous according to His way results in His acceptance and love (KJ Rev 14:13). However, choosing to live a life of wickedness in defiance of His way results in His rejection and hatred, vengeance, and wrath (KJ Dt 28:15-68, Rev 21:8).

> It is written: *The way of the LORD is strength to the upright, but destruction shall be to the workers of iniquity.* (KJ Pr 10:29)

Should one's actions align with obedience to His way, God will love and trust that individual. Should one's actions display no regard for His way, the Bible teaches that God will have no connections with that individual and allow him to live per free will, whether good or evil. And whether good or evil per worldly standards, it is **un**likely to result in a relationship with God, much less salvation, without a change in fundamental beliefs and behavior directed at being right with God.

> It is written: *In the way of righteousness is life, and in the pathway thereof there is no death.* (KJ Pr 12:28)

Since *righteousness* is another qualifier for attaining the love of God and salvation, allow Webster to remind and precisely clarify the honest facts of what being *righteous* and doing acts of *righteousness* represents.

> **Righteous:** 1.characterized by uprightness or morality; 2. morally right or justifiable; 3. acting in an upright, moral way, virtuous; 4. absolutely genuine or

wonderful. [5]

Righteousness: *1. the quality or state of being righteous; 2. righteous conduct; 3. the quality or state of being just or rightful.* [6]

Righteousness: *(synonyms) 1. [Justice] uprightness, nobility, fairness, honorable; 2. [Devotion to a sinless life] piety, saintliness, godliness.* [7]

Living a life of *righteousness* is by choice. It is what *repentance* is all about. *Repenting* is whenever one forsakes the sinful nature and becomes *righteous:* or, as the Bible at times states it, *being upright with God* (KJ Ge 6:9, Job 1:1, Ps 33:1 & 140:13, Pr 29:10). Therefore, the theme of whom God loves versus whom God hates is throughout the full context of the Bible. It has much to say about both. For example:

> It is written: *Many sorrows shall be to the wicked: but he that trusteth in the {word of the} LORD, mercy shall compass him about. Be glad in the LORD, and rejoice, ye righteous: and shout for joy, all ye that are upright in heart.* (KJ Ps 32:10–11)

---

[5] *Righteous*, Webster's Encyclopedic Unabridged Dictionary.

[6] *Righteousness*, Ibid.

[7] *Righteousness*, Charlton Laird, Webster's New Roget's A-Z Thesaurus, 3rd ed. (Boston: Houghton Mifflin Harcourt, 2003).

It is written: *Many are the afflictions of the righteous: but the LORD delivereth him out of them all. He keepeth all his bones: not one of them is broken. (However} Evil shall slay the wicked: and they that hate the righteous shall be desolate.* (KJ Ps 34:19-21)

It is written: *The LORD knoweth the days of the upright: and their inheritance shall be forever. They shall not be ashamed in the evil time: and in the days of famine, they shall be satisfied.*

But the wicked shall perish, and the enemies of the LORD shall be as the fat of lambs: they shall consume; into smoke shall they consume away.

(KJ Ps 37:18-20)

It is written: *The LORD detests men of perverse heart, but he delights in those whose ways are blameless.* (NIV Pr 11:20)

It is written: *Woe to the wicked! Disaster is upon them! They will be paid back of what their {evil} hands have done {and what their lying tongues have spoken}.* (NIV Isa 3:11)

According to Scripture, it's far better to live in a state of righteousness, resulting in **ZOE**[8], *life more*

---

[8] Kenneth E. Hagin, ZOE: *The God-Kind of Life* (RHEMA BIBLE CHURCH–Kenneth Hagin Ministries, P.O. Box 50126, Tulsa, OK, 1981), p 1.

abundantly (KJ Jn 10:10) than to do evil and follow or join deceivers, thieves, and God-haters, which, over a period, forever has dire consequences.

A † Ω

- - - - - - -

A REFLECTION OF GOD'S WAY

I. Thou shalt have no other gods before me.
      (KJ Ex 20:3, Dt 5:7, Mt 4:10)

II. Thou shalt not make unto thee any graven image, or any likeness of any thing that is in heaven above, or that is in the earth beneath, or that is in the water under the earth. Thou shalt not bow down thyself to them, nor serve them. For I the LORD thy God am a jealous God, visiting the iniquity of the fathers upon the children unto the third and fourth generation of them that hate me; and shewing mercy unto thousands of them that love me, and keep my commandments.
      (KJ Ex 20:4-6, Dt 5:8-10)

ENGRAVED IN STONE BY GOD FOR HIS ELECT

[Jesus Christ did not abolish these commandments!]
      (KJ Mt 5:17-20, 1Jn 2:3-6, Rev 14:12)

A † Ω

- - - - - - -

II. THE CREATION DECODED

The Bible opens with Moses' **allegorical** rendition of *The Creation of Planet Earth* (KJ Ge 1-2:9), written between 1450 and 1410 B.C. His story is integral to *Agape* by requiring acceptance of the undeniable facts over false beliefs. Moreover, Moses wrote the story without knowledge of the earth's development through six prehistoric ages, apocalypses, and DNA technology. Therefore, to align *Moses' Creation* with *Agape,* this chapter decodes it.

To factually outline the earth's history required modern DNA testing of archaeological discoveries that revealed the past's facts. Prolific global findings by hundreds of archaeologists overwhelmingly show that evolution over roughly six hundred million years played a significant role in plant and animal life.[9]

And since *God is the Creator of the ends of the earth* (KJ Isa 40:28), **He created evolution to advance life forms where they could eventually duplicate themselves suited to their environments.** Once they begin producing others in their image, development for that life form eventually ceases because there is no longer a need for it. Exceptions are sporadic.

Moreover, God said, as the *Creator of all life sources*, including sunlight, water, and earth, **Let the waters bring forth abundantly the moving creatures that hath life, and fowl that may fly above the earth in the open firma-**

---

[9] *Timeline of the evolutionary history of life,* WikipediA Encyclopedia, 2022.

ment of heaven (KJ Ge 1:20). It was He who commanded, *Let the earth bring forth the living creature after his kind, cattle, and creeping thing, and beast of the earth after his kind* (KJ Ge 1:24). He did **not** say, *Let me bring forth plants and animals.* Furthermore and undeniably, what He said and commanded occurred through billions of years of the earth's natural development.

Therefore, plants and animals evolving from water and land do not diminish *God as Creator of the ends of the earth* (KJ Isa 40:28). Instead, it proclaims Him as *Creator of all the elements from which life forms evolve* (KJ Ge 2:4-5). However, it voids the notion of God as a genie out of his bottle waving a magic wand, instantly creating every plant and animal in three twenty-four-hour periods, as the false literal interpretation of *The Creation* implies. Unfortunately, for years, I believed it was so because I was religious-minded and never considered that the beliefs I grew up with might not be correct.

Then, at age 33, I committed to reading every word of the Bible and have been doing so repeatedly ever since. Doing so inspired me to search deeper for the truth about God, Jesus, the Holy Spirit, and salvation (Pr 25:2, Matt 7:7, Lk 11:9). That journey evolved into THE ALPHA THROUGH OMEGA PROJECT, having many wonderful surprises. For example, setting out to correctly interpret the Bible led me on a pilgrimage of fulfillment, purpose, and spiritual development beyond what I had ever imagined.

That expedition prompted me to wholeheartedly continue my quest for the truth and examine the Scriptures more thoroughly. Then, I began seeing God's word from a new symbolical, metaphorical, and spiritual perspective far removed from being taken mistakenly, religiously, and solely literally. For example, never mentioned in the church or religious classes I attended were many facts I began reading about God, Jesus, the Holy Spirit, and salvation. Yet, I discovered those omissions were vital for establishing a relationship with God and enjoying a life of purpose and fulfillment through Him. Afterward, but very gradually, *the mysteries of God* began unfolding before me. For example,

> It is written: But do not forget this one thing, dear friends. **With the Lord, a day is like a thousand years, and a thousand years are like a day.** (KJ 2Pe 3:8)

Although this Scripture is toward the end of the Bible, it points directly to the Bible's beginning: *Moses' epic Creation of Planet Earth*. The good Lord revealed its truthful interpretation by applying the discovered facts about life on Planet Earth to the story and dividing it into sections. Far removed is that interpretation from the simplistic religious-minded literal understanding I first believed. So, experience it yourself and judge whether or not it aligns with what you have been made to think about God, Jesus, the Holy Spirit, and salvation.

GENESIS 1:1–19 / DAYS 1–4
THE FORMATION OF PLANET EARTH

Scientific discoveries revealed that the earth formed 4.54 billion years ago, with the evolution of life-producing micro-organisms dating back 4 billion years. However, life remained primarily microscopic until about 580 million years ago, when complex multicellular life arose, developed over time, and culminated in the Cambrian Explosion about 538.8 million years ago.[10]

Therefore, in **Moses' epic Creation,** each of the seven days represents an extensive amount of time, where, **With the Lord, a day is like a thousand years, and a thousand years are like a day.** However, the Scripture does not rule out that God is time-conscious in other situations throughout the Bible. Moreover, this Scripture applies specifically to the earth's beginnings to the current time.

> It is written: In the beginning God created the heaven and the earth. And the earth was without form, and void; and darkness was upon the face of the deep. And the *Spirit of God* moved upon the face of the waters. And God said, *Let there be light: and there was light.* And God saw the light, that it was good: and God divided the light from the darkness. And God called the light *Day,* and the darkness he called *Night.* **And the evening and the morning were the first day.**

---

[10] *History of the Earth,* WikipediA Encyclopedia, 2022.

And God said, *Let there be a firmament in the midst of the waters, and let it divide the waters from the waters.* And God made the firmament, and divided the waters which were under the firmament from the waters which were above the firmament: and it was so. And God called the firmament *Heaven.* **And the evening and the morning were the second day.**

And God said, *Let the waters under the heaven be gathered together unto one place, and let the dry land appear:* and it was so. And God called the dry land *Earth*; and the gathering together of the waters called he *Seas*: and God saw that it was good.

And God said, *Let the earth bring forth grass, the herb yielding seed, and the fruit tree yielding fruit after his kind, whose seed is in itself, upon the earth:* and it was so. And the earth brought forth grass, and herb yielding seed after his kind, and the tree yielding fruit, whose seed was in itself, after his kind: and God saw that it was good. **And the evening and the morning were the third day.**

And God said, *Let there be lights in the firmament of the heaven to divide the day from the night; and let them be for signs, and for seasons, and for days, and years: And let them be for lights in the firmament of the heaven to give light upon the earth:* and it was so. And God made two great lights; the greater light to rule the day, and the lesser light to rule the night: he made the stars also. And God set them in the firmament of the heaven to give light upon the earth, and to rule over the day and over the night, and to divide the light from the darkness: and God saw that it was good. **And the evening and the morning were the fourth day.**

(KJ Ge 1:1-19)

DNA Technology applied to archaeological discoveries proved that Days 1, 2, 3, and 4 of the Bible's *Creation* covered four billion years of the earth's development, including the growth of plants on Day 3 (KJ Ge 1: 11-12). Thus, four billion years was a very long time it took God to prepare Planet Earth for Day 5: animal life.

A † Ω

GENESIS 1:20-23 / DAY 5
THE EVOLUTION OF SEA CREATURES

Day 5 informs that *God commanded the waters to bring forth sea creatures, whales, and fowl of the air* (Ge 1:20-23).

It is written: And God said, *Let the waters bring forth abundantly the moving creature that hath life, and fowl that may fly above the earth in the open firmament of heaven. And God created great whales, and every living creature that moveth, which the waters brought forth abundantly, after* their kind, and every winged fowl after his kind: and God saw that it was good. And God blessed them, saying, *Be fruitful, and multiply, and fill the waters in the seas, and let fowl multiply in the earth.* **And the evening and the morning were the fifth day.** (KJ Ge 1:20–23)

The waters brought forth creatures dating back 570 million years. The time in history was known as *The Cambrian Explosion: the age of an evolutionary burst of life forms in the seas.*[11] The first known creatures the waters brought forth on Day 5 date back 558 million years. They were invertebrates known as *Dickinsonia.*[12]

Then came the Paleozoic Era, dating back 541 million years, when the waters brought forth a second invertebrate: *Nautilus.*[13] After was the evolution of *Sponges* dating back 535 million years.[14] Then came *Jellyfish* originating 500 million years ago.[15] Followed was the evolution of thousands of similar aquatic species over the next 200 million years, ending the Paleozoic Era.

---

[11] *The Cambrian Explosion,* https://evolution.berkeley.edu/the-arthropod-story/meet-the-cambrian-critters/the-cambrian-explosion/.

[12] Jeremy Rehm, *World's first animal was a pancake-shaped prehistoric ocean dweller,* https://www.nature.com/articles/d41586-018-06767-6, September 20, 2018.

[13] Alex Bolano, *Earth Timeline: From 4.5 Billion Years Ago To Today,* https://sciencetrends.com/earth-timeline-from-4-5-billion-years-ago-to-today/, March 11 – November 2, 2019.

[14] Reef Cause Team, *Sponge-like Fossil Could Be Earth's Earliest Known Animal,* https://conservation.reefcause.com/sponge-like-fossil-could-be-earths-earliest-known-animal/, September 18, 2021.

[15] *Jellyfish,* WikipediA Encyclopedia.

Fowl evolved from Theropod Dinosaurs during the Jurassic (around 165–150 million years ago). Their classic small, lightweight, feathered, and winged body design was pieced together gradually over tens of millions of years of evolution rather than in one burst of innovation.[16] Hence, *fowl* evolved from *reptiles*, while *reptiles* came from *amphibians* and *amphibians* from *fish*.

On the other hand, *whales* were first found in the fossil record approximately 52.5 million years ago (Mya) during the early Eocene in Indo-Pakistan.[17] However, *whales* were not the first mammals to evolve.

Hence, Moses' Day 5 began 558 million years ago in the Paleozoic Era by introducing the first invertebrates: *Dickinsonia*. Then came the *fowl of the air* between 165 and 150 million years ago during the Mesozoic Age. Finally came the *whales* 52.5 million years ago during the early Cenozoic Age. Therefore, Moses' Day 5 extended over three prehistoric ages, overlapping with his Day 6: **The Evolution of Land Creatures.** Noteworthy is that the Cenozoic Age is the current age determined by today's configuration of the continents.

A † Ω

---

[16] Stephen L. Brusatte, Jingmai K. O'Connor, Erich D. Jarvis, <u>The Origin and Diversification of Birds</u>, Current Biology: Volume 25, Issue 19, 5 October 2015, Pages R888-R898

[17] Mark D. Uhen, <u>The Origin(s) of Whales</u>, Annual Review of Earth and Planetary Sciences Volume 38, 2010 Uhen, pp 189-219.

Genesis 1:24–25 / Day 6's Morning: The Evolution of Land Creatures

> It is written: And God said, *Let the earth bring forth the living creature after his kind, cattle, and creeping thing, and beast of the earth after his kind:* and it was so. And God made the beast of the earth after his kind, and cattle after their kind, and every thing that creepeth upon the earth after his kind: and God saw that it was good. (KJ Ge 1:24–25)

Day 6 dates back 310 million years to the Paleozoic Age. The Carboniferous Age stood within the Paleozoic Age when the first land creatures evolved into invertebrates. These included the insects that Day 5 has as *creeping things*.

> The Carboniferous Age of the Giant Insects dates back 309 million years. Among them were griffinflies resembling giant dragonflies having a two-foot wingspan: the largest flying insects on record. They were the first animals to go airborne, but only after spending many years as water creatures. However, they became extinct after 62 million years: 247 million years ago.[18] Like the griffinflies, today's dragonflies start as water creatures known as Naiads, and, between three months and five years, depending on

---

[18] https://owlcation.com/stem/The-Carboniferous-Period-When-Giant-Insects-Ruled-the-Land-and-Sky.

water temperatures, they mature into dragonflies.[19]

Following the Paleozoic Age came the Mesozoic Era of Dinosaurs:
- The Triassic Period (252–201 million years ago),
- The Jurassic Period (201–145 million years ago),
- The Cretaceous Period (145–66 million years ago).[20]

The Mesozoic Era also included the development of the first bony fish.[21]

After 170 million years of roaming the earth, unexpected, catastrophic events resulted in the extinction of the dinosaurs, resulting in an ice age. After millions of years of recovery, the planet became habitable to new life forms, completing Moses' story with God's creation of humanity in His image. The following summarizes how the earth became suitable for modern-day humans from the Mesozoic Era of Dinosaurs.

Destroyed by the impact of a massive six-mile-wide asteroid in the Gulf of Mexico's Yucatan Peninsula and volcanic eruptions across the globe, ended the Dinosaur Age 65 million years ago. Following was darkness and an ice age of 62.5 million years. Advancing two and a half million years marked the

---

[19] *Dragonfly Life Cycle*, https://dragonflywebsite.com/dragonfly-life-cycle.cfm

[20] *The Ages of the Dinosaurs*, https://www.nhm.ac.uk/discover/when-did-dinosaurs-live.html

[21] *The Evolution Of Fish*, https://www.fossilera.com/pages/the-evolution-of-fish, 2022.

introduction of land mammals, including Woolly Mammoths that adapted to frigid conditions. Later by two million two hundred thousand years, or a mere 300,000 years ago, the first Homo sapiens, Neanderthals, evolved on the earth. [22]

Recovered have been many Neanderthal fossils, including the remains of two Homo sapiens at Omo Kabish in Ethiopia, dating back 230,000 years. Scientists quickly concluded that Omo 1 and Omo 2 were modern-day men.[23] This is likely because Africa's Bushmen [San People} date back 200,000 years.[24] Furthermore, the Bushmen are the remnants of Africa's oldest cultural group, genetically the closest surviving people to the original Homo sapiens "core" from which (some, but not all–SJ) the Negroid people of Africa emerged.[25] The same has been concluded regarding Australia's Aboriginals, who migrated from Africa.[26] [The original Neanderthals became extinct with Woolly Mammoths in 3700 B.C.[27]]

---

[22] *Human,* WikipediA Encyclopedia.

[23] *Omo Remains,* WikipediA Encyclopedia, 2022.

[24] *San People,* WikipediA Encyclopedia.

[25] *San People,* The World's Most Ancient People, https://kwekudee-tripdownmemorylane.blogspot.com/2013/06/san-bushmen-people-world-most-ancient.html

[26] M.A.Condon, *The Origin of the Australian Aborigines,* https://www.evolutioninsitu.com/the-origin-of-the-australian-aborigines.html

[27] *History of the Earth,* WikipediA Encyclopedia, 2022.

Remarkably, the San People and Aboriginals thrive today. These homo sapiens are not the people God later created on the morning of Day 6, for these indigenous people have their roots in evolution. Furthermore, their proud heritage proves that Charles Darwin's Theory of Evolution, dating back to 1859, has always been correct.[28] However, the Bible illustrates that evolution is not across the board with humans as with plants and animals. Therefore, be prepared to embrace these facts regarding the evolution of humans in contrast to others God created in His image per Genesis 1:26 and 2:7.

A ✝ Ω

GENESIS 1:26–31 / DAY 6'S EVENING GOD'S CREATION OF MODERN-DAY MAN: PHASE 1 — MORTALS

It is written: And God said {to His mate}, *Let us make man in our image, after our likeness: and let them have dominion over the fish of the sea, and over the fowl of the air, and over the cattle, and over all the earth, and over every creeping thing that creepeth upon the earth.* So God created man in his image, in the image of God created he him; male and female created he them. And God blessed them, and God said unto them, *Be fruitful,*

---

[28] Charles Darwin, *An Introduction to the Theory of Evolution, On the Origin of Species*, (Integrated Media, New York, NY., 1859).

and multiply, and replenish the earth, and subdue it: and have dominion over the fish of the sea, and over the fowl of the air, and over every living thing that moveth upon the earth. (KJ Ge 1:26–28)

And God said, *Behold, I have given you every herb bearing seed, which is upon the face of all the earth, and every tree, in the which is the fruit of a tree yielding seed; to you it shall be for meat. And to every beast of the earth, and to every fowl of the air, and to every thing that creepeth upon the earth, wherein there is life, I have given every green herb for meat:* and it was so. And God saw every thing that he had made, and, behold, it was very good. **And the evening and the morning were the sixth day.**

(KJ Ge 1:26–31)

Carefully consider all the facts here.

- God proposed to His mate to procreate.
- Together, they created others in their image: male and female.
- They were not Neanderthals but were born in the image of God: tall modern-day **vegetarian** people.
- Entrusted with free will, confined, they were **not** to any specific location.
- Without restrictions, they were given dominion over **all** plants and animals throughout Planet Earth.

The Bible and DNA Technology applied to archaeological discoveries of the remains of these truly modern-day humans reveal more about them.

- *They were giants and men of renown* (KJ Ge 6:4). It was logical for them to be giants since the earth was a place of giant animals for millions of years.
- Other than *the sons of Anak,* their ancestry is not in the Bible (KJ Nu 13:32-33).
- These giants scattered and settled throughout the earth.[29] (KJ Ge 6:1-4; Nu 13:33; Dt 2:11,20; Dt 3:11)
- They were mortals and spiritual, evidenced by their remains in enormous global mounds dating back 10,000 years.[30]
- Assuming they lived up to 1,000 years, God created their first 9,000 years ago in 7,000 B.C. as of 2000 A.D.
- They thrived before **and** after the great flood of 2448 B.C. (KJ Ge 6:1-4; Dt 2:11, 2:20, 3:11, 3:13; Jos 12:4, 13:12, 15:8, 17:15, 18:16)

Three thousand years of having dominion over Planet Earth proved they did not live up to God's expectations (Ge 6:4, Jos 13:12). Therefore, God planned the making of an **immortal** whom He would shelter from them. But first, He rested and summed up Days 1 and 2: the four billion plus years before life forms evolved.

---

[29] Richard J. Dewhurst, THE ANCIENT GIANTS WHO RULED AMERICA: The Missing Skeletons and the Great Smithsonian Cover-Up (Bear and Company, Rochester, Vermont), 2014.

[30] *Giants,* Ibid.

A † Ω

Genesis 2:1–6 / Day 7
God Rested

It is written: Thus the heavens and the earth were finished, and all the host of them. And on the seventh day God ended his work which he had made; and he rested on the seventh day from all his work which he had made. And God blessed the seventh day, and sanctified it: because that in it he had rested from all his work which God created and made.

These are the generations of the heavens and of the earth when they were created {as Day 1 *during the Hadean Eon (era) 4.5–4.0 billion years ago*[31], *and Day 2 during the Archean Eon 4.0–2.5 billion years ago*[32]}, in the day that the LORD God made the earth and the heavens, and every plant of the field **BEFORE** it was in the earth, and every herb of the field **BEFORE** it grew: for the LORD God had not caused it to rain upon the earth, and there was not a man to till the ground {**BECAUSE IT WAS NOT HABITABLE**}. But {at some point *during the Proterozoic Eon 2.5 billion to 538.8 million years ago*[33]} there went up a mist from the earth, and watered the whole face of the ground.

(KJ Ge 2:1–6)

---

[31] *Eons – The Hadean Eon*, WikipediA Encyclopedia.

[32] *Eons – The Archean Eon*, Ibid.

[33] *Eons – The Proterozoic Eon*, Ibid.

A ☦ Ω

In summarizing **Chapter II, The Creation Decoded**, God did **not** instantly create Planet Earth and every living thing. The fact is that God, as *Creator of the ends of the earth* (KJ Isa 40:28), proclaims Him as *Creator of all the elements from which life forms evolve* (KJ Ge 2:4-5). Moreover, DNA Technology applied to archaeological discoveries proves how evolution on the part of God played its role in all plant and animal life. That absolute fact is shouted aloud to scientists, archaeologists, historians, and truth seekers while denied by stone-headed prevaricators and their *worshipers of deception*.

The reality is that everything evolves. The Bible began evolving in 1445 B.C. when God met with Moses on Mount Sinai and inspired him to write its first five books. It continued developing through the centuries into the New Testament past the time of Christ. In 95 A.D., the Apostle John wrote the Book of Revelation. Hence, the evolution of the Bible spanned 1540 years, not to mention the centuries it took to bring all the documents together to form The Bible.

Think about how businesses, nations, religions, schools, and transportation evolved into what they are today. You evolved into the person you now are.

Evolution is a God-given gift that, without it, Planet Earth would be lifeless! The only exception to evolution was when God procreated with His mate around 7000 B.C. to form giants in their image: males and females (KJ Ge 1:26-28).

A ☦ Ω

III. THE WORLD LOVED BY GOD VS. THE WORLD LOVED BY SATAN

Genesis 2:7–9
God's Creation of Modern-Day Man: Phase 2 — Immortals

According to the genealogies in Genesis Chapters 5 and 11, the year is 4104 B.C., only 6,127 years ago, as of 2023 A.D., when God tried His hand at another. According to the Jewish Encyclopedia, Abram, the first Hebrew, was born in 2166 B.C. Reversing his ancestry to the year God created His immortal is 1,948 years. Add 1,948 to 2,166, and you will have 4104 B.C. [At the end of this chapter is this genealogy].

Moreover, all findings of the remains of modern-day humans beyond 4104 B.C. are not of this lineage. Instead, they belong with the mortals of Ge 1:26 or those that evolved from Neanderthals, according to Ge 1:24–25. Regarding 4104 B.C.,

> It is written: And the LORD God formed man of the dust of the ground, and breathed into his nostrils the breath of life; and man became a living soul. And the LORD God planted a garden eastward in Eden; and there he put the man whom he had formed.
>
> And out of the ground made the LORD God to

grow every tree that is pleasant to the sight, and good for food; the tree of life also in the midst of the garden, and the tree of knowledge of good and evil.

(KJ Ge 2:7-9)

Facts check:

- God formed this man from the ground dust, unlike the giants He and another bear.
- Since he came from dust, there is an excellent possibility that, like Neanderthals, evolution played a significant role in his background.
- God breathed life into his nostrils, and this man became immortal. [There is no hint of God acting this way with His first line of humans.]
- God set this genuine young man apart in the Garden of Eden rather than giving him free rein over the earth as with His giants.
- The Garden of Eden was not in the same dimension as Planet Earth, as evidenced by the *Tree of Life* and the *Tree of the Knowledge of Good and Evil* in the middle of it. [Found on Planet Earth is nothing of the sort.]

From there, the author, Moses, describes a river watering the Garden of Eden, flowing from it and separating into four headwaters (KJ Ge 2:10-14). The Garden of Eden was a prominent place, having a large river watering it and dividing it into four other rivers. The story then reveals more about the man set apart.

It is written: And the LORD God took the man, and put him into the garden of Eden to dress it and to keep it. And the LORD God commanded the man, saying, *Of every tree of the garden thou mayest freely eat: But of the tree of the knowledge of good and evil, thou shalt not eat of it: for in the day that thou eatest thereof thou shalt surely die.* (KJ Ge 2:15-17)

Out of love, God secured the well-being and safety of **the immortal He set apart** by appointing him Caretaker for His Garden of Eden. The Garden of Eden was in a beautiful world God so loved (KJ Jn 3:16). It was ideal in every aspect of climate, topography, and the *Spirit of God* that met all the needs of life within it. Additionally, the *Spirit of God* accompanied the immortal in the garden, leading and guiding him to be successful in all God wanted him to do and become. Unlike the first humans He created and settled where they pleased, God restricted His new model to the Garden of Eden. Furthermore, He informed him what he could and could not consume from the garden to keep His **immortal** Spirit alive and healthy within the man.

Hence, God tested the young man with significant responsibilities. Obedience would result in a fulfilled, enjoyable, and abundant life in the Garden of Eden, which will be—for the most part, from here on—just referred to as Eden. **Disobedience would result in the death of the immortal** *Spirit of God* **within the man.** That death—having a rippling effect—would begin with isolation from

God. Separation from God would lead to a life of strife outside Eden: the dimension *where everything imaginable was permissible but not necessarily beneficial or constructive* (NIV 1Co 10:23). Living in the world beyond Eden, where *God created giant mortals without restrictions to replenish the earth* (Ge 1:26-28), would result in aging, diseases, dissension, struggles, uncertainties, tragedies, warfare, and death.

At about that time, God recognized that *the man He set apart* needed help fulfilling his increasing responsibilities.

> It is written: The LORD God said, *It is not good for the man to be alone. I will make a helper suitable for him.* (NIV Ge 2:18)

Before making a suitable helper for him, God entrusted the man with a second responsibility: naming all animals in Eden that came to him. **He also gave the man a name.**

> It is written: Now the LORD God had formed out of the ground all the beasts of the field and all the birds of the air {adaptable to Eden}. He brought them to the {brilliant} man to see what he would name them, and whatever the man called each living creature {that the LORD brought to him}, that was its name. So, the {smart} man gave names to all the livestock, the birds of the air and all the beasts of the field {in Eden that the LORD brought to him}.
>
> But for **Adam** no suitable helper was found.

(NIV Ge 2:18-20)

The name **Adam** distinguished God's immortal from all mortals assigned to *replenish the earth* (KJ Ge 1:26-28). Moreover, as giants and mortals, none suited to smaller and wiser Adam. Therefore, God resorted to Plan B by conducting surgery on him to fulfill his need for a suitable helper. Per Moses, *God removed one of Adam's 12 ribs, and from it, He formed another immortal.* Plan C would have been to create another from dust. However, Plan B was God's solution for resolving Adam's need for a suitable helper in Eden.

> It is written: And {so} the LORD God caused a deep sleep to fall upon Adam, and he slept: and he took one of his ribs, and closed up the flesh instead thereof. And the rib, which the LORD God had taken from man, made he a woman, and brought her unto the man. (KJ Ge 2:21-22)

[It is noteworthy that although God created a woman out of Adam's rib, it did not cause his sons and grandchildren to lack any. To this day, all humans typically have 12 ribs. Adam's surgery was the same as anyone else losing a rib. For example, if you require an operation to remove a rib, it does not result in your children losing any. So, please delete the false belief that men walk around with 11 ribs while women have twelve, then catch up with Adam.]

After recovering from surgery, having been given the gift to express himself in words intelligently, Adam spoke for the first time. [The animals were forbidden of that privilege, although bestowed unique communication skills, intelligence, feelings, and instincts suited to their species.] Adam's first words focused on the suitable helper God created from one of his ribs. Additionally, Adam quickly noticed that his newly created suitable helper was not a man like himself, which God identified as a woman! However, rather than accept the woman solely as his suitable helper, zealous Adam did the unthinkable. He went two steps further: mindlessly took her as-is for his wife and trusted her. These were decisions God approved in trusting Adam with free will.

> It is written: And Adam {proudly} said, *This is now bone of my bones, and flesh of my flesh: she shall be called Woman {per God}, because she was taken out of Man.*
>
> *Therefore* {in the Kingdom of God—not at all to be confused with the world's Kingdom of Satan} *shall a man leave his father and his mother, and shall cleave unto his wife: and they shall be one flesh* (since God approved Adam's decision in making the woman his wife}. *And they were both naked, the man and his wife, and were not ashamed.*
>
> (KJ Ge 2:23-25)

As Adam's spirit developed in the SPOKEN WORD OF GOD, he recognized a third responsibility God did not have to tell him about doing. That responsibility was to inform his suitable helper regarding the restriction God placed on him. Indeed, Adam had his wife's best interest in hand. Therefore, Adam discussed with her the rule that God commanded of him. Undoubtedly, Adam was confident that obeying God's commands would result in happiness, excellent health, prosperity, safety, and uninterrupted immortality. After all, God was very clear about the consequences of disobedience. What He made clear was necessary to know and act upon to secure the prosperity and well-being Adam desired for his wife and himself throughout eternity.

The Banishment of Adam and Eve

Surprisingly, another intelligent being, metaphorically as a *serpent* dispatched from the *spirit of evil*, found his way to where Adam and his wife met with the *Spirit of God*. Amusing as the *viper* was, he recognized an excellent business opportunity through the young, adventurous, impressionable couple. Therefore, the snake looked for an opportunity where he could manipulate Adam and his wife into becoming his servants, over having them serve God in truth and righteousness as God intended.

[Consider the manipulator's point of view. Rather than allowing the woman to be of service to Adam—**should Adam always remain committed to integrity**—it would be more destructive in a world influenced by liars, having the unsuspecting couple and their descendants forever serving the *spirit of evil*. Moreover, the mission of prevaricators is to enslave honest people by having them abide by their sinful nature in defiance of God.]

In other words, by persuading Adam and his wife to attend his church, the *serpent* would encourage them and their descendants to live per free will in defiance of God rather than having to obey God's commands. Free will could lead the couple and their descendants to believe whatever liars convinced them to think about God and worldly matters. For example, a widespread free-will indoctrination among *serpents* is:

"There are no consequences for disobeying a commandment of God."

Thus, the *viper* offered a life of total and uncensored freedom. He guaranteed ecstasy through instant gratification in every aspect of survival for the couple and their descendants. Of course, the deceiver would conveniently fail to mention that by doing so, the *Spirit of God*—encouraging obedience to His life-saving way—within them and their children would die. That death would result in dire consequences, including a void throughout their lifespan mentioned earlier, whereby a devious *spirit of evil* would replace the righteous *Spirit of God*.

So, the flattering manipulator began sizing up the man and the woman to determine which would be easier to manipulate into believing his false ideology over what God commanded Adam not to do. Additionally, the one chosen would influence the other into intentionally ignoring what God commanded.

The crafty trapper knew with certainty what to expect for the couple should they fall head over heels for his propaganda: that which appeared far more appealing—as a first impression—than what God forbade. It is important to note that the prevaricator had a firsthand experience of the consequences of rebelling against God since he was a delegate for the *spirit of evil.*

Thus, being of service to the mind of sin, he knew that by rebelling against God, that God would—without grace, love, mercy, forgiveness, or hesitation—banish any and every rebel out of His kingdoms (KJ Rev 21:8 and 27). That included banishment from Eden and His Kingdom of Heaven. Instead, they would be sent into another dimension in a designated world on the wide-opened and unprotected expanse of the universe that others ahead of Adam occupied (KJ Ge 1:26-30). Should these potential insurrectionists continue in their rebellion against God, out in that wide-open expanse among others having seized it, they could be confident that shocking horrors would become their way of life.

In our dimension, the wide-open expanse of the universe was the place to which *the spirit of evil—Satan—*was appointed prince (KJ Jn 12:31, 14:30, 16:11). His royal dominion over the earth was necessary on God's part. It was to test the character of all beings of high intelligence assigned to live here (KJ Rev 22:14). Among the others were *serpents*, such as the one found in Eden, who had his eyes on God's young couple.

Knowing the peoples' natural rebellion against God's commands, the *serpent* was confident that the couple and their descendants were sure to end up as mortals outside Eden with all their predecessors. It was a place void of the *Spirit of God.* Like critters in a trap, the *spirit of evil* would eventually take control of their lives through other prevaricators making other deceptive offers. Initially, the other suggestions—as the first—would appease human lustful desires. Such would become better known as instant but consequential gratification, resulting in sin: *a transgression of God's divine law* (KJ 1Jn 3:4).

Therefore, the trapper boldly stalked the couple for the perfect opportunity to do what deceivers are best at: **manipulating the truth to entice others to disobey God's commands.** The sly manipulator sized up the woman as the one managed easier in the presence of the other and God Himself. He sized up the woman also as having more significant influence over her spouse by comparing what he entrusted her with not doing. Thus, the deceiver boldly stalked the woman with Adam at her side—God watching close by—enticing her to follow free will shamelessly: *eat freely from the tree of the knowledge of good and evil:* that which God forbade Adam—who forbade her—to do.

> It is written: Now the serpent was more subtil {crafty} than any beast of the field which the LORD God had made. And **he** said unto the woman: *Yea, hath God said, Ye shall not eat of every tree of the garden?*

> And the woman said unto the serpent, *We may eat of the fruit of the trees of the garden. But of the fruit of the tree which is in the midst of the garden, God hath said, Ye shall not eat of it, neither shall ye touch it, lest ye die.*

> And the serpent said unto the woman, *Ye shall not surely die. For God doth know that in the day ye eat thereof, then your eyes shall be opened, and ye shall be as gods, knowing good and evil.*
>
> And when the woman saw that the tree was good for food, and that it was pleasant to the eyes, and a tree to be desired to make one wise, she took of the fruit thereof, and did eat, and gave also unto her husband with her; and he did eat. And the eyes of them both were opened, and they knew that they were naked; and they sewed fig leaves together, and made themselves aprons.
>
> (KJ Ge 3:1-7)

Due to her curiosity, lust for the transcendental forbidden fruit growing on *the tree of the knowledge of good and evil,* and her belief that the trapper had something better to offer, the woman ignored both God and Adam. Not only did she touch, but she ate from the tree, became snared, and enthusiastically seduced her loving and trustworthy husband into doing likewise. Immediately, the woman's choice to shamelessly steal and share what was sacred to God and entrusted to Adam caused the death of the *Spirit of God* within her and Adam. **As promised by the *serpent*, who enticed her to steal what was sacred to God, the woman and her betrayed husband lived on in *soul, mind, and body* as mortals.**

> [Jesus identified humans as having a *spirit {heart}, soul, mind, and body.* (KJ Mt 6:22, 22:37; Lk 10:27, 11:34). The presence of God is a person's *spirit.*

Without it, a person is spiritless: dead to God, a slave to evil. A person's *soul* is the beliefs, interests, and values that drive them. The *mind* retains thoughts and emotions, wisdom and knowledge, and is subject to temptations. The *body—The Temple of God*—is the vessel that converts whatever enters it into energy and wellness, **or** feebleness, drunkenness, fatness, laziness, sickness, weakness, and premature death.]

In other words, ***a transgression of God's divine law*** left the couple with **death** as promised: **the termination of the Spirit of God within them.** Ultimately speaking, the woman, having been trapped, gave the trapper precisely what he tricked her for: descendants void of the *Spirit of God*. Destined were those descendants to become subject to the *spirit of evil* in a world outside Eden. The exception was an exceptional few choosing obedience to God's commands over disobedience. But whether obedient or disobedient, some would come to occupy the same world where a conflict between people being right with God and people hated by God would be a way of life. The location for the battle between the two would be someplace on the wide-open expanse of the universe: a place designated by God.

Nevertheless, and forever after that, the woman and her man followed the way of human nature: **servants to the spirit of evil, being void of the Spirit of God.** Though filled with instant gratification in her victory over God's command and that of her faithful husband, the woman—having trusted a liar and her husband trusting in her—

brought regrettable and immediate fear and shame to themselves. To make matters far worse, God—knowing all—passed a terrible but justified sentence on each before turning them loose in the fearsome dimension outside of Eden, which—in their case—landed them on Planet Earth.

> It is written: Unto the woman he said, *I will greatly multiply thy sorrow and thy conception; in sorrow thou shalt bring forth children; and thy desire shall be to thy husband, and he shall rule over thee.*
>
> And unto Adam he said, *Because thou hast hearkened unto the voice of thy wife, and hast eaten of the tree, of which I commanded thee, saying, Thou shalt not eat of it: cursed is the ground for thy sake; in sorrow shalt thou eat of it all the days of thy life. Thorns and thistles shall it bring forth to thee; and thou shalt eat the herb of the field. In the sweat of thy face shalt thou eat bread, till thou return unto the ground* {as an insignificant mammal void of my *Spirit*}; *for out of it wast thou taken:* **for dust thou art, and unto dust shalt thou return** {being no longer a spiritual immortal being like one of us}.
>
> (KJ Ge 3:16–19)

Because of choosing to believe in the prevaricator and acting out against God, there were no signs of a second chance for the couple to remain in Eden, much less make it to Heaven. Hence, God's earnest and reflective—but just response—to the couple's disobedience to His command distinguished the conditions of His love they failed to meet. **As promised, their violation had dire consequences.**

By fulfilling lustful desires and sinful pleasures in defiance of God, they would eventually destroy every aspect of their beings. These included the descendants of all others who failed God's test of obedience before and after Adam and his wife—including *serpents, giants, and other sons of God* (KJ Ge 6:1-4). First to go would be the *Spirit of God* within them. That **death—*the cessation of God's significant presence within the inner man and woman*—** would later be followed by the termination of their physical bodies, having transformed from immortal beings to mortal beings. To confirm all this,

> It is written: And He said unto me, *It is done. I am Alpha and Omega, the beginning and the end. I will give unto him that is athirst* {for truth out} *of the fountain of the water of life freely. He that overcometh* {lies of serpents and all other evils} *shall inherit all* {righteous} *things* {salvation}; *and I will be his God, and he shall be my son.*
>
> *But the fearful, and unbelieving, and the abominable, and murderers, and whoremongers, and sorcerers, and idolaters, and all liars, shall have their part in the lake which burneth with fire and brimstone:* **which is the second death.**
>
> (KJ Rev 21:6-8)

Unquestionably, the *second death* is the ultimate mission of the *spirit of evil* regarding its association and outcome for humanity: a reality Adam faced because he trusted in his wife's free will. Knowing that destined he was for deportation to the somewhat populated, cold, and sweaty world of uncertainty out of which God created him, Adam thought it wise to give his wife a name. That name would distinguish her from all other humanoids occupying their assigned location. Their assignment was in the world of mortals, where God found no spiritually suitable helper for Adam. So Adam named his wife *Eve*, meaning *"a life."*[34]-[dominated by the *spirit of evil*].

> It is written: And Adam called his wife's name *Eve*; because she was the mother of all living {**of their descendants bearing their likeness**—but not of all humanoids having occupancy—on Planet Earth}. (KJ Ge 3:20)

Then came the inevitable: God's banishment of both from *the perfect world He so loved* (Jn 3:16).

> It is written: Unto Adam also and to his wife did the LORD God make coats of skins, and clothed them {as a necessity for survival in the treacherous world to which he was sending them}. And {turning back to others in His image and likeness} the LORD God said {to them}, *Behold, the man is become as one of us, to know good and evil: and now, lest he put forth his hand, and also take of the tree of life, and eat, and live forever.*
>
> Therefore the LORD God sent him forth from the garden of Eden, to till the ground from whence he

---

[34] *Eve*, Webster's Encyclopedic Unabridged Dictionary.

ADAM AND EVE CAST OUT OF PARADISE

was taken.

(KJ Ge 3:21–23)

Hence, defiance of God's command cost Adam, Eve, and all their descendants a perfect life and lordship in beautiful Eden—*a world loved by God* (KJ Jn 3:16). Then, broken-hearted but just, God banished the young couple from His presence for having returned evil for good—characteristic of lowly, worthless, colluding thieves: cold-hearted, spineless, thankless, unapologetic, and ungrateful. That is how most of their descendants would turn out, resulting in being annihilated within ten generations.

> It is written: So he drove out the man {and woman, being so utterly disgusted with them}; and he placed at the east of the garden of Eden Cherubims {*celestial beings of the second order of angels*[35]}, and a flaming sword which turned every way, to keep the way of the tree of life {from them and their descendants}. [This proved that the *tree of life* was beyond the grasp of Eve and her man Adam and all other banished inhabitants residing throughout the universe outside Eden]. (KJ Ge 3:24)

However, should God have been a god of unconditional love, he would have first gone to the deceptive, manipulative *serpent* and said:

> **Good morning, preacher!** *You know I love you no matter what because my love is unconditional. And regardless of how much of a liar and manipulator you turn out to many, I will forever love you. I will relish in all the ways you configure me as a lover of all, no matter what!*

---

[35] *Cherubims*, Ibid.

For example, I especially loved how you manipulated my command in having Eve believe that the death of my life-giving spirit within her was a myth. Knowing that she would live on in the flesh for some time, void of my presence while serving as an enslaved person to you and yours in fear and shame, you were very convincing. After all, having people without me by believing they are acting freely, rather than on your behalf, is sure to produce your intentions for them: dependent upon deceivers and thieves, resulting in fear and depression, misery and regret. Also, I admired how you made light of Eve's theft, making her appear childish throughout all generations, using an apple as the forbidden fruit. That displayed how devious you were about the seriousness of what Eve boldly and shamelessly stole in my presence. Then, inspired by your lies, she dared to share it with Adam to have him held accountable for her willful act of defiance.

As far as Adam is concerned, I am so proud that he allowed Eve not only to steal the apple—as you put it—but also to have taken the lordship of Eden to which I entrusted him. In doing so, Adam proved his subjection to his wife far more significant than being obedient and subject to me. How sweet that you now have both under your control and influence!

To set straight the record, God is a gentleman. He cordially turns people over to whom they choose to believe in and obey. Hence, was His need to drive Adam and Eve from Eden. The route chosen was through the east gates of its garden: a sealed portal in the proximity of any of four headwaters leading out of Eden.

[Of the four, known are only two: the Euphrates and Tigris {KJ Hiddekel}. The Gihon Spring is outside the walls of Jerusalem, short of a river of any type. The missing other is the Pison. Nevertheless, there is a possibility that someplace along either the Euphrates (KJ Rev 9:14, 16:12) or Tigris Rivers, or where they join, or at the Gihon Spring immediately outside the walls of Jerusalem, is the mysterious sealed portal to Eden's dimension. It was through that portal that God sent Adam and Eve off to their designated place on the wide-open, unshielded expanse of the universe: home of the *spirit of evil*.]

It is a critical reminder that before their banishment from Eden, God—a gentleman that He forever is—gave Adam and Eve freedom of choice in believing in and obeying His word and command or succumbing to *serpents*. Unfortunately, Eve chose to place faith in and follow the lying viper over what her husband and God forbade. Then, she disgustingly seduced Adam into rebelling against God as she had done.

Hence, Eve's defiance of God's command had far-reaching consequences besides being banished from Eden. The fact remains that God put Adam in charge of Eden; however, Eve took ownership of both Adam and Eden. Eve didn't amuse God for defying Him and Adam. Therefore, Adam's suitable helper became a chief thief over what God entrusted him.

Hence, blind trust, tolerance, and sweetness on the part of Adam cost his lordship over Eden—a beautiful dimension by merely obeying God would have forever met all his needs. Had Adam stood fast against Eve in her defiance, things would have turned out far better for both. Unfortunately, hindsight is always wiser than foresight in all places where the *spirit of evil* occupies and defies God's way.

Hence, not long after Eve sided with the *serpent*, Adam's perfect world in Eden ceased. He transformed from an immortal—*spiritually alive with God*—to a mortal: *spiritually dead to God* in exchange for physical survival through every possible form of evil. Furthermore, set on the broad road to catastrophic obliteration after being banished from Eden were the descendants of Adam and Eve. They landed where sin had been around for a long time among mortals, void of righteousness.

> It is written: *Therefore, just as sin entered the world through one man {a serpent}, and death through sin, and in this way death came to all men, because all sinned—for before the law {any commands by God} was given {to Adam or any other humanoids in our current age}, sin was {already present among inhabitants} in the world. But sin is not taken into account when there is no law {Commandments}. Nevertheless, death {and Hell} reigned from the time of Adam to the time of Moses, even over those who did not sin by breaking a command, as did {Eve who influenced} Adam, who was*

a pattern of the {stronger and more perfect} *one to come* {Jesus Christ}. (NIV Ro 5:12-14)

Summing up his situation, Adam quickly concluded that his wife was no longer trustworthy. That caused much grief for the *few chosen* (Mt 22:14), God-fearing women of integrity for generations. Thus, God conceded to the remote possibility that only a few of Adam and Eve's descendants would listen to Him and obey His commands (KJ Dt 4:12-14, Jos 24:24, Ps 29:4 & 68:33, Jer 42:6, Da 10:9, Jn 10:27, Ac 22:9, Heb 3:7). Obeying would spare them from horrors bestowed on others, choosing to live happily ever after in sin while deeming His obedient misfits repulsive, evil, and insane.

Therefore, it was necessary to offer the descendants of Adam and Eve two profound choices. They were and forever will be:

(1) Membership to God's kingdoms through trust in the absolute truth of His undeniable Word and obedience to His Commandments,   — OR —

(2) Forever remain in bondage to the *spirit of evil* by believing in and obeying the words of *serpents* or altogether disregarding what God says, much less having anything to do with following even one of the least of His commandments. (KJ Ge 3, Dt 28:15-68)

The first identified God's requirement for a few young and old descendants who would choose to regain His life-fulfilling *Holy Spirit*. Doing so would fill the void that Adam, Eve, and their predecessors—including the *serpent*—left behind. This historical moment takes us to Abel and Cain.

A † Ω

ABEL AND CAIN

It is written: Adam lay with his wife Eve, and she became pregnant and gave birth to Cain. She said, *With the help of the* LORD, *I have brought forth a man.* {But the LORD did not respond.} Later she gave birth to his brother Abel {and said nothing to the LORD about him.} Now Abel kept flocks and Cain worked the soil. (NIV Ge 4:1-2)

The Bible was precise with whom Adam lay. That was necessary since other humanoids resided where God set Adam in that wide-open expanse of the universe, where perversion and corruption were the norms. Therefore, specifying that Adam lay with his wife confirmed Adam's commitment to his marriage. He remained faithful to Eve, regardless that she traded his perfect life in Eden, including his salvation, for instant gratification. Having engaged in several perversions through a temptation on the part of a disgusting *serpent*, Eve likewise lost her salvation.

Before Eve committed her perverted acts, she came to believe—through unconditional love—that God would quickly forgive something an adder told her was essential for her development and growth. Then, moving forward in her new environment, void of the *Spirit of God*, Eve rejoiced over the birth of her would-be evil son but remained silent over the birth of her would-be righteous son. That proved how entirely void of the *Spirit of God* she had become.

Unfortunately, farmer Cain—Eve's first son—mirrored his mother's rebellion. He went the route of the second choice. In doing so, God was not pleased with Cain or his offerings. Soon after, the *spirit of evil* caught up with him, as it did with his mother, who gave ear to a *serpent*: typical of all who believe free will, or what prevaricators falsely preach and teach about God, is superior to God's word and commands. That resulted in Cain likewise becoming void of the righteous *Spirit of God*.

As promised, being void of the *Spirit of God* has rippling effects, regardless that prevaricators would have you believe otherwise. For example, being void of the *Spirit of God*, Cain had no clue what God expected of him, regardless of what he did: a common trait of flattering defrauders in control of others unable to accomplish any righteous act. Frustrated to enormous levels, through a free will void of the *Spirit of God*, Cain became jealous of his younger brother, Abel.

Unlike Cain, Abel—one of a kind during his time—followed in the steps of his overly loving and trusting but betrayed father. Abel pleased God effortlessly, being open to the *Spirit of God*, who guided and taught all good things to him as He had done with Adam. A shepherd (KJ Ge 4:2)—favored and respected by God for having gone the route of the first choice—Abel walked and talked with God, as did Adam up to the transgression of Eve. Otherwise, as was Cain, Abel would have been clueless about how to please God.

Through free will—void of the *Spirit of God*—Cain's solution to gaining God's approval was to get rid of Abel: a typical mentality of envious *thieves, murderers, and destroyers* acting against one of God's elect (Jn 10:10). However, what Cain failed to realize was that conspiracy and theft, as well as committing a willful act of murder of a person favored and loved by God, regardless of who put him up to it, was an abomination with God, rather than a way of gaining God's approval. In other words, Cain failed to see that conspiring against, stealing from, and murdering his younger brother—favored and respected by God—would result in God hating him far more.

Hence, blinded by jealousy of **an entitlement he was not entitled to** because of greed and selfish ambition, Cain set out to murder Abel. His well-planned murder was where innocent, unsuspecting Abel felt safe and at home.

> It is written: Now Cain said to his brother Abel, *Let's go out to the field.* And while they were in the field, Cain attacked his brother Abel and killed him. (NIV Ge 4:8)

Back up a moment on behalf of righteous Abel murdered by wicked Cain. Being of a divine mind right with God—as was his father Adam—Abel did not harbor evil toward others as Cain and others envied him. As Adam never considered being betrayed by Eve, Abel never conceived of betrayal by his brother or anyone else! Committing evil or harboring evil towards others was not in Adam or Abel's *heart, soul, and mind* (KJ Mt 22:37). As did Adam, Abel shared his joy and accomplishments through God with others: the ulterior motive of extreme hatred and jealousy directed at both of them on the part of liars, in addition to *thieves, murderers, and destroyers* (KJ Mt 5:10-11, 10:21-22; Jn 10:10), and their impressionable—but enslaved—misled followers.

Filled with the *Spirit of God*, Adam and Abel looked for the good in helping others without once conceiving that those others were jealous of and repulsed by every aspect of their beings as unique individuals chosen and favored by God for being *pure in heart* (Ps 35, Mt 5:3-11). Thus, Cain betrayed Abel, as Eve betrayed Adam. However, unlike Adam, who transformed into a mortal and returned to dust, Abel retained the *Spirit of God* after being murdered and became immortalized. Why? **Answer: Abel was not swept away by an evil influence, unlike his father.** Hence, Abel was the first Biblical character to qualify for the Kingdom of Heaven, apart from unknown others, including God's angels, arriving ahead of him.

Those later following in Abel's steps would—for the most part—experience his fate: being persecuted by liars, *thieves, murderers, and destroyers* (KJ Jn 10:10). The Bible tells of the lives of a few of these astounding, one-of-a-kind repentant, righteous individuals as role models for all future generations. It also addresses their heinous adversaries. For example, immediately after Cain committed murder, the all-knowing God—whom Cain never once found favor with—confronted Cain.

> It is written: The LORD said, *What have you done? Listen! Your brother's blood cries out to me from the ground. Now you are under a curse and driven from the ground, which opened its mouth to receive your brother's blood from your hand. When you work the ground, it will no longer yield its crops for you. You will be a restless wanderer on the earth.* (NIV Ge 4:10-12)

Typical of individuals and groups who conspire against or murder the favored and loved by God and then find themselves cursed with consequences for intentional acts of evil against the righteous, Cain cried out to God for unconditional forgiveness, love, and mercy. Following in his mother's steps, he never hinted at considering the pleas of Abel as he took the life out of him. Nor did he apologize to Adam and Eve or God for having murdered Abel!

Nevertheless, Cain developed a great fear of being murdered by occupants in the world of evil he was assigned. He deserved the worst consequences for his horrific, cold-hearted act. It was that which he boldly and shamelessly believed he carried out as an act of gaining God's approval: a trend in the name of false gods passed on to others hated by God even to this day. Finally, shocking reality grabbed hold of Cain like there was no tomorrow.

> It is written: Cain {pleading his case out of fear,

having never considered dire consequences for his malicious and premeditated act of murder of one favored and loved by God} said to the LORD, *My punishment is more than I can bear. Today you are driving me from the land, and I will be hidden from your presence; I will be a restless wanderer on the earth, and whoever finds me will kill me.*

But the LORD said to him, *Not so: If anyone kills Cain, he will suffer vengeance seven times over.* Then the LORD put a mark on Cain so that no one who found him would kill him. So, **Cain went out from the LORD's presence** {like the Atheists} and lived {with a mysterious wife among other inhabitants on Planet Earth} in the {populated} land of Nod, east of Eden. {By all indications, Nod was the territory of current-day Iran, Iraq, and Syria since it was east of Eden's portal}.

(NIV Ge 4:13–16)

So, God held Cain accountable for his act of homicide of a holy shepherd of a man and brother whom He favored, respected, and loved. Thus, God cursed Cain by turning fertile lands into desert waste precisely as he said he would (KJ Ge 4:10–12). God also branded him—as a rancher brands cattle—with the identifiable symbol of a murderer (Ge 4:15).

Hence, God had Cain suffer from guilt, shame, and lack of what he and his followers crave mostly: God's unconditional love—a myth out of the mouth of *serpents* and their *worshippers of deception*. Additionally, there were no signs of anyone being upset over Cain having murdered Abel, except on the part of God. And after the murder of Abel, Seth was born to Adam and Eve, whom Eve regarded merely as Abel's replacement (Ge 4:25). Moreover, most descendants of Adam and Eve, *other sons of God, Nephilim [giants]* (Ge 6:1-4), and those of *serpents* residing on Planet Earth, immersed themselves in evil, being void of the *Spirit of God*.

> It is written: The LORD saw how great man's wickedness on the earth had become and that every evil inclination of the thoughts of his heart was only evil all the time. The LORD was grieved that he had made man on the earth {but not in all certain other places or dimensions throughout the universe}, and his heart was filled with pain. So the LORD said, *I will wipe mankind, whom I've created, from the face of the earth* . . . (NIV Ge 6:5-7)

The Lord, grieved and filled with pain, takes us to Noah, with whom He found favor (KJ Ge 6:8).

A † Ω

NOAH AND THE ARK

It is written: This is the account of Noah. **Noah was a righteous man, blameless among the people of his time, and he walked {and talked} with God.** Noah had three sons: Shem, Ham, and Japheth. (NIV Gen. 6:9-10)

And who would God recognize as righteous? Here's the answer through the leadership of an *Old Testament Prophet and Kingsman* whom you will better come to know. His name was Moses.

> It is written: *And it shall be our righteousness if we observe to do all these commandments before the* LORD *our God, as he hath commanded us.* (KJ Dt 6:25)

[Obedience to His way is supreme with God. **Obedience is a display of faith in Him.** God's blessings flow through **faith**, resulting in *Zoe: life more abundantly* (KJ Jn 10:10).]

Now, return to the time of Noah, no less than 1500 years before Moses. As expected, it was only within ten generations (KJ Ge 5, 1Ch 1:1-4) that most of Adam and Eve's descendants—*amalgamated with other humanoids on Planet Earth* (Ge 1:26-28)—became so wicked that they provoked God to destroy most all (Ge 6:1-6). An exception was Noah and his immediate family. They were among the tenth and eleventh generations of Adam and Eve's descendants. Hence, the Bible's Sovereign God indeed is, and forever will be, a God of vengeance—though filled with limited grace and mercy—to all unrepentant, unrighteous, sinful people that do evil as measured by their free-will disobedience to His commandments.

The argument is that God had yet to write out His commandments before the time of Moses. However, despite not having God's commands spelled out for them, God did make clear right from wrong with Adam, who made clear right from naughty with Eve. Hence, God illustrated that His forgiveness, grace, love, mercy, and tolerance were reserved only for the righteous in His sight. At the time, Noah and his family met that qualification. Therefore, they were found worthy of being saved from the upcoming worldwide catastrophic event God was planning.

Like righteous Abel during his brief lifetime, Noah was one of a kind during his time. Noah was the only person among many in his generation who passed God's test of *righteousness*. He had *a pure heart* (KJ Mt 5:8), *was just, and walked with God* (KJ Ge 6:9). Being *pure in heart* and *just*, Noah heard God's **still small voice** (KJ 1Ki 19:12). It was a privilege set aside for a good man. Like Abel, it resulted in knowing what God expected of him and obeying what God said.

Since all other mortals, including descendants of Adam and Eve, were beyond reproach, God set out to destroy them. That annihilation came from torrential rainfall in 2448 B.C. that lasted forty days and nights (KJ Ge 7:12, 17). It wholly submerged Planet Earth for a hundred and fifty days (KJ Ge 7:24).

Hence, Noah's choice to obey God spared the lives of Noah and his family. That included the mysterious construction—construed by God—of a massive ark [rather than a boat as the CB falsely portrays] **that would become their place of refuge for three-hundred seventy-five days** (KJ Ge 7:11, 8:14–15).

It is written: *For forty days, the flood kept coming on the earth, and as the waters increased, they lifted the ark high above the earth* (NIV Ge 7:17). [Without rudder or sails, it drifted.] *At the end of a hundred fifty days, the ark came to rest on the mountains of Ararat* (NIV Ge 8:4).

Thus, God sheltered Noah, his family, and the animals inside the ark a hundred eighty-five days after docking. That same ark—though very real—was then and forever will be a metaphor for *Genesis through Revelation*: a self-contained place of refuge for God's elect drifting through life, but guided by Him and faith [trust through obedience] in all He advises.

Similarly, the flood was and forever will be an allegory for the massive destruction of doomed worlds void of God's commands. That includes corrupt cultures and societies among nations within a world—as happened to the tenth and eleventh generations of the descendants of the Bible's Adam and Eve and all others younger and older living at the time, except for Noah's family of eight.

It is critical to emphasize that due to his acts of righteousness, while walking and talking with God, Noah was given a life-saving revelation from God that he and his family acted upon, **undeniably with the help of others**. And in doing so, God spared the lives of his wife, their three sons, and their wives. Hence, each adult in Noah's world survived or drowned per whom and what they chose to believe, trust, and obey.

ADRIFT, YET CHOSEN FOR SURVIVAL:
A Reward for Obedience

However, to make matters more terrifying, all below age twenty—regarded by God as children—had no say in choosing life or being killed. The children inherited the fate of their parents (KJ Ge 7:21-23). [In other words, only a few select children, as are adults, are destined for God's Kingdoms. Salvation for most children is primarily contingent on their parents' standing with God. Exceptions are sporadic!]

After a hundred and fifty days of floodwaters (KJ Ge 7:24), no humanoids, including children or terrestrial animals left standing, crawling, or slithering on the ground in Noah's world, survived the flood (KJ Ge 7:18-23). However, sometime after the waters began receding, plant life took root. That discovery was by a second dove Noah released after 318 days that returned with an olive leaf in its beak (KJ Ge 8:1-13).

A ☦ Ω

In summarizing this chapter, **THE WORLD LOVED BY GOD vs. THE WORLD LOVED BY SATAN** started in 4104 B.C., roughly 2,896 years of God's giant sons and daughters having dominion over **all** the earth without restrictions. It was the year God decided to create another modern-day man due to His disgust of His *perverted giant sons* who became known as *men of old* (KJ Ge 6:4).

Unlike the giants, this new man, created from ground dust (KJ Ge 2:7), was designed smaller and as an immortal possessing God's spirit. Also, unlike the giants, he was confined to the mysterious mega *Garden of Eden* and given charge over it. This garden was not in Planet Earth's dimension. It grew *the tree of the knowledge of good and evil, which was off-limits to the man, lest he surely dies* (KJ Ge 2:17). It also grew *the tree of {eternal} life* (KJ GE 3:22). Most importantly, the Garden of Eden was the home of God's evolution, *where out of the ground evolved every beast of the field and every fowl of the air* (KJ Ge 2:19) *as on Planet Earth over millions of years.*

But even with all the man had and had to do, *God determined it was not good for him to be alone* (KJ Ge 2:18). So, He put the man to sleep, extracted a rib from him, and miraculously created a woman with his bone. And without breathing into her nostrils or involving water or dust, she became a living being God brought to the man as his helper (KJ Ge 2:21–22).

But then came a preacher who convinced the woman that God's unconditional love approved her to eat good and evil fruit, which she shared with her man. That resulted in the couple's discovery that God is not an unconditional lover since God banished them from Eden. But the worst was yet to come upon them and their descendants, having been stripped of God's immortal spirit: **annihilation**.

Hence, earning God's approval comes down to two factors: whom we believe, trust, and obey, and what we do with what we believe, trust, and follow. Having the *Spirit of God* in the inner person is one led in righteousness and truth. Being void of the *Spirit of God* is one guided by the *spirit of evil* in opposition to God's way. Hence, free will on the part of humanity, in and of itself, is a myth. *We either serve the Spirit of God in righteousness or help the adversaries of God in wickedness* by *using freedom as a cover-up for evil* (KJ Heb 10:26–27; NIV 1Pe 2:15–16).

Additionally, know with certainty reserved is God's limited forgiveness, grace, love, mercy, and tolerance. All are for the few He recognizes as His elect for living according to His principles. Therefore, regardless that countless millions claim God to be unconditionally and madly in love with them, as did Adam and Eve and the people of Noah's world, it does not confirm that He is happily in love with them.

DESCENDANTS OF NOAH'S SONS:
Japheth, Shem, and Ham [36]

[The Bible credits Japheth, Shem, and Ham as fathers of nations, not fathers of the five races. However, and undoubtedly, their descendants bore children by women of various races.]

Japheth was Noah's elder son (KJ Ge 10:21). *He was born when Noah was 500 years old* (KJ Ge 5:32). *He is the father of the Europeans & people of India: Gentiles of two distinct races* (KJ Ge 10:1-5).

Japhethites include Gomer/Germany, Magog/Russia, Javan/Greece (Gen. 10:2 – "white"-skinned people), and Madai-Medes/India (Gen. 10:2 – "dark"-skinned people).

*Noah's blessing on **Japheth** was far-reaching for all of his descendants. The **Japhethites** were known for their intellectual activity.*

Shem was born when Noah was 503 (KJ Ge 11:10, 7:11). *Shem* is *the father of the nations of the Ancient Near East. They are Assyrians, Babylonians, Israelites, Lydians, Persians, and Syrians* (KJ Ge 10:21-31). *Moreover, Judaism, Islam, and Christianity also sprang from Shem's line. The **Semites** were mainly known for their religious zeal.*

[Of the line of **Shem** was **Peleg**, born 2347 B.C.; *in his days was the earth divided* (KJ Ge 10:25). This

---

[36] *The Descendants of Shem, Ham, and Japheth*, Bible History.com

divide was not Planet Earth breaking apart as it did during the Carboniferous period of the giant insects (359-299 million years ago). Instead, it referred to the clever people of Babel around 4300 years ago, who were divided into nations by God and scattered to designated territories (KJ Ge 11:1-9).

Abram (2156-1981 B.C.), named by God as *Abraham, the first Hebrew*, was also of the line of *Shem* (KJ Ge 11:10-27).] His son, *Isaac,* was the *Child of Promise* (KJ Ge 17, 21). His grandson, *Jacob,* **father of 12 sons (tribes) born to four wives** (KJ Ge 29-30), was named by God *Israel,* meaning, *"for as a prince hast thou power {wrestled} with God and with men, and hast prevailed"* (KJ Ge 32: 24-30). *Israel* also means *"the person or nation to whom God presents himself"* (KJ Ge 35:9-10).

Ham was Noah's youngest son (KJ Ge 9:24), *born when Noah was around 506 years old. Ham is the father of the nations of Africa and The Far East* (KJ Ge 10:6-20): *multiple races. Hamites include Cush/Ethiopia, Mizraim/Egypt, Phut/Somalia, Ptolemais/Libya (Gen. 10:6 - "dark"-skinned people), and also Sinites/Chinese (Gen. 10:17 - 10:17 - "yellow"-skinned people). The Hamites were known for their physical endurance.*

Ham's fourth son, Canaan, was prophetically cursed by Noah because after disembarking the ark, Ham gazed at Noah's drunken nakedness (KJ Ge 9:18-27).

A ✝ Ω

ADAM TO ABRAM GENEALOGY
1,948 YEARS

BIRTH	NAME	FATHER'S AGE
4104 BC	ADAM	{MADE FROM DUST}
3974 BC	SETH	ADAM @ 130
3869 BC	ENOS	SETH @ 105
3779 BC	CAINAN	ENOS @ 90
3709 BC	MAHALALEEL	CAINAN @ 70
3644 BC	JARED	MAHALALEEL @ 65
3482 BC	ENOCH	JARED @ 162
3417 BC	METHUSELAH	ENOCH @ 65
3230 BC	LAMECH	METHUSELAH @ 187
3048 BC	NOAH	LAMECH @ 182
2456 BC	SHEM	NOAH @ 502
2448 BC		THE GREAT FLOOD
2446 BC	ARPHAXAD	SHEM @ 100
2411 BC	SALAH	ARPHAXAD @ 35
2381 BC	EBER	SALAH @ 30
2347 BC	PELEG	EBER @ 34
2317 BC	REU	PELEG @ 30
2285 BC	SERUG	REU @ 32
2255 BC	NAHOR	SERUG @ 30
2226 BC	TERAH	NAHOR @ 29
2156 BC	ABRAM	TERAH @ 70

Adam to Abram Genealogy
1,948 Years

LIFE SPAN	REFERENCES
ADAM: 930 YRS	(Ge 2:7, 5:1-5)
SETH: 912 YRS	(Ge 5:6-8)
ENOS: 905 YRS	(Ge 5:6-11)
CAINAN: 910 YRS	(Ge 5:9, 12-14)
MAHALALEEL: 895 YRS	(Ge 5:13, 15-17)
JARED: 962 YRS	(Ge 5:12, 15-17)
ENOCH: 365 YRS	(Ge 5:18, 21-24)
METHUSELAH: 969 YRS	(Ge 5:22, 25-27)
LAMECH: 777 YRS	(Ge 5:26, 28-31)
NOAH: 950 YRS	(Ge 5:28-29, 9:28-29)
SHEM: 600 YRS	(Ge 5: 32, 10: 21, 11:10-11)
DURING NOAH'S 600TH YR	(Ge 7:6)
ARPHAXAD: 438 YRS	(Ge 11:10-13)
SALAH: 433 YRS	(Ge 11:11-15)
EBER: 467 YRS	(Ge 11:14-17)
PELEG: 243 YRS	(Ge 11:16-19)
REU: 237 YRS	(Ge 11:18-21)
SERUG: 230 YRS	(Ge 11:20-23)
NAHOR: 148 YRS	(Ge 11:22-25)
TERAH: 205 YRS	(Ge 11:24-28, 32)
ABRAM: 175 YRS	(Ge 11:26, 25:7)

IV. ABOMINATIONS THAT CAUSE DESOLATION

DESTITUTE
Wading through the consequences of abominations generate far more significant challenges than merely walking in the rain.

Def: Abominations that cause Desolation—*A despicable misuse of the Temple* [any worship location] *of the Lord during a time of great trouble—an event foreseen and foretold* [twice] *by the prophet Daniel* [concerning the end of times and discussed twice by Jesus Christ].[37]

ABOMINATIONS THAT CAUSE DESOLATION, as recorded in the Bible, offer additional evidence that God's love is conditional. For if God's love was unconditional, noting would be an abomination in His sight. Such is not the case since God is aware whenever anyone

---

[37] ***Abominations that Cause Desolation,*** Nelson's New Illustrated Bible Dictionary, Ronald F. Youngblood, gen. ed.; F. F. Bruce and R. K. Harrison, consulting editors; Herbert Lockyer, gen. ed. of the original ed. (Nashville, Tn.: Thomas Nelson Publishers, 1995).

attempts to misuse worship locations to mislead His people. Referring to such, Daniel, a youthful *Old Testament Prophet, and Kingsman*—favored by God—was told of its coming.

> It is written: *And from the time that the daily sacrifice shall be taken away, and the abomination that maketh desolate set up, there shall be a thousand two hundred and ninety days.* (KJ Da 12:11)

Apart from a literal meaning concerning the abandonment of truth in the churches, the 1,290 days is an allegory for the window of opportunity entrusted to every human being to be at home in God's undeniable Word: read, study, believe, and obey *Genesis through Revelation*. Jesus reiterated that prophecy.

> It is written: *When ye therefore shall see the abomination of desolation, spoken of by Daniel the prophet, stand in the holy place—whoso readeth, let him understand* {truth and reality}. *Then let them which be in Judae'-a* {the *few chosen* by God} *flee into the mountains* {the truth of God's word}. (KJ Mt 24:15-16, Mk 13:14)

A † Ω

SEARCHING FOR TRUTH

Over the years, I attended various churches to discover as much as possible about the Bible's God, whom I came to fear, know, love, serve, and trust. And although I gained some knowledge while attending many of those churches, I also discovered that beliefs and teachings about Him sometimes differed like night and day. In making comparisons, I found that the primary reason for those differences is that Scripture lends itself to being misinterpreted—whenever stripped of its full context—to cater to and condone various demonic behaviors and philosophies.

Hence, the misrepresentation of Bible Scripture, intentional or not, falsifies reality and truth. It is *Liars Syndrome*, whereby manipulated facts into lies, resulting in misled congregations believing they are heaven-bound when, in fact, they are all hell-bound.

Thus, defying the truth about God comes with dire consequences.

> It is written: *Thou shalt not take the name of the* L<small>ORD</small> *thy God in vain; for the* L<small>ORD</small> *will not hold him guiltless that taketh his name in vain.* (KJ Ex 20:7)

The most common violation of this Third Commandment is via snippets that alter the Scriptures' intended meaning, revealed only in its full context. Hence, the entire context of any subject indicates the truth regarding its matter. [T<small>HE</small> A<small>LPHA THROUGH</small> O<small>MEGA</small> P<small>ROJECT</small> reveals God's intended truth in *Genesis through Revelation*.]

Sequestering the full context of Scripture opened the floodgates for hundreds of religions, cults, and governments worldwide. They often use corruption, entertainment, gimmicks, and God or His Bible to bait a critter's trap. Doing so attracts uninformed followers, seeking approval among others like themselves, believing whatever they falsely make God be apart from who He is.

Exposing God's intentions is doing to Scripture what honest investigators set out to do in solving cases. They gather all the good, bad, and ugly facts and expose hidden mysteries to settle lawsuits to have justice served. Filled with good, bad, and ugly truths inspired by Jehovah, Christ, and the Holy Spirit is the Bible: the reason it has tremendous credibility!

That takes us to the Book of Daniel and his vision of what is taking place in many worship locations: clergy pretending to be of service to God while being of service to Satan. Hence, the revelation given to Daniel over 2600 years ago steers directly to exceedingly evil forms of worship conducted by men and women masquerading as *angels of light* when they are servants of evil (KJ 2Co 11:14-15). Biblically and metaphorically referred to as *serpents*, these are *prevaricators* (KJ Ge 3, Ps 91:13, Mt 23:33).

The abominations these *serpents* have caused, due to intentionally falsifying God's word, have driven out the *Spirit of God* in all locations where these impostors preside. This void, resulting in abolishing the truth and other unimaginable crimes, has rippling effects on church congregations made to believe in deception. Furthermore, by all indications, now is when the daily sacrifice—intended worship to God—has been certified as abolished throughout much of the land: fulfillment of prophecy (KJ Da 12:10-11).

To illustrate this profound truth, I will enlighten you concerning six other abominations that cause desolation according to God's word. However, these are not all the abominations that stir God to wrath.

Before pursuing these, I cannot over stress that these six and others used as *a cover-up for evil are considered freedom* (NIV 1Pe 2:15-16). However, regardless that politicians and their clergy may condone, endorse, and practice these abominations, God's vengeance always catches up with them (examples: KJ Ps 94:1, 99:8, 149:7; Pr 6:34). [Vengefulness on the part of God is not something heard from deceivers manipulating Scripture. Key Biblical words such as *vengeance* are omitted from their vocabulary because they nullify God as having unconditional love.]

Thus, the following six, and all other abominations, are nothing more than illusions about God having unconditional love. They must be exposed as evil to establish a love relationship with God and qualify for His kingdoms. Doing so is a matter of choice because freedom of choice is God's will for humanity in every aspect of life. For those who heed God's way,

> It is written: And he {Solomon upon completion of the temple} said, LORD *God of Israel, there is no God like thee, in heaven above, or on earth beneath, who keepest covenant and mercy with thy*

servants that walk before thee with all their heart. (KJ 1Ki 8:23)

It is written: *Let your heart therefore be perfect with the* LORD *our God, to walk in his statutes, and to keep his commandments, as at this day.* (KJ 1Ki 8:61)

On the other hand, believed to be the best solutions for a growing evil and overpopulated world among *the enemies of God* are **abominations that cause desolation** (KJ Ro 1:18-32, Php 3:18, Jas 4:4). Moreover, the Bible teaches that these abominations are forever **un**acceptable to God. That alone causes the Bible to be rejected by *many called* to His kingdoms. Among the *many called*, destiny has it that only a *few* choose to overcome these and all other repulsive acts abhorred by God. Those *chosen few* understand that a love relationship with God is *a commitment to continue wholeheartedly in His way* (NIV 1Ki 8:23, 61).

That strikes a nerve with many relying on the love lie about God. That lie is:

"Since God's love is unconditional, there is no need to continue wholeheartedly in His way."

The totality of Scripture voids that mainstream lie.

Before presenting any abominations per God, allow me to assure you that I fell victim to atrocities where all I had left was the Bible to comfort me. And even as lowly as I became, God's living word spoke directly to me every time I read page after page without skipping any part. Hence, this is what I discovered about *sinfulness*—often referred to as *backsliding*—(KJ Jer 2:19, 3:6, 8, 11, 12; Hos 4:16, 14:4) while at the same time being zealous for the Bible:

> ***No matter the degree to which it instantly gratifies, sin never earns God's endorsement: damnation, yes; love and good fortune, no!***

And without God's consent, one can forget about His kingdoms. Per the Bible, that alone has proven to cost the salvation of many people, falsely believing God loved them and their children unconditionally (ex: KJ Dt 9). That truth and reality could have spared the souls of many now burning in Hell.

Therefore, by sharing what I experienced because of abominations—**as regarded by God**—I hope you will see that I'm **not** out to deceive anyone. For example, considering the God factor, I could not hide backsliding, regardless of how discreet I believed I was in keeping things to myself! You can expect the same should you forsake Satan's world and act upon the undeniable facts of God's word. Your past may haunt you for some time, and nothing you do will go unnoticed as God makes you transparent. On the contrary, should you reject the truth of God's word, you will fit in Satan's society. Unfortunately, fulfillment in life you will never find.

And why is it necessary to admit having been a horrible backslider? Answer: It is to give hope in knowing that

God speaks to us through His life-giving Word to *draw near to him* (Jas 4:8) that we may be *born again of His Spirit* (Jn 3:5), that which Eve aborted by believing a *serpent* and Adam destroyed to placate Eve. Having God speaking to us through His life-giving Word is contingent upon our reading, studying, believing, and obeying it: **TRUE FAITH**. Then, and only then, by **GRACE**, He may transform us into one of His *elect* (Eph 2:8): *a new creation* hostile to the sinful nature of our past (KJ 2Co 5:17). And although we all fall victim to enticing illusions, there is no place in God's kingdoms for unrepentant sinners. There is no place for excuses to continue in the sins of our youth nor to conspire against the righteous for choosing repentance and becoming holy for God.

> It is written: *For thou* {Job's sinful accusers} *writest bitter things against me, and* {falsely attempt to} *makest me to possess the iniquities of my youth* {which are no longer a part of my being}. *Thou puttest my feet also in the stocks, and lookest narrowly unto all my paths; thou settest a print upon the heels of my feet.* (KJ Job 13:26–27)

Hence, the Bible testifies that one does **not** sin by rebuking liars who slander them and bullies who try to enslave them. Evil people—out to **discredit** God's repentant *elect* of whatever—are *designated for condemnation* (NCV Jude 4), **NOT THE OTHER WAY AROUND!** Thus, *worshipers of deception* who regard righteous people as their problem expose the reality of their sins, a bias toward evil: bribery, deceit, greed, hatred, idolatry, murder, and theft.

> It is written: {Since I, David, repented} *Remember not the sins of my youth, nor my transgressions: according to thy mercy remember thou me for thy goodness' sake, O Lord.* (KJ Ps 25:7)

Now, wade through a few of Satan's abominations intended to drive out the *Spirit of God* among His people.

A ✝ Ω

The Abomination of Deception
~Lies Paralyze ~

> It is written: ***An unjust man is an abomination to the just*** {righteous}***: and he that is upright in the way*** {commandments} ***is abomination to the wicked.*** (KJ Pr 29:27)

Of the many churches I attended, the false belief and teaching that God's love is **un**conditional were common to all but one Bible, faith-based church. The universal abomination among all others was, *"God loves you, but not the sin in you."* Therefore, I wanted to know the truth because when I heard that repeatedly, my spirit would become very unsettled to the point that I would have to walk out of those services. So, I searched and found that God never once separates who a man, woman, or child is apart from their actions. In other words, God identifies people by their actions: *deceivers, devils, friends, murderers, serpents,* and other names that make the two one. Jesus touched on these many times. For example,

> It is written: *Give not that which is holy unto the dogs, neither cast ye your pearls before swine, lest they trample them under their feet, and turn again and rend you.* (KJ Mt 7:6)

If God's love is adamantly unconditional and loves everyone by discarding their sins, why would Jesus refer to only a few as *friends* while others to Him are *dogs* and *swine?* The answer is that Jesus made those distinctions to separate the few he loved from the people he hated and were doomed to hell. This lesson was not about dogs and pigs. Instead, Jesus used the terms *dogs* and *swine* as metaphors for abominably corrupt, unrepentant, cold-hearted people recognized for their heinous actions and beliefs.

And so—allegorically speaking—it turns out that all who read *Genesis through Revelation* come to a fork in the road. The top-rated broader **left road** leads to a metropolis named **Bible Deception**. The much less traveled, narrower **right path** leads to a small village called **Bible Truth**. Putting this in perspective, Eve and Cain took the broad road to **Bible Deception**, while Abel and Noah took the far less traveled route to **Bible Truth**.

Hence, it is not surprising that history, religion, worship, and divine prophecy have independently and altogether proven that most Bible skimmers take the left fork to **Bible Deception**. There, they collaborate to dissuade others from journeying down the right to **Bible Truth**. Hence, it should not be shocking to God's *chosen few* that many who complete a Bible journey ending in **Bible Deception** often come to hate **Bible Truth**.

Why? Here's the answer. Like the sly trapper in misleading Eve about what God commanded, most discover that the truth about Him, such as *JEALOUS* (KJ EX 34:14) and *VENGEFUL* (KJ Dt 32:35, Na 1:2, Ro 12:19, Heb 10:30), do not agree with their desired lifestyles, nor what they want to believe and teach about God as love. About them,

> It is written: *For such are false apostles, deceitful workers, transforming themselves into the apostles of Christ. And no marvel; for Satan himself is transformed into an angel of light. Therefore it is no great thing if his ministers also be transformed as the ministers of righteousness; whose end shall be according to their works.* (KJ 2Co 11:13-15)

Thus, these false apostles, manipulative clergy, and deceitful workers, masquerading as Apostles of Christ and servants of righteousness, presiding over many believed to be devout Christians, do everything in their power to keep the truth from being known among the *many called* by God. Therefore, only a *few* who discover and obey the full context of God's undeniable Word, through sincerity and self-determination in finding it, *are chosen* for His divine gifts and kingdoms. Furthermore, falling for whatever comes out of **Bible Deception** never has, never does, and never will dissuade God one iota in how he passes judgment on all. In other words, a million lies—having evolved into various established traditions designed for unrepentant sinners—never will amount to an ounce of truth, much less salvation.

Hence, regardless of what deceivers out of **Bible Deception** choose to preach, teach, and have their congregations falsely believe, God holds everyone accountable for their love relationship with Him. Earned it is by gaining knowledge of and belief in the complete Bible and choosing to *continue wholeheartedly in His way* (NIV 1Ki 8:23). Also,

> It is written: *And {I, Nehemiah} said, I beseech thee, O LORD God of heaven, the great and terrible God, that keepeth covenant and mercy for them that love him and observe his commandments . . .* (KJ Ne 1:5)

> It is written: *He that hath my commandments, and keepeth them, he it is that loveth me: and he that loveth me {by obeying my commands} shall be loved of my Father, and I will {then and only then} love him, and will manifest myself to him.* (KJ Jn 14:21)

Those profound Old and New Testament Scriptures conflict with deception associated with unconditional love. Unconditional love voids God's commandments, making no one accountable in their love relationship with Him. Why? The answer is twofold: (1) **obedience to His commandments is an expression of our love and respect for Him** (KJ Dt 11:1, Jn 14:15, 23-24), and (2) unconditional love has no boundaries. Hence, the notion of God the Father and Jesus separating who people are from their sins and having unconditional love for everyone—as Eve and Cain so believed about God—leads to exceedingly evil societies having abolished God's commandments. Thus, living according to God's principles in the Old and

New Testaments gives hope and protection to repentant over-comers stepping away from mainstream lies.

> It is written: *The hand of our God is upon all them for good that seek him; but his power and his wrath is against all them that forsake him.* (KJ Ezr 8:22)

> It is written: *He that hath an ear, let him hear what the Spirit saith unto the churches; He that overcometh shall **not** be hurt of the second death.* (KJ Rev 2:11)

Hence, God identifies and judges all by our actions. Guided are actions according to beliefs. Both expose the *soul* of each individual. *Choosing to continue wholeheartedly in His way* (1Ki 8:23) demonstrates a person filled with truth and discernment of right from wrong. Therefore, should you plan to enter the Kingdoms of God, those are ample reasons to avoid putting blind trust in any worship services without a thorough and correct understanding of the Bible.

A † Ω

THE ABOMINATION OF HOMOSEXUALITY

Homosexuality—referred to numerous times throughout the Bible as an **abomination**—is a Bible word not once found in Strong's Exhausted and Expanded [Main] Concordances of the Bible. **One must ask:**

> *Why would researchers for the Bible's number one concordance omit homosexuality?*

Answer:

People void of the Spirit of God will do everything possible to suppress the truth.

These prevaricators have no shame regardless of where they disguise themselves as servants of righteousness while pretending to serve God. Psychopathic they are!

Hence, manipulating the truth about God results in not such honest men and women filling the shoes of prevaricators. Living in denial of what the Bible teaches regarding homosexuality and God's vengeance leaves the floodgates of deception open for generations. Such denial is the basis behind Satan's unconditional love. So, be truthful and face the **abomination of homosexuality** throughout human history.

Although I contended with this abomination, homosexuality **without repentance** is idolatry that disqualifies people from God's kingdoms! Homosexuality in the sight of God—not Satan's world—is an addiction, illusion, and perversion: a severe mental illness that terminates the *Spirit of God* within unrepentant souls (KJ Ro 1:22-28).

Overcoming homosexuality is required to enter the Kingdoms of God. Overcoming homosexuality and all other abominations per God are acts of repentance. There are no substitutions for repentance over what God regards as evil. Therefore, regardless that the root of most homosexuality stems from any and every form of child abuse—acknowledged or concealed, recognized or unrecognized, remembered or forgotten—for one's salvation, overcoming it is required. This requirement is evident in both the Old and New Testaments.

Found are facts opposing immorality in the Old Testament: **that which Jesus Christ did not abolish**. For example, destroyed were Sodom and Gomorrah around 2100 B.C. for their homosexuality (KJ Ge 18-19). The reason was its addictive, adverse, degrading, destructive, idolatrous, and hostile effects toward holiness, especially among the few living to please God. [Such a person, living in Sodom by choice, was Lot, Abram's nephew (KJ Ge 13)].

God's revenge on the people of Sodom and Gomorrah came from a heavenly storm that carried molten sulfur above the two kingdoms. Before releasing the burning sulfur on the inhabitants living in Sodom and Gomorrah, two death angels (KJ Ge 19) scanned the territory for individuals worthy of having their lives spared from a very agitated God. The angels rescued Abram's nephew Lot, his wife, and their two daughters. Doomed were all remaining at Sodom and Gomorrah for condoning homosexuality or engaging in it.

Unfortunately for all children living in Sodom and Gomorrah, their fate was in the hands of their parents: *death by burning with molten sulfur*. This stark reality reaffirms that not all children belong to God: the truth deceivers would not want you or your children to discover, much less believe (KJ Ge 18-19, Dt 2-3).

The New Testament also addresses the abomination of homosexuality. There, homosexuality is referred to as *perversion, degrading of one's body, and sexual impurity. It causes a buildup of the wrath of God, unleashed from Heaven, against all who condone or engage in homosexu-*

ality without repenting (KJ Ro 1:18-32).

Serpents that favored or engaged in homosexuality without repenting led to same-sex marriages and to committing other adulterous abominations in many worship locations and localities. Concerning all who conduct same-sex marriages or practice other atrocities, such as playing up to deceivers,

> It is written: *Who knowing the judgment of God, that they which commit such things are worthy of death, not only do the same, but have pleasure in them that do them.* (KJ Ro 1:32)

A ✝ Ω

The Abomination of Disobedience

Now, pick up with the plight of the four survivors fleeing Sodom and Gomorrah, about whom you just read. Here, *Lot, Lot's wife, and their two daughters* were right with God. Therefore, the *death angels* allowed them to escape from Sodom to a nearby small village called Zoar. Zoar would be shielded from the molten sulfur storm since God recognized the few residing there as righteous in His sight. One of two of God's *death angels*—dispatched for the task of destroying both Sodom and Gomorrah—*warned the four not to look back as they escaped to Zoar* (KJ Ge 19:15-17).

Unfortunately—like Eve—*Lot's wife* couldn't shake off a temptation in defiance of what the angel commanded while escaping to Zoar: **look back**. Hence, regardless of the reason or need, her resistance to looking back provoked God. And although He spared her life from the molten sulfur storm for being one of His, *He held her accountable and instantly killed her by transforming her defiant breathing body into a pillar of salt* (KJ Ge 19:1–26).

Noteworthy is that this was a case where Lot's adult daughters had a choice in following in the steps of their reluctant father, defiant mother, or rebellious fiancés among homoerotics in the Kingdom of Sodom (NIV Ge 19:12–16). Fortunately for them, the two chose to follow their father. Unfortunately, their fiancés decided to remain in Sodom and experienced God's deadly vengeance and wrath with all the other remaining inhabitants of both kingdoms. **However, soon after Sodom and Gomorrah met up with doomsday, Lot's two daughters made their father drunk to commit incest, resulting in each bearing a cursed illegitimate son:** *Moab, father of the cursed Moabites, and Benammi, father of the doomed children of Ammon* (KJ Ge 19:29–38, Zep 2:8,9).

A † Ω

THE ABOMINATION OF DOUBT AND FEAR

Look at another abomination after the destruction of Sodom and Gomorrah, causing God to move against people he hated. It occurred in 1446 B.C. over Israel's refusal to enter the *Promised Land* (KJ Nu 13–14), also known as *the land of* {Ham's son} *Canaan* (KANE un). The event involved up to a million and a half people coming out of Egypt as Hebrew slaves.

To fully understand the historical magnitude of this

Biblical event, allow Nelson to enlighten you about *the land of Canaan—the Promised Land*—since it is often at the core of current and world events.

> **The** *Promised Land—a beautiful territory of* [abundance in] *purple* [dye]*—was where Canaan settled. Canaan was the fourth son of Ham.* [Recall that Ham was the third of three sons born to Noah, who survived the Great Flood by being one of eight people on Noah's Ark. However, Canaan is not to be confused with Adam and Eve's son, Cain, who settled in Nod with a mysterious wife.]
>
> *Ham's descendants included the Jebusites, Zemarites,* and the Philistines (KJ Ge 10:6-20)]. [*They became collectively known as Canaanites. The Canaanites were a tribe of people who conspired against God. Unfortunately, they settled throughout the land that God would come to promise to Abram, his wife Sarai, and descendants of their miracle child of promise, Isaac* [descendants of Noah's obedient son, Shem (KJ Ge 11:10-32)].[38]

Concerning their escape from Egypt, where the Israelites resided for four hundred and thirty years (KJ Ex 12:40-41), while adhering to God's voice, Moses—appointed by God as their divine leader—acted upon what God said. Moses, therefore, sent the leader from each of Israel's twelve tribes to spy on the inhabitants of the *Promised Land*. On their journey, they saw giant humanoids, **up to thirteen feet tall**—a tribe of *Nephilim* from a primitive race known as *Rephaites* in addition to *Canaanites* (KJ

---

[38] *Ham's descendants,* Nelson's New Illustrated Bible Dictionary

Ge 6:4; Nu 13:32–33; Dt 2:10–12 and 20–21, 3:1–11; Am 2:9). Fearful, ten of the twelve returned with a doubtful and negative report. Only Caleb of the tribe of Judah and Joshua [Oshea] of the tribe of Ephraim insisted that the take-over was possible with the help of God. They knew God fiercely hated the *Nephilim* and *Canaanites;* otherwise, He would not have commanded the Israelites to drive them out and possess their territory. He had His justified reasons!

> It is written: *Speak not thou in thine heart, after that the* Lord *thy God hath cast them out from before thee, saying, For my righteousness the* Lord *hath brought me in to possess this land: but {rather} for the wickedness of these nations the* Lord *doth drive them out from before thee. {It is} Not for thy righteousness, or for the uprightness of thine heart, dost thou go to possess their land: but for the wickedness of these nations the* Lord *thy God doth drive them out from before thee, and that he may perform the word which the* Lord *sware unto thy fathers, Abraham, Isaac, and Jacob.* (KJ Dt 9:4–5)

Due to the faithless mindset of ten of the twelve who came across the fearless Canaanites and Rephaites, outvoted by ten votes were Caleb and Joshua. Hence, cast by popular vote was the decision not to cross into the Promised Land (KJ Nu 13:17–33 and 14:1–23). *Unfortunately for the entire Israelite nation, infuriated was God. Why?* **He has little to no interest in political correctness or popularity for fearful liars who rebel against His commands.** *He immediately killed the ten doubters, whom He quickly came to hate, regardless of whether they followed in the* *steps of the twelve patriarchs as leaders of the twelve tribes of Israel* (KJ Nu 14:36-38).

Furthermore, all others wandered for a long time: one year, for each of the forty days, tribal leaders went out to spy (KJ Nu 14:34). Moreover, He had all 603,550+ remaining men qualified to serve in Israel's army who left out of Egypt and were twenty years old and up (KJ Nu 1:45-47), *die in the wilderness because of trusting the doubters over doing what He commanded* (KJ Nu 14:28-30). Hence, only Joshua of the tribe of Ephraim and Caleb of Judah—rewarded for what they tried to have their Israelite brothers, sisters, and cousins do forty years earlier—went into the Promised Land forty years late. The multitude included the children who left out of Egypt forty years earlier and their children.

[God was **not** time-conscious for the billions of years of the earth's evolution. However, He became aware of time as of 4104 B.C. upon His creation of Adam. Therefore, when He passed a forty-year sentence on the Israelites 2,658 years later, that forty-year sentence meant not one day short or one day beyond forty years. *The Israelites left out of Egypt in 1446 B.C., the day following the Passover* (KJ Ge 11-12), *and they crossed into the Promised Land forty years later in 1406 B.C., the day after the Passover* (KJ Jos 5:6-12).]

A † Ω

THE ABOMINATION OF ARROGANCE

Before the Israelites finally moved into the *Promised*

Land, God commanded Joshua, leader of the new Israelite generation, to have all occupants of the *Promised Land*—whom he hated—annihilated. The *Canaanites* and the *Rephaites*, feeling secure in the land they occupied as free-will thinkers, resulted in an arrogant, blissful lifestyle. The only problem with their evil ways, fueled by deception, was having been void of the *Spirit of God* (KJ Nu 14:9). Thus, they created the saying, *"What you don't know can't hurt you."* *"What you don't know can't hurt you"* is what you better find out before reaching the point of being annihilated: precisely what became of them.

In other words, high-minded arrogance in a fantasy world of rapture [pleasure], evil ideology, and ecstasy on the part of the original inhabitants of the *Promised Land* resulted in letting down their guard. After all, who would dare come against *giants* who occupied the *Promised Land* **before and after** the great flood of 2448 B.C. and were descendants of the original mortals God created and frightened away Israel's little spies forty years earlier? Nevertheless, the *Canaanites* and *Rephaites* failed to realize they did not intimidate God. Instead, He set out to annihilate them with the help of a *Kingsman* in charge of thousands: Joshua (Jos).

Hence, know that God does not change His mind to destroy unrepentant nations once determined they are! The only exceptions are:

> (1) allow the righteous few to escape to safety as He allowed with Noah's family of eight and with Lot and his two daughters before their incest episode,

OR

(2) to have a *Kingsman* convince Him otherwise, as did Moses in the Israelite camp during their forty years of wandering in the wilderness.

God's command to Moses and Joshua—to destroy or drive out all humanoids residing in the *Promised Land*—was an acknowledgment that those inhabitants had reached the point of abandonment with God. Biblically speaking, they reached Omega: their point of extermination.

> It is written: {The LORD said to Moses:} *And ye shall divide the land by lot for an inheritance among your families: and to the more ye shall give the more inheritance, and to the fewer ye shall give the less inheritance: every man's inheritance shall be in the place where his lot falleth; according to the tribes of your fathers ye shall inherit.*
>
> *But if ye will not drive out the inhabitants of the land from before you; then it shall come to pass, that those which ye let remain of them shall be pricks in your eyes, and thorns in your sides, and shall vex you in the land wherein ye dwell. Moreover it shall come to pass, that I shall do unto you, as I thought to do unto them.*
>
> (KJ Nu 33:54–56)

Indeed, the LORD held to His promise since Israel ran in fear of the *Canaanites* and *Rephaites* under Moses. However, after the death of Moses, the new generation overwhelmingly went forth as God commanded.

> It is written: Now after the death of Moses the servant of the LORD it came to pass, that the LORD

spake unto Joshua the son of Nun, Moses' minister, saying, *Moses my servant is dead; now therefore arise, go over this Jordan {River}, thou, and all this people, unto the land which I do give to them, even to the children of Israel. Every place that the sole of your foot shall tread upon, that have I given unto you, as I said unto Moses. From the wilderness and this Lebanon even unto the great river, the river Euphrates, all the land of the Hittites, and unto the great sea {Mediterranean} toward the going down of the sun, shall be your coast.*

There shall not any man be able to stand before thee all the days of thy life: as I was with Moses, so I will be with thee: I will not fail thee, nor forsake thee. Be strong and of a good courage: for unto this people shalt thou divide for an inheritance the land, which I sware unto their fathers to give them. Only be thou strong and very courageous, that thou mayest observe to do according to all the law, which Moses my servant commanded thee: turn not from it to the right hand or to the left, that thou mayest prosper whithersoever thou goest.

This book of the law shall not depart out of thy mouth; but thou shalt meditate therein day and night, that thou mayest observe to do according to all that is written therein: for then thou shalt have good success. Have not I commanded thee? Be strong and of a good courage; be not afraid, neither be thou dismayed: for the Lord thy God is with thee whithersoever thou goest {PROVIDED YOU OBEY!}.

(KJ Jos 1:1-9)

By obeying God's command to drive out all humanoids who possessed the *Promised Land*—apart from a few **select** individuals residing there—the Israelites, under Joshua's steadfast and fearless leadership, remained in God's grace. However, once Joshua's generation passed away, leaving a few remaining nations to annihilate, the Israelites ignored God's commands (KJ Jdg 2:6-15). That had a profoundly adverse rippling effect on Israel to this day, precisely as God so promised it would (KJ Nu 33:55-56, Jos 24:20). For starters, it resulted in their losing the divine protection of God, who brought their ancestors out of Egypt and worked miracles among them.

Hence, the Bible teaches that God denies safekeeping and assurance to most, regardless of claiming to be shielded by Him. For example, doing what is humanitarian or politically correct in opposition to God, such as refusing to serve justice against the wicked, will provoke His anger and wrath against such people. That is a Divine Law that never fails over time. *As in days of old, God will turn His back on rebellious, ill-informed fools who blindly trust liars, thieves, murderers, and destroyers* (KJ Dt 28, Jos, Jdg, 1Sam, 1Ki, 2Ki, Ro 1:18-32, 1Co 10:1-13).

A † Ω

The Abomination of Child Sacrifice

It is written: **Thou shalt not murder** (NIV Ex 20:13).

Def: **Human Sacrifice**—*a pagan rite in which a human being, often the firstborn child, was offered to a god to* *atone for sin or secure the god's favor.* {The Bible's} *God distinctly prohibited the Hebrews* {and His people throughout the ages} *from imitating their heathen neighbors by offering up children as sacrifices.*[39] (KJ Lev 20:2–5; Dt 18:10; 2Ki 3:26–27, 16:3, 21:6; Jer 19:4–6 and 32–35).

God prohibits taking the lives of children among the people He recognizes as His. Sparing them was illustrated early on when He forbade Abraham from offering up his second son Isaac, **Child of Promise,** as a sacrifice (KJ Ge 22:1–19). On the contrary, He cares less about the children of the adversaries who forsake His commands (KJ Ex 11–12, Eze 9:3–6, Mt 13:38–40).

God caring less about the children of heathens takes us to the abomination of child sacrifice through abortion, a highly profitable business worldwide. Abortion also proved to be the most effective means of exterminating Caucasians in the USA, with the passage of Roe vs. Wade in 1973. Should you live in the USA, attend the next pro-abortion rally in your location. There, you will find a handful of people of color, if any, among a packed house of cold-hearted Caucasian women protesting the murder of perfectly healthy, unborn children.

According to accurate statistics, people of color are far less enthusiastic about having their unborn children aborted. Murdered are many more unborn Caucasian children than any other race in the USA.

---

[39] *Child Sacrifice,* Nelson's New Illustrated Bible Dictionary

Caucasian abortions accounted for are as high as three million yearly, Hispanics under a million, Blacks hover at 500,000, and all others are near zero.[40]

Ironically, Roe vs. Wade intended to reduce the population of people of color. However, by *Divine Law*, no one escapes the consequences of his actions (Ester, Isa 3:11, Daniel, Rev 20:13)! Hence, the curse of Roe vs. Wade fell mostly on unwanted Caucasian children. [Roe vs. Wade was enacted in 1973 under President Richard M. Nixon—impeached afterward, Congress, and an even worse Supreme Court. In 2022, overturned was Roe vs. Wade, resulting in madness: forcing heathens to have children they despise, leading to doomsday by overpopulation and wickedness.]

Discounting illness, rape, and other circumstances, abortion is child sacrifice. Hence, Christians avoid aborting legitimate children regardless of justified carnal and satanic reasons to murder a perfectly healthy baby. However, that's not so for children born of pagans. For example, Judas Iscariot was one such child, regardless that Jesus chose him as an apostle. In the end, Christ referred to him as a *"devil"* (KJ Jn 6:70) and cursed him by saying,

> *"It would have been better had he never been born."* (KJ Mk 14:21)

Furthermore, history illustrates that human sacrifice

---

[40] Wm. Robert Johnston, *Abortions in the United States by Race*: www.Johnstonsarchive.net/policy/abortion/USA_abortion_by_race.html. (2019).

is tolerable within demonic cults, gangs, evil regimes, religious fanatics, and many claiming insanity after committing violent crimes. Moreover, while often granted undeserved mercy and grace to these criminals at the public's expense, little or no justice is served to their victims. **There is an underlying mystery for the unfair practice of allowing undeserved mercy and grace to real criminals while being merciless to the falsely accused. Revealed it would be.**

A † Ω

In summary, **ABOMINATIONS THAT CAUSE DESOLATION** are all about the defiance of God. Living abominably—as a Bible believer—is inviting major trouble. Living abominably—as a Bible hater—is a means of fulfilling one's devious desires and ending up in Hell. Therefore, no matter how thin you slice evils, giving in to abominations leads to the second death (KJ Rev 2:11, 20:14, 21:8).

Next, the Bible teaches that God has no regard for most people because they have no genuine desire for Him, much less have to obey His righteous, life-sustaining commandments. Ironically, and without looking themselves in the mirror, these *worshipers of deception* falsely regard His *elect*, who rely on Him and express love to Him by adhering to His commands, often as deplorable and worse (Mt 5:10-12). These slandering nefarious souls hypocritically stand paranoid for Satan against any who oppose their corruption and demonic ideologies. Also, attempting to save *devils* has dire consequences because, per Jesus Christ,

> It is written: *"It would have been better had they never been born."* (KJ Mk 14:21)

Expounded in the next chapter and AGAPE, Part B, is that revealed mystery.

Hence, **ABOMINATIONS THAT CAUSE DESOLATION** should only concern Bible believers. Otherwise, it is hypocritical for Bible deniers—good or evil—to display remorse over wickedness that causes extinction unless their inner being [soul] is agitated over God's laws.

Annoyed by God's principles, it brings to mind something to consider. Shocking as this may sound, it is not the government's responsibility to display *The Ten Commandments* publicly. That responsibility rests with the people in charge of God's churches! After all, are not church grounds the most appropriate places to find monuments of God's expectations? ABSOLUTELY! Then why aren't they there? Did Christ unconditionally abolish God's rules for the mainstream? NEVER! God's commandments are an expression of His love. **Obeying them demonstrates commitment, faith, and trust because it expresses gratitude, love, and respect to Him, which Jesus modeled how to fulfill as *the Way*** (KJ Jn 14:6, Ro 13:8-10). Any church abolishing God's commandments—*the Way*—is a satanic church. Bible-believing Christians must avoid these.

V. DESTRUCTIVE FORCES OF SATAN

DESOLATION

It is written: *Eloi, Eloi, lama sabachthani?*
—which means,
My God, My God, why have you forsaken me? (NIV Mk 15:34)

© *Yaroslav Gerzhedovich*

To fully understand the magnitude of *AGAPE*, the *many called* by God must come to grips with the reality that numerous evil forces are out to destroy civilized humanity for one reason or another. Those demonic forces play significant roles in the lives of all who forsake God's principles, knowingly or unknowingly.

Therefore, regardless that someone forsakes God unknowingly all are held accountable for *righteousness and the truth of His Word* (KJ Ps 37:39, 96:13; Eph 5:1-21; 1Th 4:1-12). Both are conditions for one's salvation. It is the same whenever someone unknowingly drives through a stop sign and injures or kills others. Since the driver did not obey the law by stopping, regardless of all reasons or excuses under normal circumstances, that person remains accountable for the death, destruction, injuries, and grief he inflicted on others.

Hence, this chapter is devoted to understanding and coming to grips with a shocking reality. It concerns demonic forms of human annihilators while striving to instill more in-depth principles of *AGAPE* in overcoming all evils. Meeting those conditions saves lives! Unfortunately, *only a few out of many* (Mt 22:14) heed those conditions. They are individuals warranted by ALPHA AND OMEGA — **Genesis through Revelation: The First and the Last, The Beginning and the End, Jesus Christ** (Rev 22:13). So, pursue these phenomena and how they affect humanity.

A ✝ Ω

SUPERNATURAL ANNIHILATORS

The Bible teaches about set times when demonic beings cause death and destruction supernaturally. Thus, extermination by demonic creatures raises a fundamental question:

> *How is it possible to predict and recognize the extermination of people by forces of evil or by God?*

To answer that profound life and death question, one must first become familiar with the *spirit of evil* and its vast array of *deceivers* and *manitous* introduced and discussed throughout the Bible. Collectively, the Bible refers to these and their constituents as *enemies* or *adversaries of God* (NIV Heb 10:26–27). They include *serpents, devils,* and *demons,* of which there are variations, and their followers: *worshipers of deception.* Now, examine and distinguish each of these destructive forces of evil.

A † Ω

THE ENEMIES OF GOD
1. Serpents

> It is written: {Speaking to His disciples, Jesus said} *Behold, I give unto you power to tread on **serpents and scorpions**, and over all the power of the enemy: and nothing shall by any means hurt you.* (KJ Lk 10:19)

As a book filled with figurative language, the Bible is intriguing. For example, expressions such as *adder, asps, brood of vipers, blind guides, cobras, dogs, dragons, pigs, lions, scorpions,* **serpents**, *swine, tempters, and thieves* are metaphors used by Jesus Christ and the Prophets. They used these to identify all deliberately engaged in misrepresenting God's complete, undeniable, rightly interpreted Word. Such prevaricators are **unrepentant** people that God and Jesus undoubtedly hate and will continue to condemn throughout eternity.

> It is written: *For their rock is not as our Rock, even our enemies themselves being judges. For their vine is of the vine of Sodom, and of the fields of Gomorrah: their grapes are grapes of gall, their clusters are bitter. Their wine* {fraud, misleading preaching and teaching as well as conducting demonic ceremonies, such as same-sex marriages} *is*

> *the poison of dragons, and the cruel venom of asps Is not this laid up in store with me, and sealed up among my treasures?* (KJ Dt 32:31-34)

The answer to that profoundly spiritual question is emphatical: *"NO!"* The truth is that those facts have been *God's Spoken Word* throughout eternity. Unfortunately, whenever *serpents* take charge of the churches, they falsify the full context of the Scriptures with lies and snippets. Unbeknown to their congregations, many evolve into *worshipers of deception*, regarding the Bible as contemptuous compared to brainwashed. Hence, God's regard for *vipers* {KJ Mt 12:34} is lower than animals because they believe and instill deceit about Him and slander righteous people who oppose them. In addition to *pulpit serpents*, they include politicians fabricating lies, reporters falsifying news, and all other corrupt souls in authority.

So, look now at how God, through allegory, addressed a typical *serpent:* a metaphor for the humanoid that tempted Eve through deception.

> It is written: And the LORD God said unto the *serpent, Because thou hast done this, thou art cursed above all cattle, and above every beast of the field; upon thy belly shalt thou go, and dust shalt thou eat all the days of thy life. And I will put enmity between thee and the woman, and between thy seed and her seed; it shall bruise thy head, and thou shalt bruise his heel.* (KJ Ge 3:14-15)

Now, open your eyes and ears so that you may see and

hear the true meaning of the allegory using the noun *serpent* as a metaphor. Here, you discover the *serpent* as being a charming but abominable manipulative human being, falsely misleading Eve in the presence of Adam and God Himself.

> It is written: And the LORD God said unto the *serpent* {a man of comprehension}, *Because thou hast done this* {influenced Eve who persuaded Adam to defy my command}, *thou art cursed above all cattle, and above every beast of the field* {individuals and groups void of God's spirit}; *upon thy belly shalt thou go, and dust shalt thou eat* {being forever denied the Kingdoms of God and Heaven} *all the days of thy life: And I will put enmity* {hostility, hatred, ill will, animosity, antagonism[41]} *between thee and the woman, and between thy seed and her seed; it* {the righteous} *shall bruise thy head* {bring to justice}, *and thou shalt bruise his heel* {persecute}. (KJ Ge 3:14–15)

Time for a review! The *serpent* that spoke lies to tempt Eve was abominable and flattering. He was a human being, filled with trickery and manipulation. How is it possible to know that for sure? Biblically, and reaffirming what was said, the noun, *serpent*, is a metaphor for an intentional bald-faced liar, parallel to *dragons, asps, a brood of vipers, and cobras* God condemned to Hell.

It is written: *Their wine is the poison of dragons*

---

[41] *Enmity*, Websters Encyclopedic Unabridged Dictionary.

{psychopaths}, *and the cruel venom of asps {cobras-sociopaths}.* (KJ Dt 32:33)

Those appearances of intentional liars—driven to provoke God's people to anger or to entice them to act out against God's commandments—prove just how bold these genuinely wicked people are, even in the presence of God. Falsely hailed as *angels of light* by massive numbers of *worshipers of deception*, they are the heroes of evil (KJ 2Co 11:14-15).

Hence, the narrow road to salvation includes recognizing possible *serpents* presiding over the church or religious and government classes you attend. Without thorough Bible knowledge, even the brightest minds will likely be unaware of the truth. Why? It is because, if under the spell of liars, **"What you do not know cannot hurt you"** is their primary strategy of enslavement.

A ✝ Ω

----

2. Devils

It is written: *The thief {devils} cometh not, but for to steal, and to kill, and to destroy: I {Christ} am come that they {God's elect} might have life, and that they might have it more abundantly.* (KJ Jn 10:10)

Def: **Devil**—*1. a subordinate evil spirit at enmity with God, and having power to afflict humans both with bodily disease and with spiritual corruption. 2.*

an atrociously wicked, cruel, or ill-tempered person. 3. a person who is very clever in wickedness.[42]

It is written: Then was Jesus led up of the Spirit into the wilderness to be tempted of the ***devil***. And when he had fasted forty days and forty nights, he was afterward an hungred. And when the tempter came to him, he said, *If thou be the Son of God, command that these stones be made bread.*

But he answered and said, **It is written, Man shall not live by bread alone, but by every word that proceedeth out of the mouth of God.**

Then the ***devil*** taketh him up into the holy city, and setteth him on a pinnacle of the temple, And saith unto him, *If thou be the Son of God, cast thyself down: for it is written, He shall give his angels charge concerning thee: and in their hands they shall bear thee up, lest at any time thou dash thy foot against a stone.*

Jesus said unto him, **It is written again, Thou shalt not tempt the Lord thy God.**

Again, the ***devil*** taketh him up into an exceeding high mountain, and sheweth him all the kingdoms of the world, and the glory of them; And saith unto him, *All these things will I give thee, if thou wilt fall down and worship me.*

Then saith Jesus unto him, **Get thee hence, Satan:**

---

[42] *Devil*, Websters Encyclopedic Unabridged Dictionary..

> *for it is written, Thou shalt worship the Lord thy God, and him only shalt thou serve.*
>
> Then the *devil* leaveth him, and, behold, angels came and ministered unto him.
>
> (KJ Mt 4:1-11)

Kingsmen—*truth seekers*—are not *devils*, as *serpents* and their *worshipers of deception* would have you believe. The Bible makes known who the anti-Christ genuinely are; however, it takes the wisdom of God's complete Word to recognize *devils* and *serpents*. For example,

> It is written: Jesus said unto them {the clergy}, *If God were your Father, ye would love me: for I proceeded forth and came from God; neither came I of myself, but he sent me. Why do ye not understand my speech? Even because ye cannot hear my word.*
>
> *Ye are of your father the devil {Allah}, and the lusts of your father ye will do. He was a murderer from the beginning, and abode not in the truth, because there is no truth in him. When he speaketh a lie, he speaketh of his own: for he is a liar, and the father of it.*
>
> (KJ Jn 8:42-44)

Although addressing the clergy out to destroy Him, Jesus made clear that statements coming from very high-profile preachers, teachers, evangelists, and their fool-hearted followers are full of loopholes. For example, they quickly claim that *"Jesus loves you unconditionally"* or that *"God *does not hate you."*

Let me clarify the Bible: Who's to say that *"Jesus loves you"* and that *"God does not hate you"* should you engage in lying, stealing, murdering, or destroying? I assure you that only *serpents, devils,* and *constituents* speaking their native languages would make liars, thieves, murderers, and destroyers believe that Jesus and God love them unconditionally. The second lie that these prevaricators use to support their first lie is: *"God separates who a person is from what a person does."* Nothing could be further from Bible facts! (Ps 92:7; Isa 3:11; Rev 20:12-13, 15; Rev 22:12-14)

First, God is a gentleman. He does not enforce *His Spoken Word*—*Rhema*—on the clergy who embed lies among their fool-hearted constituents, such as, *"Jesus loves you no matter what."* Such individuals stand grossly out of order with God, Jesus Christ, and the Holy Spirit. Such accommodating deception is among the numerous abominations that cause desolation.

In John 8:42-44, Jesus left no room for forgiveness or mercy on the part of prevaricators who intentionally led to Hell, *many called* to God's kingdoms. Why? It is because *Jesus came to destroy the works of devils* (KJ 1Jn 3:8): precisely who and what all other *devils* are out to protect.

> It is written: *Little children, let no man deceive you: he that doeth righteousness is righteous, even as he is righteous. He that committeth sin*

is of the devil; for the devil sinneth from the beginning. For this purpose the Son of God was manifested, **that he might destroy the works of the devil** {not condone it nor save the world}. *Whosoever is born of God doth not commit sin; for His seed* {God's Spirit} *remaineth in him: and he cannot sin because he is born of God. In this the* {few} *children of God are manifest, and the* {many} *children of the devil.* **Whosoever doeth not righteousness is not of God, neither he that loveth not his** {obedient God-fearing Bible believing} **brother.** (KJ 1Jn 3:7-10)

It is essential to point out that since *serpents* often subject themselves to the desires of *devils* in charge, *serpents* cannot belong to the Kingdoms of God any more than can *devils*. For example, all *vipers* leading God's people into worshiping the gods of unconditional love while desecrating worship locations all fall into that category. The only escape is to reject and abhor these highly influential, sometimes famous individuals and groups, out to void God's way. Unless one does, he may never become qualified to go home to be with the Lord, regardless of what his obituary and religion may claim.

Therefore, using Bible language, examine a few well-known *devils* and decide if the love of God and the Bible's Jesus applies to all, no matter what. When murdered for no justifiable reason, such as children doing the right thing by attending school or people enjoying an outing or traveling, you can be sure their assailants came out of the Kingdom of Satan. Here are five examples of the six *devils* involved:

(1) The satanic influence was the driving force behind *eighteen-year-old seniors Dylan Klebold and Eric Harris, who engaged in the murder of countless fellow students and teachers at Columbine High School in Columbine, Colorado, on April 20, 1999. Their aftermath—far short of the 600+ they planned to gun down—left twelve fellow students and a teacher shot dead while wounding twenty-one others.*[43] before finally doing the right thing by taking their own lives.

(2) The satanic influence was the driving force behind *James Holmes' massacre at the Century Movie Theater in Aurora, Colorado, on July 20, 2012. On sight, Holmes killed 12 people while wounding 70 others. What spared the lives of many was that Holmes' assault rifle jammed. Holmes, who lived on [at taxpayers' expense], was convicted of 24 counts of first-degree murder, 140 counts of attempted first-degree murder, and one count of possessing explosives.*[44]

(3) The satanic influence was the driving force behind twenty-year-old *Adam Peter Lanza, who—before committing suicide—fatally shot his mother, then went on and riddled the bodies of twenty first-graders and six educators with as many as eleven bullets each. His deadly*

---

[43] *Columbine Massacre*, WikipediA Encyclopedia, Wikimedia Foundation (San Francisco, Ca.)— as well as Fox News (12 11 Avenue of the Americas, New York, NY).

[44] *Century Movie Theater Massacre*, Ibid.

assault occurred on December 14, 2012, at peace-loving, unsuspecting Sandy Hook Elementary School in Newtown, Connecticut.[45]

(4) The satanic influence was the driving force behind *twenty-eight-year-old Co-Pilot Andreus Lubitz, who intentionally flew Germanwings Airbus Flight 9525 head-on at full throttle into the French Alps on March 24, 2015. His act of premeditated mass murder and suicide resulted in the horrifying deaths of 144 passengers, including 16 tenth graders — 14 girls and two boys — and their two teachers.*[46]

(5) A replica of the Sandy Hook massacre occurred at *Robb Elementary School in Uvalde, Texas, on May 24, 2022, by an 18-year-old devil, Salvador Ramos, leaving dead two teachers, nineteen students, and himself* (Epoch Times).

For months, Klebold, Harris, Holmes, Lanza, Lubitz, and Ramos freely chose to form partnerships with others who influenced them with fantasies of mass murder among members of their own or nearby communities. As highly intelligent and decisive murderers they freely chose to become by reading, studying, believing, and obeying all the elements necessary to execute mass murder among people in their own or nearby communities, they fulfilled their mission as *devils.* Their betrayal of their own or nearby communities reflected Judas Iscariot, a man Christ also referred to as a *devil* since he was a liar, a thief, a murderer, and a destroyer (KJ Jn 6:70–71).

---

[45] *Sandy Hook Elementary Massacre,* Ibid.

[46] *Germanwings Airbus Flight 9525 Crash,* Ibid.

The remaining question is not why Klebold, Harris, Holmes, Lanza, Lubitz, and Ramos committed mass murder of innocent and helpless people among whom they lived. Instead, it was more about who they initially turned to and idolized for guidance in making it happen. If you are willing to accept the possibilities to that profound question, you might fumble over the answer.

The harsh reality of their mass murders is that these *devils* did not act alone. How is it possible to know that? It is from others that we learn human behaviors and patterns. That reflects far back when Cain learned—**from someone else**—how to murder Abel. Hence, they were well-trained executioners and not judges and juries.

Art of Massacre is what these young psychopathic *devils* carried out (KJ Jdg 8:28-9:6). *Art of Massacre* is premeditated, cold-blooded murder of innocent, unarmed, and unsuspecting people. It has no regard or regrets for the innocent lives it destroys. That includes children of any age, parents, educators, athletes, the elderly, and people in the workforce. It also entails unarmed military comrades commanded to trust an enemy who infiltrates their ranks and sets out to murder them. Unlike the Art of War, the *Art of Massacre* is unconditional, unlimited, and without boundaries. Therefore, those engaging in the *Art of Massacre* do not heed the law. Furthermore, although such disguise themselves as *angels of light* and humanitarians, they are evil-minded people with a destructive and deadly mission riddled with anger, deception, fantasies, greed, hatred, lies, power, religion, vengeance, and likely out for fame. Self-centered they are.

Art of Massacre begins with a host, either human or spiritual, who recruits aspiring, young but often rejected loners, tested to become potential executioners of others in their own or nearby communities. Given the respect and attention, these sometimes dismissed loners often long for but never receive or perceive from local people, they are fed all the evidence or lies necessary to influence themselves to believe that people in their communities, schools, or workplaces are nuisances. After months of encouragement, these harmless young recruits transform into *lonely wolves*, willing to carefully plan and execute as many people living among themselves as possible. They are then wholly esteemed into believing that their deadly mission is an act of heroism or an action of God, remembered forever.

Think back on Cain made to believe that he would gain God's approval by murdering his brother, Abel, whom God loved. Thus, Klebold, Harris, Holmes, Lanza, Lubitz, and Ramos followed in Cain's steps under the influence of evil, lawless, anti-Christ perpetrators.

As cooperation increases to kill members of their communities through increasingly false promises and secrecy on the part of their host, these lone wolves move up in rank to that of *devils on a deadly mission*. Hence, the *Art of Massacre* is whenever unsuspecting amateur *devils* on a fatal mission kill people in their own or nearby communities. The highest level of the *Art of Massacre* is for a host to have his enemies destroy each other. Ironically, that dooms the executioners, as well as their victims, because, as Jesus put it allegorically,

> It is written: *Ye are the salt of the earth: but if the salt have lost his savour, wherewith shall it be salted? It is thenceforth good for nothing, but to be cast out, and to be trodden under foot of men.* (KJ Mt 5:13)

However, there is still more shock to their cause. The death of the executioners leaves no opportunity for their interrogation! Allegorically speaking, it kills two birds with one stone: reap what you have sown while the mastermind returns to being a drone. There, drones take on fresh recruits and begin another cycle of *Art of Massacre*. Thus, the cold-blooded murders that Klebold, Harris, Holmes, Lanza, Lubitz, and Ramos effectively committed against innocent people in their own or nearby communities resulted in zero casualties to the masterminds behind their atrocities. The masterminds they came to esteem, respect, and trust started them down their journey of cold-blooded murder. That put them all at having committed the ultimate act of the *Art of Massacre*.

From a spiritual aspect, *Art of Massacre* goes as follows: On the event day, the host abandons his highly-trained *devils*, leaving them without a trace. There, the highly-trained *devils* find themselves in the place they feared most. They then convince themselves that they are out serving in the best interest of humanity, seeking revenge, or merely doing the will of God. Out of pride, while being committed to murder at the point of no return and abandonment, they view themselves as martyrs without any other options. Martyrdom is their reward, but it is no longer a fantasy. That is where suicide often takes its deadly toll if they have not already been killed or taken into custody. It is no less whenever an evil host forces young people—one way or the other—to carry out the ultimate sacrifice as a suicide bomber or some other means of mass-murdering through self-annihilation.

Hence, the *Art of Massacre* leads to one primary question concerning the same somewhat forgotten and cleaned-up massacres at Columbine High School, Century Movie Theater, Sandy Hook and Robb Elementary Schools, and Germanwings Flight 9525:

> *Who or what got them started with a passion for killing helpless, innocent, unsuspecting people among whom they lived?*

That is a crucial question to find out. Why? It is because, by all indications, their horrendous actions were only models of what lies ahead for God-forsaken communities and nations. How is it possible to know that with certainty? The answer: Whenever deception about God takes hold, kind and innocent people become vulnerable to *devils*, demonized synergy, and other forms of destruction as God withdraws Himself from their communities.

Not to be confused with lone sheep out to please God through righteousness, *devils* start as *lone wolves*. The *psychopaths* they are, *lone wolves* set out to satisfy their egos by proudly lying, stealing, and destroying. And in communities where God has withdrawn Himself, *lone wolves* will develop into *devils*. Once established, they go out roaming here, there, and everywhere, doing what *devils* cherish: to instill fear by destroying and killing.

> It was precisely what Ali Muhammad Brown randomly carried out in 2014. He started in Seattle, Washington. On April 27, Muhammad gun-downed Leroy Henderson. On June 1, he gun-downed Ahmed Said and Dewone Anderson-Young. He then drove cross-country, where on June 25, he cold-heartedly gun-downed Brendan Tevlin, a nineteen-year-old Caucasian All-American Honors Student from Livingston, New Jersey. *Art of Massacre also occurred in Las Vegas in ten minutes on October 1, 2017, as high-powered bullets rang out into a crowd of thousands, gunning down 59 while injuring 850 others.*[47]

Hence, the *Art of Massacre* is regularly the ultimate act of terrorism synergized in God-forsaken nations. Rejoicing supporters of the executioners minimize such heinous acts with excuses like: *"This type of thing happens in big cities."* Biblically speaking, they are a *brood of vipers*.

Had Klebold, Harris, Holmes, Lanza, Lubitz, Ramos, Brown, and other heartless assassins invested time and energy in God's word, they may have become mighty warriors for God rather than lone wolves for Allah. Why? It is because all were fearless but misguided individuals committed to their cause. It is the type of commitment God's

---

[47] *Las Vegas Massacre*, WikipediA Encyclopedia.

saints need to expose the truth and power of His Word without apologies or fear. Instead, their acts of murder proved how ultimately a success the *adversaries of God* have become (NIV Heb 10:26-27). Like Cain—void of the *Spirit of God*, the illusionary teaching and inspiration of cobras led them to believe that Jesus unconditionally forever would love them but frowned upon their deeds.

While on *devils*, beware that mental illness—such as insanity—is not a Biblical excuse in executing the *Art of Massacre* or any other form of the heartless murder of innocent people. What is true is that people who engage in cruel, premeditated crimes must face justice. **Not one of God's Bible-believing, *Spirit-filled*, law-abiding followers should ever set out to condone, empathize with, tolerate, or find excuses for *devils*. No one should set out to forgive or show mercy to them, all of which would reliably result in a backlash, at some point or another, whenever giving in to the *enemies of God*!**

Recall the backlash for giving into evil in Paris, France, on Friday the 13th, in November 2015? According to CNN, murdered were 130 innocent, peaceful, unarmed people, while 494 others were injured: 98 in critical condition. Hence, God is not looking for excuses to condone and protect *devils* disguised as *angels of light* (KJ 2Co 11:14-15). By allowing such, there are no second chances for innocent lives caught in the crossfire on the part of psychopaths out to gun down innocent, law-abiding people. It all boils down to this expressed best in allegory.

To believe that you can allow a Rattlesnake into your

country, home, or public office, and through kindness, love, and its distribution of propaganda at your expense—whom it is out to destroy—that it will transform into Prince Charming looking out for your best interest.

Once allowed into your territory, regardless of how much kindness you show and toy with a Rattlesnake, it will forever be a Rattlesnake out to strike you dead. Once it completes its deadly mission, other prominent vipers influence Satan's media and are allowed to condone other heinous acts of murder. For example, other prevaricators would piously broadcast the following without shame after a massacre:

"Now is the time for all to be more compassionate, more tolerant, and more understanding to our Leftist Movement and Islam."

That condones their atrocities for permission to enter another's business or public office, expand their territory, and repeat what evils they have been doing for centuries. *Vipers* will never transform into charming princes looking out for your best interest, regardless of electing them as President, Governor, or any other high office. Turning loose their deceptive propaganda in school districts under siege through bribery becomes their breeding ground for the *Art of Massacre,* as do violent video games.

The Bible teaches there is no grace, forgiveness, or mercy on the part of God and Jesus against individuals who bask in evil without remorse. Reserved are grace, forgiveness, and compassion on the part of God for the few He recognizes as being *poor in spirit* (KJ Mt 5:2): having a passion for *every word out of the mouth of God* (NIV Mt 4:4).

Therefore, murderers like James Holmes, spared at the cost of **$400,000 yearly** for up to 3,330 years under obnoxious and nauseous laws to Colorado's overburdened taxpayers, are not and never can be forgiven. Devil's lying and willful acts of *stealing, murdering, and destroying* (KJ Jn 10:10) are what they see as fulfillment. If you believe it is not so, then study up on Judas Iscariot: a name ideally suited for the doings of *devils* like James Holmes—*is* a *scar* and *riot on humanity*—doomed to Hell per Jesus Christ! Hence, no one should have been out to save James Holmes or any other devils, for that is an abomination in God's sight. Like Cain, pleading with God over Abel, Holmes lied by pleading not guilty because of insanity. Unfortunately, one pious juror parading as an *angel of light* said *"NO!"* to his execution. Colorado's message:

> *"We provide first-class accommodations to our heartless, demonic murderers; however, should you become a victim of one of our distinguished killers, don't expect any help from Colorado."*

Similarly, a prison chaplain out to save *devils* discovered that harsh reality at the Polunsky Texas State Penitentiary in Livingston on May 9, 2000. He blindingly put trust in charming Juan Salvez Soric, scheduled for a justified execution that July. Extending his arms for prayer and salvation into Soric's cell—an abomination to God—the foolish trusting chaplain's hands were tied with sheets as

Soric came near to severing the chaplain's hands and arms with razor blades before being rescued too late. Served to Soric was justice by execution on July 26, 2000: a significant upset for the *enemies of God* but a great victory for Texas taxpayers in doing the will of God. The big question is: **DID THE PREACHER LEARN A LESSON THAT COST HIS LIFE? DO NOT PRAY FOR THE SALVATION OF** *DEVILS:* **EXECUTE THEM BY THE UNDENIABLE WILL OF GOD. ABSOLUTELY!** (Ecc 3:3; Mt 26:24) Who wants *devils* in Heaven? *Serpents* and other *devils*. That's who! Most certainly not God, Jesus Christ, or the Holy Spirit. What about you?

Prayed for release and God's blessings are the thousands of individuals wrongly accused, jailed, and some executed because of false witnesses and assumptions without scientific (DNA) evidence: very heartbreaking. Included are all wrongfully incarcerated for protesting stolen elections and other unchecked evils of devils in charge. That is God's expectation; otherwise, praying for the release and salvation of devils deserving punishment will get you the horrors you deserve. Never sympathize or toy with devils!

Devils are not limited to being cold-blooded murderers by any imagination. Without shame, *devils use freedom as a cover-up for evil* (NIV 1Pe 2:15–16). These are individuals proudly engaged in deception, theft, and other violations of God's way. As heartless thugs, they conspire against the righteous via blackmail, bribery, flattery and manipulation, slander, social media, liberal programming, stealing, and other evils. They bear no consciousness or guilt over their vigilante and perverted evil acts. Why? Integrity is no part of their existence, although they may attend church regularly, work in government, and preside over their county's corrupt but elite Squatter's Club.

Living next door to these esteemed by the community and possessing much of everything they want can be challenging but victorious because *Jesus Christ came to destroy the works of devils* (KJ 1JN 3:8). Even though they are wealthy and employed by the CIA or serve as a preacher, it does not give them the right to violate you. Blinded are they by arrogance, greed, and pride. Their boldness demonstrates confidence in corrupt routine achievements over decades with innocent, unsuspecting, honest, hard-working people they defrauded. Their trademarks are *lying, stealing, destroying, and murdering* (KJ Jn 10:10). They are a classic example of *"swine"* (KJ Mt 7:6), as Jesus calls them, *using their authority as a cover-up for evil* (NIV 1Pe 2:15–16).

A † Ω

----

3. Demons

Def: **demon**—*1.an evil spirit. 2.an evil passion or influence.*[48] [King James identifies *demons* as *devils* in some cases.]

---

[48] *Demon,* Webster's Encyclopedic Unabridged Dictionary.

It is written: *For our struggle is not against flesh and blood, but against the rulers, against the authorities, against the powers of this dark world and against the spiritual forces of evil (demons) in the heavenly realms.* (NIV Eph 6:12)

For the most part, *demons* are a type of *manitou*.

Def. **Manitou:** *supernatural being that controls nature; a spirit, deity or object that possesses supernatural power.*[49]

Demons are destructive forces known as *demonic manitous*. There are two main types: *mind-possessing manitous* and *storm manitous*. God's *elect* needs to recognize both types and distinguish their differences. Though unseen, *demonic manitous* can induce mass destruction, for that is their sole purpose of existence. Amazingly, the Bible teaches how to overcome both types; however, defeating them is impossible without believing they exist. Therefore, should you sincerely desire to overcome *demons*, I challenge you to learn as much about them as possible through the hidden and spiritually coded interpretation of *Genesis through Revelation*.

Their ancestry began with Lucifer (KJ Isa 14:12-15, Mt 16:23, Eph 6:12). Creating chaos and madness is their mission. Avoiding their devastation is possible through *complete obedience to the Commandments of God* (Dt 28:15-68), *together with correct beliefs about Jesus Christ and the Holy Spirit* (1Jn 3:8), *in addition to fasting and*

---

[49] *Manitou*, Ibid.

prayer (Mk 9:17-29). If achieved, they can cause *demons*, like death angels, to **pass over** one or many on their days of wrath. Here and now, you may understand how they co-exist and thrive and how to avoid and overpower them. Read on to examine both types.

A ✝ Ω
- - - - - - -

3a. Storm Manitous

Like mighty wrecking balls on the loose, *demons controlling the weather* can destroy communities. They are known as *storm manitous*. *Storm manitous* violently oppose peace. The Bible illustrates the effects of *storm manitous* and how to overpower them. For example, the following episode with *storm manitous* involved Jesus and his followers.

It is written: And the same day {after an amazing sermon about God's *elect*}, when the evening was come, he {Jesus} saith unto them, *Let us pass over unto the other side.* And when they had sent away the multitude, they took him even as he was in the ship. And there were also with him other little ships.

And there arose a great storm of wind, and the waves beat into the ship, so that it was now full. And he was in the hinder part of the ship, asleep on a pillow: and they awake him, and say unto him, *Master, carest thou not that we perish?*

And he arose, and rebuked the wind, and said unto the sea, **Peace, be still.** And the wind ceased, and there was a great calm.

And he said unto them, *Why are ye so fearful? How is it that ye have no faith?* And they feared exceedingly, and said one to another, *What manner of man is this, that even the wind and the sea obey him?*

(KJ Mk 4:35–41)

When Jesus, filled with supernatural powers, spoke to the winds and waves, He addressed *storm manitous* that stirred the wind and water to a furious state. Ironically, His young, faithless, and inexperienced disciples—in an early stage of spiritual development—**were terrified** at Him for having done what they called Him to do: **save their lives!**

Terrified is the typical response whenever God moves to action through one of His calming storms. The reason is hatred for God, lack of knowledge of the truth, or being overcome by the magnitude of the miracles God works through *Kingsmen*.

Calming storms minimize demonic activity, which can agitate devils throughout corrupt communities. It explains why many have inner fear or outright hatred, without a known justifiable cause other than slander, directed at a Bible admirer or *Kingsman* whom they cross paths with or perhaps settle in their community. They have no clue that God put him there to *destroy their works* (1Jn 3:8). His presence exposes evil. However, long-established, cold-hearted, wicked people will *strike at the heel of God's servant* at any and every opportunity (NIV Ge 3:15).

Truth in the matter concerning divine supernatural power over storm manitous or any other forces of evil is that **dis**believing that Jesus came as a role model or that He is an unconditional lover and forgiver of *devils* and *serpents* prevents victory. It will not happen, regardless of how many sinners beg God to comfort them by singing *Kumbaya*.

That is where **certain** seminaries play their destructive roles, having taken God's promising young aspiring saints down that left fork to **Bible Deception**. Rather than men and women wanting wholeheartedly to serve God in His way, they become indoctrinated in religion as *serpents*.

On the other side of disbelief and disobedience are *Kingsmen*. *Kingsmen* will consistently *continue wholeheartedly in God's way* while being persecuted by prevaricators, those who are terrified by truth, and by others condemned by God. For example, it's what Jesus, His apostles, and Paul experienced from terribly evil clergy people and their *worshipers of deception*: slandered, jeered, spit upon, and eventually executed, except for John.

A ✝ Ω

3b. Mind-Possessing Demonic Manitous

Mind-possessing demonic manitous will bind you to do evil. They will entice you to go against God's way by having you disgrace yourself, hoping to have you stripped of everything you own and represented, then imprisoned and killed. They will torment and tear you apart from family and close friends. Moreover, once you give in to them, exposed, you will be with nothing but shame, guilt, and total disgust for yourself, should you be among the *many called* by God. All alone—as one called by God—you will have to change beliefs and behaviors, should you be fortunate enough to overcome and survive the aftermath of *demons*. Without a doubt, Klebold, Harris, Holmes, Lanza, Lubitz, Ramos, Brown, and other mass murderers were possessed with *demonic manitous* at the point of no return, as they willfully carried out the *Art of Massacre*.

In addition to what you have learned thus far concerning *mind-possessing demonic manitous*, I am going to share my experience dealing with them, being confident that you will learn profound and shocking lessons from what you read. In my situation, the closer I drew to God through His complete Word, the greater *demons* tormented me. *Demonic torment* made me fully understand why highly religious individuals become mass murderers. Killing others and self is what *demons* want you to accomplish, as acts of murdering at random violate the sixth commandment: **THOU SHALT NOT MURDER** (CB and NIV Ex 20:13, Dt 5:17).

Coming into this revelation, as an avid Bible reader and believer, I desperately needed to remain as active as possible to avoid them as much as possible. In my case, when I finally took time out for myself from work or chose to read the Bible—out of nowhere—multiple demonic voices, filled with perversions, would sometimes flood my mind. Their after-effect had a very tight band around my head—the likings of migraine headaches—which was relieved by submitting to them: perhaps identical to gaining relief from any and every self-destruct addiction.

I eventually learned through the Bible that I was dealing with *external evil spirits* that desired to become *internal*. Through my belief in **every Word of God** (KJ Dt 8:3, Mt 4:4), with a sincere desire to rid myself of these unseen perverted beings and their destructive and shameful enticements, I searched and found the answers (KJ Mt 7:7-8). However, acting on those Biblical solutions counts; otherwise, a pretentious desire to change for the better is vainglorious.

By acting upon correct Bible solutions through determination and persistence, I would—over many years—hope to overcome [exorcize] every evil thing in my life that the world belonging to the *spirit of evil* had to offer. The solution to reaching that goal reflected Psalm 23 for the need to fill my cup Biblically, leaving no room for demonic possession or other evils per KJ Mt 12:43–45. So, instead of backing off with the Bible in fear of possible suicide or the *Art of Massacre*, **I did the unthinkable. I went in the opposite direction. I engulfed myself in reading, studying, and believing** *every spoken word of God* (Mt 4:4) **regularly and continued doing so from then on.**

For example, between September 1996 and June 2004, I became very accustomed to reading the New Testament softly in an audible voice *while walking with the Lord in the cool of the day* (KJ Ge 3:8). I did this on a two-mile, tree-covered path, less traveled near Greens Bayou: a mile west of Greenspoint Mall in Houston, Texas. I lived in a small one-bedroom apartment at Bayou Crossing Apartments for those eight years. I reached the point where I could read and walk for hours. For example, on Saturdays, without tiring, I could read and walk from 8 a.m. to around 5 p.m., with a short lunch break, covering—for example—all four Gospels of Matthew, Mark, Luke, and John. How many miles I walked, I haven't a clue. That was unimportant; however, I remained in perfect health throughout those eight years.

The purpose was that I emerged myself in the Bible

to, at some point, have it first in my life. However, things would get far worse before they got better, portraying me as a hypocrite. Why? The answer is in the New Testament.

> It is written: *For the Word of God is quick, and powerful, and sharper than any two-edged sword, piercing even to the dividing asunder of soul and spirit, and of the joints and marrow, and is a discerner of the thoughts and intents of the heart.* (KJ Heb 4:12)

Therefore, I remained focused on learning how to overcome demonic temptations, particularly those that wreaked havoc in my life. Living embarrassed and humiliated because of backsliding summed up my life to the tenth degree. Created was awareness from my passion for God's commandments and the truth of His Word. Otherwise, I would have been clueless and shameless regarding my sins and how to please God: the perfect equation for falsely believing in God as having unconditional love.

Nevertheless, while submerging myself in the Bible as much as possible, the good Lord raised me throughout those eight years. I overcame many challenges thanks to Him and the blessed work I enjoyed. However, reestablishing myself did not immune me from the curse of loneliness in my private life.

Around that same time, I was assigned a new position and moved to Humble, Texas. Moving to Humble—saturated with diverse places I was disgustingly attracted to for companionship—brought severe challenges outside my profession. It reminded me of Lot, choosing to live in Sodom, torn between perversions and doing the will of God, separated by a fragile fine line.

Therefore, to overcome the loneliness, I devoted myself to the Bible and worked ten to twelve-hour days at my new campus for the success of my students and the overall school I served. I also worked at Park 'N Fly during the weekends, holidays, and summers. Hence, I chose not to go online to collaborate with the *enemies of God* in learning skills in the *Art of Massacre*. Having the Bible as my number one and only trustworthy personal friend, I chose to do something constructive with my spare time: serve others by driving shuttle buses for Park 'N Fly.

However, upon leaving Park 'N Fly late into the night, I occasionally frequented places I should have avoided. Each time, a *still small voice* would plead with me not to go, but I allowed feelings to get the best of me. **That disappointed the *Counselor of Truth* and me repeatedly.** How and why the *Counselor* stayed with me was beyond comprehension at the time, for I certainly felt undeserving of His true friendship.

Overtaken by two new companions that I did not want—but desperately needed—every time I went where I should not have gone became customary. The two were *Guilt* and *Regret*, which I could not hide despite my creativity. Hence, I begged the good Lord to free me from temptations in the name and fullness of Jesus and through the Holy Spirit. Moreover, although in excellent physical health, I even sought treatment from a medical doctor to remove specific desires from my very healthy biological being, to which he laughed and said, *"You are perfectly normal."* That was highly encouraging from the world's medical point of view; however, it did not bring peace to my spirit.

I sincerely wanted to please God rather than the *spirit of evil* or allow sinful temptations to get the best of me. Calling God to my rescue, here is what the *Spirit of Truth*, in a *still small voice* (KJ 1Ki 19:12), told me so clearly that I will never forget or lose sight of:

Stephen, I cannot take sinful pleasures from you or anyone else. Where I am is holy ground, and you are to be holy unto me: the reason for my commandments. There is no room for any form of sin in my kingdoms. At some point, you will need to choose between me and your sinful pleasures. Therefore, it is not up to me, Jesus, the Holy Spirit, doctors, or the wind to stop you from backsliding. That's all up to you! You know my commandments, as you discovered all of them in Genesis through Revelation. The choice to obey or not is in your court, not mine. **The death and resurrection of Christ only atone for the sins of my elect: sincerely self-controlled repentant people pursuing righteousness instead of continuing to gratify their sinful desires. Therefore, go and sin no more** (KJ Jn 5:1–15, 8:3–11).

That was eye-opening compared to my religious indoctrinations: *"Bless me, Father, for I have sinned,"* and then bragging about it with, *"Lord, you know I'm a sinner."*

In June 2008, I retired from public education with thirty years of service that went by in a flash. I went to work full-time at Park 'N Fly, where I was moved to collections for a couple of months before resigning. My resignation resulted from a couple of very sly young liars manipulating me to let them leave Park 'N Fly in a vehicle without a pay stub because they claimed it got lost. Their lesson of manipulation took me a while to learn that all too trustworthy and impressionable Christians must comprehend and never forget to avoid demonic and costly entrapment:

> *Letting down your guard by living in denial or being too accommodating, too sweet, too stupid, too tired, too tolerant, too trusting, too gullible, and too empathizing can get you into much trouble. It can cost your job, good reputation, or even your life!*

As soon as the shysters drove off, the burden of guilt settled heavily on me. The following day, the episode came back to embarrass me with management, where I apologized, offered to pay their unpaid fee, and resigned. And did either of those prevaricators return to my aid? NEVER!

A † Ω

Occults: Satan's Den

Through experiences in overcoming demonic temptations, I attest that individuals seeking the occult soon discover that toying with *demons* and following *devils* is not rewarding: sensational for a brief period and often deadly—ABSOLUTELY! Unfortunately, for every decent but ill-informed person joining an occult or any other type of evil regime, regret eventually sets in at the point of no return. That's a result of having no connection with the truth about God during loneliness and difficult times while foolishly turning to idols and charming *devils* and *serpents* for companionship (KJ Ro 1:18-32, Php 3:18-19, Jas 4:4). And once hooked, there is often no escaping from their evil grasp where fear of what they might do to traitors imprisons.

On the other hand, should a person have a passion for God's word and be willing to endure *longsuffering* (KJ Gal 5:22), God will provide a window of opportunity to overcome demonic temptations. Don't be ashamed of your misery and rejection if you are such an individual (KJ Mt 10:22, Mk 13:13). **God is calling you: a call you should answer and express your faith and love in Him by obeying Him!**

A † Ω

In summarizing this chapter, **DESTRUCTIVE FORCES OF SATAN**, you are likely better informed about *demons, devils, and serpents*. The following reviews each.

Demons are either *mind-possessing* or *storm manitous*; though unseen, they induce massive destruction. Avoiding their devastation is through *belief in their existence* (KJ Eph 6:12), *fasting and prayer* (KJ Mt 17:21), *and liv-*

ing wholeheartedly according to God's principles (NIV 1Ki 8:23, 61).

Devils are people who willfully violate the innocent and God's commandments. Through greed and corruption, they thrive. Cold-hearted, scandalous, and intrigued as vigilantes of organized crimes are what they are. Their selfish, persistent, cruel schemes include bullying, conspiring with others like themselves, deceiving, destroying, flattering, intimidating, slandering, stealing, and worse. They are a classic example of *people who pervert freedom as a cover-up for evil* (NIV 1Pe 2:15–16).

In politics, *devils*—as do *serpents* in churches—falsely pose as *angels of light*, portraying evil as good. There, they gain popularity among all void of the *Spirit of God*. They influence idiots with propaganda like wanting equality for all self-proclaimed deprived souls while basking in bribes, blackmail, and corrupt elections. Those are their means of remaining influential for decades as multi-millionaires. Focused are they on abolishing Biblical values such as righteousness, which they hate. Their ballyhoo intimidates and creates chaos because that's what *devils* do best. They evade truth at all costs because deception is their existence. Their organizations appear to have no Master Plans, but indeed they do. For example, with Leftists, it goes like this:

We are here to form an exceedingly corrupt, immoral, poverty-stricken, perverted Union. We accept bribes, ensure domestic violence, erase his-

tory, and establish injustice through Communism and Socialism. We lie to gain control with the help of corrupt elections. We abolish the common defense, promote warfare, increase welfare, and secure the anti-Christ ideology and curses to ourselves and our prosperity. Moreover, we ordain and proclaim this Bill of Evils for our rise to power and the downfall of Christianity and Democracy.

With *devils* as neighbors despising you and coveting the property you buy upright, challenging are they with unlimited resources and connections. They may work at the CIA and own apartments or serve as a fraudulent preacher and be dead set on defrauding you of your ownership, as I experienced in two places. First and foremost, they will have zero respect for you and the legal process. They will covet what is yours and go to extremes to steal it. Their premeditated strategies are always identical: flattery to gain trust, then manipulating you to believe you are subject to them, is how they begin to take control. Bullying follows.

Once you wise up to their aggression and begin resisting them, they will conspire with others to destroy your character to have you removed from their territory. They will become malicious in frustrating, humiliating, intimidating, and slandering you. With the help of other unscrupulous influential *swine* in high places like themselves, their corruption involves the removal of property markers and placing squatter's signs (their addresses) on your property. It includes leaving parked vehicles in front of your home or property. They will defecate on your driveway at night to certify their squatter's status. They and theirs will trespass, vandalize, and conduct business on your property. Their corruption also includes running surveillance and stalking you, lying about their ownership of what belongs to you, and having satellite images falsified, showing fake pictures of their private road across the front and down the middle of your property.

However, because God hates *devils [liars, thieves, destroyers—squatters]*, regardless of how much church they attend and work in the highest level of law enforcement, **Hell is their destiny.** Do not pray for their salvation unless you want to burn in Hell with them. **If you obey God's way, your victory over them is promised** (KJ Dt 28:1–14). So consider the following in having God ally with you against devilish neighbors, and remember that **God sees all!**

Cursed are them for removing property markers.

It is written: *Cursed be he that removeth his neighbour's landmark.* (KJ Deut 27:17)

Stand tall with the Word of God against them.

It is written: *Be strong and of good courage: be not afraid, neither be thou dismayed: for the* LORD *thy God is with thee whithersoever thou goest.* (KJ Jos 1:6-9)

Remain confident that God shall fulfill His prom-

ises. At the height of their glory, doomed are they.

It is written: *When the wicked spring as the grass, and when all the workers of iniquity do flourish, it is that they shall be destroyed forever.* (KJ Ps 92:7)

Disaster is upon them.

It is written: *Woe to the wicked! Disaster is upon them! They will be paid back for what their {evil} hands have done* {and lying tongues have spoken}. (NIV Isa 3:11)

Be patient. God will take them out!

It is written: *Thus saith the* LORD *against all mine evil neighbours, that touch the inheritance which I have caused my people Israel* {God with us} *to inherit; Behold, I will pluck them out of their land.* (KJ Jer 12:14)

Never repay evil for evil.

It is written: *Do not repay anyone evil for evil. Be careful to do what is right in the eyes of everybody. If it is possible, as far as it depends on you, live at peace with everyone. Do not take revenge, my friends, but leave room for God's wrath, for it is written: "It is mine to avenge; I will repay," says the Lord.* (NIV Ro 12:17-19)

Pray for justice in having what they set out doing to you fall back on them! (Ester, Daniel)

Best regarded are *serpents* as prevaricators misleading others in God's word. As bald-faced lying preachers, teachers, evangelists, and prophets, they violate the **Third Commandment.** Doing so leads to a violation of all other of God's commandments.

> It is written: *Thou shalt not take the name of the L*ord *thy God in vain; for the L*ord *will not hold him guiltless that taketh his name in vain.* (KJ Ex 20:7)

The correct interpretation of the Third Commandment is not to misrepresent God. Claiming and teaching that God's love is unconditional misrepresents God. Teaching children that God loves them but not their sin **misrepresents God.** God knows and judges all by our actions!

Serpents abhor righteousness. Being righteous voids their devilish ideologies that instill that humankind cannot be exemplary. They form a trinity, with the *spirit of evil*, in deceiving humanity that often hails them as great evangelists, messiahs, philosophers, preachers, prophets, and saviors, particularly for—but not restricted to—anti-Christians, who refer to their kind as *"Leftist Christians."* Since nothing in their devious minds angers them more than *righteousness*, they stereotype God's holy people as bigoted, fascist, racist, and self-righteous: precisely who and what they are as Satan's Leftists.

A † Ω

VI. DESTRUCTIVE FORCES OF GOD

It is written: *The* Lord *is a man of war; the* Lord *is his name.* (KJ Ex 15:3)

Similar to the destructive forces of Satan, there are times when the good Lord will cause massive annihilation and destruction, confirming that His love is highly conditional. These destructive forces are as far removed from the gods of unconditional love as Heaven is from Hell. Nevertheless, they exist!

Like a good king, God will do and command whatever is necessary for overcoming forces of evil once they are held in checkmate by Him: that is, their point where forgiveness, grace, love, mercy, and tolerance are abolished (ex. KJ Dt 28:15-68). The time of abolishment is when the clergy, in the fullness of *serpents*, repeatedly teach about their one-sided carnal rendition of an utterly false, unconditional, always forgiving, forever graceful, infinitely loving, and ever merciful God. Believing in their rhetoric is ominous and leads societies to abolish God. Abolishing God causes Him to exterminate them. This highly destructive side of God creates a healthy balance in His judgment of humanity. It makes Him equally loving and vengeful.

It is written: *God is jealous, and the* Lord *revengeth; the* Lord *revengeth, and is furious; the* Lord *will take vengeance on his adversaries,* **and he reserveth wrath for his enemies.** *The* Lord *is slow to* *anger, and great in power,* **and will not at all acquit the wicked:** *the* L ORD *hath his way in the whirlwind and in the storm, and the clouds are the dust of his feet.* (KJ Na 1:2–3)

Therefore, to rid Himself of people held in checkmate by Him, that is, the majority who have no intentions of ever following in His way, known has been Almighty God to defeat, silence, and annihilate them through any of three means. Apart from the destructive forces of Satan, including drugs and alcohol, natural disasters, sickness, suicide, and euthanasia enthusiasts, they are as follows:

> 1) **Kingsmen** [apostles, prophets, seers, and warriors] These *elect* are righteous and trustworthy leaders. Integrity is their existence. Living according to God's principles sustains them. They have no fear of evildoers and follow God's lead in destroying demonic strongholds.
>
> 2) **Death Angels** *annihilate the wicked to serve justice and uphold righteousness on God's orders.*
>
> 3) **God personally** *is jealous and will not leave the wicked unpunished.*

Read on to investigate these three means by which the Lord quells His enemies, apart from the satanic forces discussed in the previous chapter.

1. PROPHETS AND WARRIORS
Example: Moses

Born to Amram and Jochebed, Moses was a descendant of Noah, Shem, Abraham, Isaac, Jacob, and Levi (KJ Ge 11:10-32), down to Kohath. Jochebed was the sister of her husband's father, Kohath! In simple terms, Amram married Aunt Jochebed and begot Moses (KJ Ex 6:6-20, Nu 26:58-59)!

Moses had several one-on-one encounters with God. During two of these, God spoke, wrote, and rewrote the Ten Commandments on two sides of two stone tablets. He handed them to Moses for the Israelites to live by (KJ Ex 20:1-21, 31:18, 32:15-16; Dt 5:1-22, 10:1-5). With obedience, the nation would prosper, enjoy abundance, be victorious over its enemies, secure its well-being, and live happily ever after (KJ Dt 8:1-18, 28:1-14). Disobedience met catastrophic disasters (KJ Dt 8:19-20, 28:15-68).

Nelson's New Illustrated Bible Dictionary cites Moses, *inspired by God*, as a remarkable leader:

> **MOSES** [MOE zez]—*the Hebrew prophet who delivered the Israelites from Egyptian slavery and was their leader and law-giver during their [forty] years of wandering in the wilderness.* **Moses was a leader so inspired by God that he formed a united nation from a race of oppressed and weary slaves.** *In the covenant ceremony at Mount Sinai, he founded the religious community known as Israel, where God wrote the Ten Commandments. As the interpreter of those covenant*

laws, he organized the community's religious and civil traditions. His story is in the Old Testament Books of Exodus, Leviticus, Numbers, and Deuteronomy.[50]

Moses lived one-hundred twenty years, whereby three forty-year periods define his lifespan. The following is a summary of each. Knowledge of these is a necessary component of *AGAPE*. It illustrates the type of individual God searches throughout the universe to find the perfect candidate to fulfill His will. Such individuals are *wholeheartedly committed to His way that He can bet on* (NIV 1Ki 8:23, 61 and Job 1–2). And, whenever moved by the *Holy Spirit, they destroy the works of devils* (KJ 1Jn 3:8).

THE FIRST FORTY-YEAR PERIOD [1526—1486 B.C.] began with the birth of Moses in Goshen [outside Rameses / Avaris] and his adoption at three months by a young princess, **Bithiah** (bih-THIH-uh). [The Jewish Encyclopedia tells of Bithiah, married to **Mered, a descendant of Judah: the lineage of Christ** (KJ 1Ch 4:1 and 17–19).]

Concerned over the explosive population of Hebrews in Goshen, Bithiah's father, Pharaoh [King] Ahmose I [1550—1525 B.C.], ordered the drowning in the Nile of all Hebrew newborn boys (KJ Ex 1:22). However, God's plan for those Hebrew infants conflicted with Pharaoh's plan to kill them. The following is how it turned out for Moses.

---

[50] *Moses*, Nelson's New Illustrated Bible Dictionary.

Bithiah was the daughter of Pharaoh [Ahmose I], identified in the Midrash with Moses' foster-mother. Explained is her name: God said to her, "You have called Moses, your son, although he was not your son. Therefore I will call you my daughter ["Bithiah" = "bat," daughter; "Yah," God], although you are not my daughter" (Lev. R. i. 3; Meg. 13a; and elsewhere).

Bithiah bathed in the Nile because, having a skin disease, she could bathe only in cold water; yet she had hardly touched the casket in which Moses lay when her sickness left her while all her maidens met instant death. She then knew destined the boy was for greatness (Pirḳe R. El. xlviii.; Ex. R. i. 23). Healed by surprise when she barely touched the casket, Bithiah chose to keep the Hebrew baby as her own and named him Moses, saying, I drew him out of the water (KJ Ex 2:10).[51]

Upon deciding to keep Moses as her own, Bithiah needed someone to assist with the baby. Aware of that need, Moses' sister Miriam appeared to the princess, offering to get one of the Hebrew women to fill her need. Moreover, due to circumstances, no one in Pharaoh's household dared to express a concern that the woman chosen for the task, Jochebed, was the infant's mother (KJ Ge 2:1-10).

During these forty years, Moses grew into manhood in the house of *Bithiah* under the reign of three other

---

[51] *Bithiah,* Jewish Encyclopedia: The unedited full-text of the 1906 Jewish Encyclopedia.

pharaohs: Amenhotep I (1525—1504 B.C.), Thutmose I (1504—1492 B.C.), and Thutmose II (1492—1479 B.C.).[52] There, Moses became wise in all the ways of the Egyptians during a time of massive construction of storage cities inspired by Joseph: Pitham (Pi-Atum) and Raamses (Pi-Ramesses) (KJ Ex 1:11). [The city of Raamses is **not** to be confused with the reign and accomplishments of *"The Great Ramesses II"* two-hundred + years later (1279—1212 B.C.).]

THE SECOND FORTY-YEAR PERIOD [1485—1446 B.C.] began when Moses rescued a fellow Hebrew whom an Ancient Egyptian slave driver beat. Being a witness to the abuse of his people on the part of the Ancient Egyptians, Moses took matters into his own hands and served justice by murdering the abuser (KJ Ecc 3:3). Moses ran for his life and set out for Midian when word got out about it.

> It is written: And it came to pass in those days, when Moses was grown, that he went out unto his brethren, and looked on their burdens: and he spied an Egyptian smiting a Hebrew, one of his brethren. And he looked this way and that way, and when he saw that there was no man, he slew the Egyptian and hid him in the sand.

> And when he went out the second day, behold, two men of the Hebrews strove together: and he said to him that did the wrong, *Wherefore smitest thou thy fellow?* And he said, *Who made thee a prince*

---

[52] *Pharaoh Timeline*, World History Encyclopedia.

and a judge over us? Intendest thou to kill me, as thou killedst the Egyptian? And Moses feared and said, *Surely this thing is known.*

Now, when Pharaoh {Thutmose II} heard this thing, he sought to slay Moses. But Moses fled {approximately 300 miles from the city of Rameses} from the face of Pharaoh. He dwelt in the land of Midian {near Mt. Sinai}, and he sat down by a well {belonging to Jethro, known as Reuel, who would become his father-in-law and shelter for the second forty-year period of his life}.

(KJ Ex 2:11–15)

While in Midian, Moses married Zipporah, a daughter of Jethro, an Ethiopian black priest, **not Hebrew**. Zipporah gave birth to their son, *Gershom. Gershom* symbolizes *being an alien in a foreign land* (KJ Ex 2:21–22). *Gershom* was similar in meaning and pronunciation to *Goshen:* the populated territory outside of Egypt, the place of Moses' birth, where the Israelites settled as aliens under Joseph 350 years before Moses' birth (KJ Ge 46 & 47). Zipporah later gave birth to a second son, Eliezer: a name symbolic of, *My father's God was my helper; he saved me from the sword of Pharaoh* (KJ Ex 18:4).

Toward the end of this second forty-year period, God spoke to Moses on Mount Horeb {Sinai} in the form of a burning bush. There, he informed Moses that he was to return to Egypt and command Pharaoh {Thutmose III (1458—1425 B.C.)} to release the Israelites. [Although having served the Egyptians for 320 years before the birth of Moses, the Israelites became significantly deprived under Pharaoh Thutmose III during these 40 years: a ramification of Moses obeying God.]

It is written: Now Moses kept the flock of Jethro his father in law, the priest of Midian: and he led the flock to the backside of the desert, and came to the mountain of God, even to Horeb {Sinai}. And the angel of the LORD appeared unto him in a flame of fire out of the midst of a bush: and he looked, and, behold, the bush burned with fire, and the bush was not consumed.

And Moses said, I will now turn aside, and see this great sight, why the bush is not burnt. And when the LORD saw that he turned aside to see, God called unto him out of the midst of the bush, and said, Moses, Moses. And he said, Here am I.

And he said, Draw not nigh hither: put off thy shoes from off thy feet, for the place whereon thou standest is holy ground. Moreover he said, I am the God of thy father, the God of Abraham, the God of Isaac, and the God of Jacob. And Moses hid his face; for he was afraid to look upon God.

And the LORD said, I have surely seen the affliction of my people which are in Egypt, and have heard their cry by reason of their taskmasters; for I know their sorrows; And I am come down to deliver them out of the hand of the {Ancient} Egyptians {whom He hated}, and to bring them up out of that *land unto a good land and a large, unto a land flowing with milk and honey; unto the place of the* {descendants of Noah's youngest yet disgraceful son, **Ham** (KJ Ge 9:18-25)} *Canaanites, and the Hittites, and the Amorites, and the Perizzites, and the Hivites, and the Jebusites* {where also resided Nephilim: *giants* that were descendants of Anak (KJ Nu 13:32-33)}. *Now therefore, behold, the cry of the children of Israel is come unto me: and I have also seen the oppression wherewith the Egyptians oppress them. Come now therefore, and I will send thee unto Pharaoh* {Thutmose III} *that thou mayest bring forth my people the children of Israel out of Egypt.*

And Moses said unto God, *Who am I, that I should go unto Pharaoh, and that I should bring forth the children of Israel out of Egypt?*

And he said, *Certainly I will be with thee; and this shall be a token unto thee, that I have sent thee:* **When thou hast brought forth the people out of Egypt, ye shall serve God upon this mountain** {location God would come to write out His Ten Commandments}.

(KJ Ex 3:1-12)

The end of Moses' second forty-year period extended through Israel's departure from Egypt: a movement involving as many as two million Hebrew and Egyptian refugees that became best regarded as *Exodus* (Ex).

The Exodus occurred in 1446 B.C. It began after God imposed ten destructive miracles through Moses against the Ancient Egyptians to have Pharaoh {Thutmose III} release the Hebrews from his control. And since God loves **not** all children, the tenth miracle imposed death on all the firstborns of the Ancient Egyptians and firstborns of all their livestock: **not** something they would have been proud to admit, much less maintain its records. Nevertheless, it was a final blow when Pharaoh finally ordered the release of the hundreds of thousands of Hebrews under his control.

Upon their release, Moses led the Israelites and company {300 miles back} to Midian, where he had been for the past forty years—the location of Mount Sinai. It is time to recall that God instructed Moses to rendezvous with him at Mount Sinai to have the Hebrews worship him there.

This dramatic second period concluded with God parting the waters of the *Sea of Reeds* [*Yam Suph* in Hebrew]. Based on facts and Biblical maps, Nelson cites the event as follows:

> *A solid east wind from the desert began to blow on the water's surface, described more fully as a reed sea (Ex 15:22) or lake of papyrus reeds. Earlier versions of the Bible mistakenly translated the phrase as the Red Sea, but this name describes an enormous oceanic gulf* [208 miles wide and 1398 miles long] *far to the southeast where papyrus reeds do not grow. The concentrated, hot winds miraculously parted the marsh waters and*

dried a significant path so the Israelites could flee.[53]

What happened is that God hardened Pharaoh's heart. Thus, Pharaoh Thutmose III regretted setting free his hundreds of thousands of enslaved Israelites. Therefore, the king had his entire army pursue the Israelites to have them return. This dynamic episode ended as God miraculously dried the marsh to provide an escape route on dry land for the Israelites. The course landed them in Shur, a vast territory east of the *Sea of Reeds* and the *Red Sea*. After the Hebrews crossed over, God returned the waters, bogging down Pharaoh's pursuing army, resulting in all drowning (KJ Ex 14): justice served!

THE THIRD FORTY-YEAR PERIOD [1447—1406 B.C.] took in the years the Israelites remained wandering in the desert. It resulted from forsaking God's straightforward command to occupy the *Promised Land* (KJ Nu 13–14), a journey that should not have taken 8 weeks (Dt 1:2-3). Nevertheless, before they made their fatal decision, God intercepted the Israelites at Mount Horeb as promised.

There, God met with Moses—forty days and nights—and wrote His *Ten Commandments* on two sides of two stone tablets (KJ Ex 31:18, 32:15-16). Afterward, God had Moses return to the people because idolatry was throughout the camp (KJ Ex 32:7-10). Filled with anger upon eying pagan worship, Moses tossed the tablets from the mountain, likely at the newly molded golden calf

---

[53] *Exodus,* Nelson's New Illustrated Bible Dictionary..

PORTRAYAL OF MOSES WITH THE TEN COMMANDMENTS

celebrated as a god below. The toss broke both tablets to pieces at the foot of Mt. Sinai (KJ Ex 32:19).

Under pressure, Aaron, the brother of Moses, formed the golden calf from plundered Egyptian gold (KJ Ex 32:21-24). It ignited a separation of God's loyal Hebrews from idol worshipers destined for immediate death. Thus, God's deadly vengeance led by Moses resulted in the instantaneous massacre of 3,000 reveling infidels involved with starting up idol worship (KJ Ex 32:27-28). A fatal plague annihilated the remaining 24,000 insurgents (KJ Ex 32:35, Nu 25:9). Additionally, the episode resulted in Moses seeking the LORD another forty days and nights with two new stone tablets for God to rewrite His Ten Commandments (KJ Ex 34:1-3, Dt 10:1-5).

To complicate matters, shortly after the return of Moses from being with God the second time, ten of the twelve tribal leaders—sent into the *Promised Land*—returned with a fearful and negative report (KJ Nu 13-14). Fear—*false evidence appearing real*—which the ten instilled among the Israelites because of their encounter with *giants*, delayed Israel's entry into the *Promised Land* for the last forty years of Moses' life. *Apart from Joshua and forty-year-old Caleb, who displayed no doubt of success in marching forth as God commanded* (KJ Nu 13:30, Jos 14: 6-9), *lost was all hope of entering the Promised Land to forty years of wandering: one year for each day the twelve went out to spy* (KJ Nu 14:34).

Now, review the facts about Moses! First, since Moses killed an enemy of God at the right time (Ecc 3:3)—*to defend against evil, serve justice, and uphold righteousness*—he became a hero in God's sight while remaining the enemy of Pharaoh. Unlike Cain, who was held accountable for the murder of his brother, Abel—a child of God—by murdering the slave-beating Ancient Egyptian, Moses did what was right with God but wrong in the mind of *Pharaoh, devils, pulpit serpents,* and their *worshipers of deception.* It is what Able should have done in self-defense: killed Cain.

Although having a speech impediment, God saw that Moses, a courageous man of action and integrity to be trusted, was a powerful and influential *Kingsman* (KJ Ex 4:10–17). Per the Jewish Encyclopedia cited earlier, anointed was Moses to do miraculous wonders starting at birth. First recorded when he was three months old, God healed his stepmother, Bithiah, while causing the instant death of all of her maidens.

Then Moses—at age forty—having killed an abusive Egyptian slave master has had far-reaching implications among the *many called* by God throughout the ages. Those implications include but are not limited to the following:

- Any chosen individual by God who kills a person attempting to bring severe bodily harm to them, members of their family, or any other righteous person is a hero in God's sight. (Ecc 3:3)

- Members of a jury that convicts a person to death **based on scientific evidence (DNA)** for having murdered someone favored and loved by God are heroes in God's sight. [Upholding the Death Penalty—whenever and wherever warranted—is a requirement of God's. (KJ Lev 10:1–3; Nu 21:1–3; Ecc 3:3, Ac 5:1–11, 12:21–24)]

- Men and women enlisted in the Armed Services or serve in law enforcement to preserve the Kingdom of God and bring justice against the forces of evil are heroes in God's sight. (Ecc 3:3)

- Rebuking criminals **based on scientific evidence (DNA)** and serving justice, including administering the death penalty, are not sinful acts. (Ecc 3:3)

A ✝ Ω

- - - - - - -

2. Death Angels and Guardian Angels

It is written: *Because thou hast made the* LORD, *which is my refuge, even the most High, thy habitation; there shall no evil befall thee, neither shall any plague come nigh thy dwelling. For he shall give his **angels** charge over thee, to keep thee in all thy {righteous} ways. They shall bear thee up in their hands, lest thou dash thy foot against a stone. Thou shalt tread upon the {corruption of the} lion and {lies of the} adder: the young lion (evil aggressors) and the dragon (devils) shalt thou trample under feet.* (KJ Ps 91:9-13)

According to Scripture, it is evident that every person is either loved or hated by God. *By making Him your dwelling through the full context of His Word—where is found the truth, He will love you. He will command His angels to guard you in all your righteous ways* (NIV Ps 91:9-12). However, there are challenges to His favoring you. For example:

It is written: *Yea, truth faileth, **and he that depar-***

teth from evil maketh himself a prey {of the wicked}: *and the* LORD *saw it, and it displeased him that there was no judgment* {passed onto the wicked for persecuting his righteous *elect*}. (KJ Isa 59:15)

The primary question is:

How do you make the Lord your dwelling, to have Him dispatch His angels to guide and guard you in all your righteous ways, over being destroyed by death angels?

Far removed from the gods of unconditional love and their one-sided, only loving, graceful, merciful false Jesus that defrauders glorify and have theirs worshiping to no avail is the answer to that mystery. Therefore, please be introduced to God's *death angels* to learn how to have them bypass you.

When provoked to anger by individuals and massive numbers of people engaging in immorality, corruption, and willful defiance of His way, God has dispatched *death angels* to destroy them. To God, it is a mere expeditious disposal of easily identifiable tall weeds that attempt to take over one or all His gardens.

Found in the Old Testament, God dispatched *death angels* to kill massive numbers of people where evil dominated throughout Sodom and Gomorrah, ancient Egypt, and among heathens and traitors that rebelled against Him in the Israelite camp during the forty-year Exodus (KJ Ge 18–19, Exodus, 1Co 10:1–10). Elsewhere in the Old Testament, King David lost seventy thousand innocent-unsuspecting men in three days to a *Death Angel* for going beyond the will of God (KJ 1Ch 21).

An example of a *Death Angel* appearing in the New Testament, where is found miraculous appearances of *angels* on several occasions, is as follows:

> It is written: And upon a set day Herod {Agrippa I—grandson of Herod the Great, the Ascalonite}, arrayed in royal apparel, sat upon his throne and made an oration unto them. And the people gave a shout, saying, *It is the voice of a god, and not of a man.* And immediately the angel of the Lord smote him because he gave **not** God the glory: and he was eaten of worms, and gave up the ghost. (KJ Ac 12:21-23)

Hence, contrary to all false beliefs, God's angels are truthful messengers, warriors, and annihilators dispatched to destroy the arrogant wicked. They bring unannounced—but deadly surprises—to people God judges as evil. Whenever that occurs, there's no longer a discussion concerning right and wrong or who lives and dies! Therefore, be reminded that God's unconditional love is a myth. Once luck plays out on the part of all persistent evil minds, death and hell become eminent, one way or the other.

A † Ω

----

3. God as Destroyer

It is written: *For, behold, the* LORD *will come with*

> *fire, and with his chariots like a whirlwind, to render his anger with fury, and his rebuke with flames of fire. For by fire and by his sword will the* LORD *plead with all flesh:* **and the slain of the LORD shall be many.** (KJ Isa 66:15-16)

Therefore, look at a couple of Biblical examples of people killed by God while not losing sight of the many others He destroyed throughout the ages. This first example occurred during the last forty years of Moses' life while out in the desert. It involved two of his nephews from the *Levitical Priesthood* and their father, Aaron.

> It is written: And **Nadab** and **Abihu**, the sons of Aaron {Moses brother}, took either of them his censer and put fire therein, and put incense thereon, and offered strange fire before the LORD, which he commanded them not. And there went out fire from the LORD, and devoured them, and they died before the LORD.
>
> Then Moses said unto Aaron, *This is it that the* LORD *spake, saying,* **I will be sanctified in them that come nigh me, and before all the people I will be glorified.**
>
> And Aaron held his peace {after his sons were consumed by fire for having chosen a manner of worship that was **un**acceptable with God}.
>
> (KJ Lev 10:1-3)

Putting this in perspective is that it's best to worship God per His will (NIV 1Ki 8:23, 61). Likewise, it's best not to associate with churches that do not. The big question is:

Do you know if the church you are attending follows God's protocol or has chosen a manner of worship unacceptable to Him?

There are three simple methods of finding that out!

(1) Study your Bible cover to cover!

(2) Are God's Ten Commandments ingrained in the lives of the congregation? If not, B E W A R E !

(3) If a church instills God and Jesus as having unconditional love, it is a satanic church hated by God. They violate the Third Commandment by misrepresenting the Father, Son, and Holy Spirit. [A violation of the Third Commandment leads to a breach of all the other commandments.]

Revealed also in the New Testament is the wrath of God. For example, in the Book of Acts, shortly after the Resurrection of Jesus Christ, believers had come together to share some of what they owned with fellow Christians. This case involved a husband and wife, *Ananias* and *Sapphira,* who agreed to give to **The Way—*a community of believers in the risen Christ*—**what they earned by selling a portion of their property (KJ Ac 5:1-10). **Unfortunately, the couple had second thoughts and held back some of what they publicly agreed to give.**

It is a shockingly sad story that turns many people away from the honest, loving, but **vengeful** God (KJ Isa 34:8, 35:4, 47:3; Jer 50:15 and 28). Moreover, it is a profound warning among the *few chosen* by God not to steal what you oblige yourself to give God. God expects obedience and honesty. Showing mercy, forgiveness, and tolerance to *Ananias* and *Sapphira* would have discredited the integrity of the community since what they tried to get away with was regarded by God as having lied to and blasphemed the Holy Spirit: an unforgivable act and open rebellion against the Kingdom of God on Earth.

> It is written: *But he that shall blaspheme against the Holy Ghost hath never forgiveness, but is in danger of eternal damnation.* (KJ Mk 3:29)

Thus, God did what He is swift and good at: killing those who provoke Him to anger for defying Him.

> It is written: But a certain man named Ananias, with Sapphira his wife, sold a possession, and kept back part of the price, his wife also being privy to it, and brought a certain part, and laid it at the apostles' feet.
>
> But Peter said, Ananias, *Why hath Satan filled thine heart to lie to the Holy Ghost, and to keep back part of the price of the land? Whiles it remained, was it not thine own? And after it was sold, was it not in thine own power? Why hast thou conceived this thing in thine heart? Thou hast not lied unto men, but unto God.*
>
> And Ananias hearing these words fell down, and gave up the ghost: and great fear came on all them that heard these things. And the young men arose,

wound him up, and carried him out, and buried him.

And it was about the space of three hours after, when his wife, not knowing what was done, came in. And Peter answered unto her, *Tell me whether ye sold the land for so much? And she said, Yea, for so much.*

Then Peter said unto her, *How is it that ye have agreed together to tempt the Spirit of the Lord? Behold, the feet of them which have buried thy husband are at the door, and shall carry thee out.* Then fell she down straightway at his feet, and yielded up the ghost: and the young men came in, and found her dead, and, carrying her forth, buried her by her husband.

And great fear came upon all the church, and upon as many as heard these things.

(KJ Ac 5:1-11)

Other than being presented as a reminder to fulfill one's voluntary financial commitment to what he perceives represents the SPOKEN WORD OF GOD {Rhema}, know that God is eventually vengeful to all wicked people (KJ Eze 24:8, 25:14 and 17; Mic 5:15). Your safety, prosperity, and salvation depend on it because you do not want to be among *worshipers of deception* whenever God unleashes His wrath.

You must understand and know with certainty that the forces of evil are out to defraud you of God's blessings and promises, your heritage and children, your freedoms, and everything else in your life. Their purpose is to destroy God's values, using their authority as a cover-up for evil. Biased and prevaricators are they toward Atheism, Communism, criminals, homosexuals, illegals, Islam, and Socialism, portraying evil as good and good as evil. They also make God a myth where fearing Him is a joke.

Hence, without understanding and accepting the complete Word of God in full context, people are often influenced into believing any and every lie in place of truth and God's intentions. The following Scriptures testify to these facts.

> It is written: *The simple believeth every word: but the prudent man looketh well to his going.* (KJ Pr 14:15)

> It is written: *A wise man feareth, and departeth from evil: but the fool rageth, and is confident.* (KJ Pr 14:16)

> It is written: *The simple inherit folly: but the prudent are crowned with knowledge.* (KJ Pr 14:18)

Now, regarding that false teaching as *fearing God is a joke*, the following speaks volumes about having a respectful fear of God and its relation to divination.

> It is written: And Samuel {a seer of God's (1Ch 9:22)} said {to King Saul concerning Saul losing his kingship for having disobeyed God's orders},

> *Hath the* LORD *as great {a} delight in burnt offerings and sacrifices,* **as in obeying the <u>voice</u> of the** LORD**? Behold, to obey is better than sacrifice, and to hearken than the fat of rams.** *For rebellion {against God} is as the sin of witchcraft, and stubbornness is as iniquity and idolatry. Because thou hast rejected the word of the* LORD*, he hath also rejected thee from being king.* (KJ 1Sa 15:22-23)

Did you notice that *rebellion against God* rather than fearing God *is like the sin of witchcraft* [divination] *and stubbornness* [arrogance] *like the evil of idolatry?* Some, in this case, witches, turn that into a lie, having skimmed or picked away at the Bible by falsely claiming, "The Bible is a book of sorcery;" and, "Fearing God is divination" [Valerie Love and Calvin Witcher.] Setting aside their lies, take a truthful glimpse of what a respectful fear of God is.

> It is written: *The fear of the* LORD *is clean, enduring for ever: the judgments of the* LORD *are true and righteous altogether.* (KJ Ps 19:9)

> It is written: *The fear of the* LORD *is the beginning of wisdom:* **a good understanding have all they that do his commandments:** *his praise endureth for ever.* (KJ Ps 111:10)

> It is written: *The fear of the* LORD *is to hate evil: pride, and arrogancy, and the evil way, and the froward mouth, do I hate.* (KJ Pr 8:13)

It is written: *The fear of the* LORD *prolongeth days: but the years of the wicked shall be shortened.* (KJ Pr 10:27)

It is written: *The fear of the* LORD *is a fountain of life, to depart from the snares of death.* (KJ Pr 14:27)

So, the big unanswered question is:

How does God know that a person fears Him?

The answer is very straightforward throughout the Bible. I hope that you and yours will never forget it.

A person displays his fear of God by repenting (KJ Mt 4:17) ***and continuing wholeheartedly in His way.*** (NIV 1Ki 8:23, 61)

Where does that put the bulk of humanity having nothing to do with God's principles? The simple and truthful answer is: ***Having no fear of God!*** Having no fear of God is what *serpents* instill about unconditional love. Here's an example:

Let's say you sincerely believe God loves you because you attend church, but you keep backsliding due to a lousy addiction. Never forget this profound truth: Each time you backslide—which I have done many times to my regret—you are sending a message to the LORD that you have no fear of Him. And where there is no fear of the LORD, His vengeance is an ongoing phenomenon among such foolish *worshipers of deception*.

In other words, we jeopardize our lives, possessions, and

salvation whenever we backslide or attend worship ceremonies that do not align with the truth of God's undeniable Word: that which the Bible warns about repeatedly. For example, God obliges humanity with whatever it chooses to believe in and obey. However, following Him leads to His blessings and kingdoms, while evil leads to curses like drought and Hell (KJ Dt 28: 1-68).

> It is written: *The priests said not, Where is the LORD? And they that handle the law knew me not: the pastors also transgressed against me, and the prophets prophesied by Ba'-al* {sun gods & storm gods} *and walked after things that do not profit.* (KJ Jer 2:8)

> It is written: *They have belied* {lied about} *the LORD, and said, It is not he; neither shall evil come upon us; neither shall we see sword nor famine:* **And the prophets shall become wind, and the word is not in them: thus shall it be done unto them.**
>
> *Where thus saith the LORD God of hosts, Because ye* {Kingsmen} *speak this word* {of truth against the wicked}, *behold,* **I will make my words in thy mouth fire,** *and this people* {void of the truth who hate you as} *wood, and it shall devour them.*
>
> (KJ Jer 5:12-14)

There is no mistaking! Qualifying for the Kingdoms of God without *continuing wholeheartedly in His way* is a myth (NIV 1Ki 8:23, 61). That alone determines the fate of the clear majority who worship all false gods, including gods of unconditional love: Hell bound! But it does not stop there because how can anyone believe they are Hell bound by believing and worshiping false gods? Answer: They cannot until it is too late, and find themselves screaming out:

> "Here I am burning in Hell regardless of having attended church all my life. How could I have been so blinded by what I chose to believe about the Lord? This torment just can't be happening to me! Rescue me! Someone, please rescue me!"

There is no answer. God warned Moses, and Moses warned the Ancient Israelite Nation to annihilate heathens wherever they would settle. Hence, it was the Israelites' freedom of choice—as it is every human being—to follow deceivers or obey God's Commandments.

> It is written: *When thou art come into the land which the* Lord *thy God giveth thee, thou shalt* **not** *learn to do after the abominations of those nations* {the Lord hates}. *There shall* **not** *be found among you anyone that maketh his son or his daughter to pass* {burn alive} *through the fire* {or abortion clinic except for unusual circumstances}, *or that useth divination, or an observer of times, or an enchanter, or a witch, or a charmer, or a consulter with familiar spirits, or a wizard, or a necromancer* {magician involved with the deceased}. *For all that do these things are an abomination unto the* Lord: *and because of these abominations, the*

LORD *thy God doth drive them out from before thee.*
{But} **Thou shalt be perfect with the** LORD **thy God.**

(KJ Dt 18:9-13)

King Solomon, filled with the wisdom of God, initially followed in the wise steps of his father, King David. Although Kings David and Solomon both engaged in life in the fullness of God, both experienced the consequences of committing the fullness of backsliding via adultery and polygamy. Learning from his right and wrong of everything he found possible to do, Solomon put to pen his wisdom. He authored the Bible's books of Proverbs, Ecclesiastes, and Song of Solomon. The following best sums up his first respect for the LORD.

> It is written: *Let us hear the conclusion of the whole matter:* **Fear God, and keep his commandments: for this is the whole duty of man.** *For God shall bring every work into judgment, with every secret thing, whether it be good, or whether it be evil.* (KJ Ecc 12:13-14)

Paul of the New Testament reiterated God's warnings to the *many called* by God that God's love is highly conditional. Meeting the conditions of God's unfailing love distinguishes the *few chosen* for His kingdoms from many left behind who will never qualify. It's all spelled out. For example,

> It is written: *Now the works of the flesh are manifest, which are these;* Adultery, fornication, uncleanness, lasciviousness, idolatry, witchcraft,

*hatred {for righteousness}, variance, emulations {cloning}, wrath, strife, seditions, heresies, envyings, murders, drunkenness, revellings, and such like: of the which I tell you before, as I have also told you in time past, that they which do such things shall **not** inherit the kingdom of God.*

*But the fruit of the Spirit is love {**for righteousness**}, joy, peace, **longsuffering**, gentleness, goodness, faith, meekness, temperance: against such, there is no law.*

(KJ Gal 5:19–21)

A ✝ Ω

In summarizing **THE DESTRUCTIVE FORCES OF GOD,** you are either with or against God. Being with Him has its requirements: read, study, believe, and obey per the full and intended context of the Bible! Doing so will result in heavenly beings serving you while heathens shall hate and persecute you. On the other hand, by making God out as a myth, which nullifies His way, the heathens will love you and make you a slave to them. Also, turning your back to God will rise into a moment of instant gratification, followed by both forces of evil and celestial beings out to destroy you.

A REFLECTION OF GOD'S WAY

III. Thou shalt not take the name of the LORD thy God in vain; for the LORD will not hold him guiltless that taketh his name in vain.

(KJ Ex 20:7, Dt 5:11, Mt 5:34-36, Mk 3:29)

[This monumental commandment forbids misrepresenting God, Christ, the Holy Spirit, and the full context of Scripture. Unfortunately, misrepresentation has led to a massive violation of all God's commandments. Hence, likely doomed are all living in violation of this commandment.]

IV. Remember the Sabbath day by keeping it holy. Six days you shall labor and do all your work, but the seventh day is a Sabbath to the LORD your God. On it you shall not do any work, neither you nor your son or daughter, nor your manservant or maidservant, nor your animals, nor the alien within your gates. For in six {allegorical} days, the LORD made the heavens and the earth, the sea, and all that is in them, but he rested on the seventh day (2Pe 3:8). Therefore, the LORD blessed the Sabbath day and made it holy.

(KJ Ex 20:8-11, Dt 5:12-15, Mk 2:27-28)

ENGRAVED IN STONE BY GOD FOR HIS ELECT

[Jesus Christ did not abolish these commandments!]

(KJ Mt 5:17-20, 1Jn 2:3-6, Rev 14:12)

A † Ω

VII. THE FAVORED BY GOD

It is written: And all Israel from Dan even to Beersheba knew that **Samuel** was established to be a prophet of the LORD. And the LORD appeared again in Shiloh: **for the LORD revealed himself to Samuel** in Shiloh by the word of the LORD. (KJ 1Sa 3:20–21)

It is written: Now God had brought **Daniel** into favour and tender love {kindness} with the prince of the eunuchs. (KJ Da 1:9, 6:22, 9:23, 10:11 and 19)

It is written: The angel {Gabriel} went to her {**Mary**} and said, *"Greetings, you who are highly favored! The Lord is with you."* (NIV Lk 1:28)

Throughout the Bible, seen is God favoring specific individuals above all others. The following episode is a perfect example. It is in the Old Testament's Book of Numbers. This example portrays Moses challenged by his brother Aaron, married to Elisheba (KJ Ex 6:23), and their sister Miriam. Aaron and Miriam challenged Moses out of jealousy and because he was married to an Ethiopian, Zipporah. She was a black woman from the line of Ham (p. 45) rather than a Hebrew as themselves from the line of Shem (KJ Nu 12:1–5). Recall that after Moses murdered the Egyptian, he escaped 300 miles from the city of Rameses to Midian near Mount Sinai. There, he remained for forty years with the family of Reuel, the Ethiopian priest. Reuel gave his daughter Zipporah to Moses in marriage. Furthermore, God favored Ruel's Ethiopian family for sheltering Moses.

> It is written: And Miriam and Aaron spake against Moses because of the Ethiopian woman whom he had married: for he had married an Ethiopian woman. And they said, Hath the Lord indeed spoken only by Moses? Hath he not spoken also by us? **And the Lord heard it.** (Now the man Moses was very meek, above all the men which were upon the face of the earth.)
>
> And the Lord spake suddenly unto Moses, and unto Aaron, and unto Miriam, *Come out ye three unto the tabernacle of the congregation.* And they three came out.
>
> And the Lord came down in the pillar of the cloud, and stood in the door of the tabernacle, and called Aaron and Miriam: and they both came forth. And he said, *Hear now my words: If there be a prophet among you, I the Lord will make myself known unto him in a vision, and will speak unto him in a dream.*
>
> ***My servant Moses is not so, who is faithful in all mine house.*** *With him will I speak mouth to mouth, even apparently, and not in dark speeches; and the similitude of the Lord shall he behold: wherefore then were ye not afraid to speak against my servant Moses?*

And the anger of the Lord was kindled against them; and he departed. And the cloud departed from off the tabernacle; and, behold, Miriam became leprous, white as snow: and Aaron looked upon Miriam, and, behold, she was leprous.

And Aaron said unto Moses, *Alas, my lord, I beseech thee, lay not the sin upon us, wherein we have done foolishly, and wherein we have sinned. Let her not be as one dead, of whom the flesh is half consumed when he cometh out of his mother's womb.*

And Moses cried unto the Lord, saying, *Heal her now, O God, I beseech thee.*

And the Lord said unto Moses, *If her father had but spit in her face, should she not be ashamed seven days? Let her be shut out from the camp seven days, and after that let her be received in again.*

And Miriam was shut out from the camp seven days: and the people journeyed not till Miriam was brought in again. And afterward the people removed from Hazeroth, and pitched in the wilderness of Paran.

(KJ Nu 12:1–16)

Question: *Why does God favor a few individuals above others that appear contradictory to other Scriptures, implying that God loves everyone equally?* (KJ Ac 10:34, Ro 2:11, and Col 3:25)

Discovered is the answer to that mystery in the dual interpretation of the Bible: the mainstream versus the suppressed and spiritually coded historical and literal aspects, in conjunction with its symbolical and metaphorical interpretations. Mainstream interpretations emphasize God as not expressing favoritism to have everyone believe that God loves all unconditionally without bias, particularly the wicked. But what does the Bible honestly say about this matter? The answer is in the suppressed **full context** of Scripture; otherwise, it misleads! Acts 10:34 is a perfect example to which I'm referring. In its case, Scripture is out of context through missing words. For example:

> It is written: Then Peter said, *Of a truth I perceive that God is no respecter of persons:* (KJ Ac 10:34)

At first glance, you find Peter—one of Jesus' apostles—saying that *God does not show bias.* The truth is that Acts 10:34 standing alone is misleading. Why? It is because it is void of critical life-giving-spiritual components that share its intended interpretation. Discovered are those missing components in Acts 10:35, altering it from misleading to truthful. And so, continuing where we left off:

> It is written: *But in every nation he that feareth him, and worketh righteousness {obey His commandments}, is accepted with him.* (KJ Ac 10:35)

Now connect Acts 10:34 to 10:35. There alone, you will discover that *God is no respecter of evil people while favoring and accepting all who fear Him and follow His righteous ways.*

> It is written: Then Peter said, *Of a truth I perceive that God is no respecter of {wicked} persons: But in every nation he that feareth him, and worketh righteousness, is accepted with him.* (KJ Ac 10:34-35)

Acts 10:34-35 reaffirms the Old Testament with whom God finds favor. Again, *they are* [repentant] *people who fear Him and do what is right* (KJ Ge 18:19, 2Sa 8:15). They resound throughout the Bible. [Living according to God's principles is doing like the Prophets: *to continue wholeheartedly in His way* (NIV 1Ki 8:23, 61).]

Look at a close friend of Peter's Acts 10:34-35. That close friend is the Apostle Paul, who also stated that *God does not show favoritism* in his letter to the Romans. Standing alone, Paul's Romans 2:11 is open to deception, as is Peter's Acts 10:34. However, God's intended message is discovered in what—in this case—precedes Romans 2:11 rather than what follows as in Acts 10:34; otherwise, the two are identical. Witness this truth for yourself.

> It is written: *For there is no respect of persons with God.* (KJ Ro 2:11)

Now, add what **precedes** Romans 2:11 and discover **God's truthful meaning in the full context of the Scripture**, as with Acts 10:34-35. Testify it to others you care about making it to Heaven and *avoiding the second death* (KJ Rev 2:11, 20:14, 21:8).

> It is written: *To them who by patient continuance in well doing seek for glory and honour and immortality,* {they will reap} *eternal life. But unto them*

> *that are contentious, and do **not** obey the truth, but obey **unrighteousness**, {there shall be} indignation and wrath, tribulation and anguish, upon every **soul** of man that doeth evil: of the Jew first, and also of the Gentile. But glory, honour, and peace, {will be given} to every man that worketh good, to the Jew first, and also to the Gentile. For there is no respect of {evil} persons with God.*
>
> (KJ Ro 2:7–11)

Here, Paul, as did Peter, clearly points out whom God favors versus whom He hates and how he pays out each. For example, *God will give eternal life to the few who seek glory, honor, and immortality **by persistence in doing good**. However, there will be wrath, anger, trouble, and distress for self-seekers who reject the truth and follow evil.*

Now, look at the full context of another related Scripture: Colossians 3:25. Here, Paul reinforces God as favoring and granting well-being and salvation to all who dedicate their work and lives to Him while dooming evildoers.

> It is written: *And whatsoever ye do, do it heartily, as to the Lord, and not unto men; knowing that of the Lord ye shall receive the reward of the inheritance: for ye serve the Lord Christ. But he that doeth wrong shall receive for the wrong which he hath done: and there is no respect of {wicked} persons.* (KJ Col 3:23–25)

Should God exhibit love to all who do wrong, wouldn't you agree that *salvation* would be the same for those He finds favor as with those He hates as the signs of *serpents* and their *worshipers of deception* attest to one and all, which read, **"Jesus loves you?"** Of course! It would be: precisely what the *enemies of God* have theirs believing! But, that is not at all the case, say, like *sunshine* and *rainfall* (KJ Mt 5:45) bestowed to one and all per God.

Moreover, Jesus addressed the clergy for their false teachings, which angered them to do away with the real Him. America lost being in God's grace because of this!

> It is written: *Isaiah was right when he prophesied about you hypocrites; as it is written:*
>
> *These people honor me with their lips, but their hearts are far from me. They worship me in vain; their teachings are but rules taught by men.*
>
> *You have let go of the commands of God and are holding on to the traditions of men.*
>
> And he said to them: *You have a fine way of setting aside the commands of God in order to observe your own traditions!*
>
> (NIV Mk 7:6-9, Mt 15:7-9, Isa 29:13)

Thus, I hope you are beginning to recognize the significance of having to read, study, believe, and obey God's complete Word on your own. Repeatedly, you should if you aspire to qualify for His kingdoms and avoid *the second death*—Hell (KJ Rev 2:11, 20:14, 21:8). Why? The Bible makes known whom God loves versus those He hates and dooms. It defines righteousness and evil and defies the lies of *pulpit serpents*, demonic religions, and other cults.

Hence, without correct knowledge and belief in the full context of *God's Spoken Word*, most are highly likely to fall for any and everything heard out of *pulpit serpents, devilish politicians,* and *the fake media* without ever coming upon the truth about God. Therefore, by familiarizing yourself with God's complete Word, you would quickly recognize that while most of the clergy suppress the full context of Scripture as much as possible, they choose what they want, throw out the rest, and carve a path to Hell.

For example, people of the Jewish faith remain focused on the Five Books of Moses: *Genesis, Exodus, Leviticus, Numbers, and Deuteronomy.* On the other hand, Gospel people remain concentrated in the Gospels: *Matthew, Mark, Luke, and John.* Some find comfort in the *Psalms* or the *Epistles of Paul.* Other approaches to the Bible—most involving snippet preaching and teaching—evolved into demonic religions and non-denominational churches across the globe! However, not a single incomplete approach to the Bible expresses ALPHA AND OMEGA: ***the fullness of Christ, which He referred to as the manifestation of Himself, including "the way, the truth, and the life"*** (Jn 14:6, Rev 1:8).

Three years before making that proclamation, He corrected a tempter—*serpent* and *devil* all in one—out to destroy Him with Deuteronomy 8:3 from the Old Testament.

> It is written: *Man{'s spirit} doth not live by bread only, but by every word that proceedeth out of the*

mouth of the LORD *doth man{'s spirit} live.* (KJ Dt 8:3, Mt 4:4)

There are several questions to consider, knowing that the undeniable facts about God and Jesus encompass ALPHA AND OMEGA—*Genesis through Revelation: the First and the Last, the Beginning and the End,* **every word of the Lord.**

1) Where do you stand with reading the complete Bible at least once?

2) Is the full context of God's word and obedience to His commands your guiding light?

3) Do you believe God is unconditionally in love with the human race no matter what?

4) Who is your Jesus? Do you regard him as a stand-alone, unconditional, all-loving savior without substance, void of the Commandments of God? Is your Jesus void of the Old Testament, apart from the full context of the Bible? **All are *serpent* lies that will take you straight to the second death!**

5) If you are uncertain or not at peace with God, what will you do about it?

I will cover this dynamic topic in more detail in Chapter XV: MISLEADING THROUGH SNIPPETS!

A † Ω

In summarizing **THE FAVORED BY GOD,** know God *favors* all who *continue wholeheartedly in his way* (NIV-1Ki 8:23, 61). He supports all who obey His commands, a theme throughout ALPHA AND OMEGA. **But don't take my word for it.** He prefers you read, study, and believe it. To encourage you in that direction, consider the following Scriptures signifying the importance of living according to His righteous principles—over following prevaricators.

> It is written: *For thou, LORD, wilt bless the righteous; with favour wilt thou compass him as with a shield.* (Ps 5:12)

> It is written: *By this I know that thou* {Almighty God} *favourest me,* **because mine enemy doth not triumph over me.** (KJ Ps 41:10-11}

> It is written: *A good* {righteous} *man obtaineth favour of the LORD: but a man of wicked devices* {such as officials using corrupt voting machines} *will he condemn.* (KJ Pr 12:2)

God indeed has favorites, including righteous non-Jews. He is biased toward the few that first and foremost *repent* (KJ Mt 4:4) and *continue* {on} *wholeheartedly in His way* (NIV 1Ki 8:23, 61). Likewise, it never fails that—at some point in time—God contends with evil people who humiliate, intimidate, slander, steal from, and physically harm those He favors (KJ 2Ki 2:23-25, Esther, Ps 34:17-20, Ps 35-37, Eze Chpt 9, Da Chpts 3 and 6, Ac 12:21-23).

VIII. UNFAILING LOVE VS. UNCONDITIONAL LOVE

INTRIGUED

It is written: *Draw nigh to God, and {only then will} he will draw nigh to you.* (KJ Jas 4:8)

Now consider the genuine love relationship God desires of His followers, Himself, and people throughout His kingdoms. In relationships, at least two involved must express love to one another. No Exceptions! In other words, regardless of whether someone has a passion for you while you do not care for them, a love relationship does not exist. Why? It is because love is a two-way association having common ground. It's the same with God. The Bible states that God certainly does not have a connection with most people. Instead, His love extends only to the few having a passion for His way, as expressed throughout His correctly interpreted Word.

Hence, it is up to every twenty-year-old and older desiring membership to God's kingdoms to develop an association with Him per His conditions, not the other way around! Furthermore, Scripture holds people accountable for acquiring God's love. For if they refuse to draw near to Him through *the truth* [His complete and correctly interpreted Word], in conjunction with *the way* [obedience to His life-saving commandments], he most certainly will **not** connect with them (KJ Jer 29:13, Jn 14:6).

The Bible teaches that God's higher order of love is *unfailing love.* It is the opposite of Satan's *unconditional love* (CB and NIV Ex 15:13; Ps 6:4, 13:5, 18:50, 21:7, 31:16, 32:10, 33:5, 51:1, 107:15 and 31, 119:41 and 76, 143:8 and 12; Isa 54:10). Moreover, having heard repeated lies concerning God having *unconditional love,* I inquired of the Lord by asking: *"What is unfailing love?"* I asked that question because **unfailing love** was throughout the Chronological and NIV Bibles. **However, nothing was found or hinted at God expressing *unconditional love* in the Scriptures of the CB, King James, NIV, NCV, or The Living Bibles. Hence, *the unconditional love myth*** annoyed me. Through the *Spirit of Truth,* the Lord said:

> *Unfailing love is my kind of love. It's the highest order of holiness I have given humankind to live by* (NIV Pr 19.22). *Unfailing love—expressed through obedience to my commandments* (KJ Jn 14:21, 23-24)—*is*

love that cannot backslide; in other words, I cannot sin against myself. I cannot lie, steal, or cheat; however, you found that I will safeguard the sanctity of my Kingdoms with whatever is necessary, as a responsible and good father out to protect his family from a destroyer: precisely what I look for in my few.

Through the *Spirit of Truth*, the Lord spoke on:

*My **unfailing love** is what I want parents to teach their children for their well-being so that they may become members of my smaller but obedient Kingdom on Earth: a prerequisite for getting into my much larger Kingdom of Heaven. **Unfailing love is holy and pure.** Defined in my Word (NIV 1Co 13:4–8) are the conditions of my unwavering love in its purest form:*

*Love is patient; love is kind. It does not envy; it does not boast; it is not proud. It is not rude; it is not self-seeking; it is not easily angered—**but most certainly can be**—and it keeps no record of wrongs of those few who sincerely **repent** of their sinful pleasures and believe in the truth of my Word. **Love does not delight in evil but rejoices with the truth.***

Each condition defines the boundary between good and evil. Each is a condition that I want my followers to display and teach. Obedience to the commandments is how I distinguish the few I choose to be my own.

*That explains **the unfailing and conditional love** I want to make known to everyone. As the Bible points out repeatedly, no one will be exempt from learning and obeying the quali-*

fications for entering the Kingdom of Heaven.

Unfailing love has borders and expectations. Unconditional love is pretentious and has no limits or expectations. It often results in every misguided aspect of one's dark and hopeless pagan life: lying, stealing, cheating, murdering, idolatry, covetousness, and immorality. Moreover, pagan rhetoric condones it all, beginning with Jesus loving you unconditionally and discarding your sins no matter what.

On the truthful side of that coin, unfailing love is a display of integrity. Unconditional love has no integrity. It is deception-based, whereby evil flows everywhere, like lava from a volcano. Do what you want to do, believe whatever you want, and let the good times roll against the will of God. When tragedy strikes, you often hear these dead spirits passing blame, crying out something like:

"*I just can't believe God let this happen.*"

Faced with lying, stealing, cheating, and destruction on the part of the sinful people of the world, Jesus, dying on the cross, put it this way:

Eloi, Eloi, lama sabachthani? — which, interpreted is, M*y* G*od*, *my* G*od*, *why hast thou forsaken me?* (KJ Mk 15:34)

In other words, while nailed to a cross, experiencing excruciating pain, Jesus expressed how people who abandon God end up having God forsake them. When tragedy strikes, most cannot possibly accept why God allowed terrible things to happen to them. They look for excuses and blame others rather than look in a mirror and blame themselves. Their denial and false accusations include forsaking God's way while attempting to lay siege on *Kingsmen: honorable people of integrity* (KJ Ge 18:19, 2Sa 8:15), *having the Spirit of Christ destroying the works of devils* (KJ 1Jn 3:8).

The excuse for forsaking the spiritual truth of God's word and commandments may be *enemies of God*, peer pressure, or freedom of choice not to believe in the facts. Nevertheless, everyone throughout the universe setting out for the Kingdom of Heaven is held accountable by God in the reality of His word and obedience to His commandments: bar none!

> It is written: *Let the field be joyful, and all that is therein: then shall all the trees of the wood {His elect} rejoice before the* Lord: *for he cometh, for he cometh to judge the earth: he shall judge the world with righteousness, and the people with his truth.* (KJ Ps 96:12–13)

Evaluated according to obedience to God's commandments is credible judgment. It begins with *repentance* followed by *integrity* through *holiness, righteousness, and truthfulness:* **God's principles.** Moreover, God assesses each according to our knowledge of, belief in, and respect for the fullness of His word. The whole context of Scripture—*the full armor of God*—makes those facts about Him and true faith of primary importance for salvation.

A ✝ Ω

SATAN'S CHURCHES AND IDEOLOGIES

Now, discover how *serpents* persuade congregations into forsaking the truth. But before moving forward, let me make it clear that by no means are all clergy people prevaricators. By no factor would I make such judgment of individuals serving God—as He intended—as their way of life. Godly men and women who preach and teach Bible truth—*the full armor of God*—welcome being monitored by what they preach and teach because facts and Bible faith are their honorable existence. THE ALPHA THROUGH OMEGA PROJECT does not question these masters of God's word; instead, it is to esteem them.

However, it is the responsibility of all adults intending to earn salvation to discover the truth, whether inspired by a spokesman of God or misled by *serpents*. These include seminary students who want to serve God and demand Bible truth over concoctions of what religious schools falsely make God out as being. Unfortunately, many become—as Jesus put it—*"twice as much a son of Hell"* (NIV Mt 23:15) for being brainwashed in idol worship, immorality, religious lies, satanic rituals, snippets, superstition, and worthless traditions in place of the full context of the entire Bible.

Getting people to see the truth about God is one of the objectives of THE ALPHA THROUGH OMEGA PROJECT: to move the *many called* to read, study, believe, and obey God's word on their own. Then, if found to be under the spell of deceivers, be set free to have *life more abundantly* (KJ Jn 10:10): God's intended plan for His people. That would include being at home in the Bible with excellent health, happiness, prosperity, success, *and victories over the enemies of God* (KJ Ps 41:11)! **However, persecution is always part of the package.**

Therefore, being made to believe having *life more abundantly* is evil, as the *enemies of God* profess to all except themselves, then it is past time to administer the left foot of fellowship to some church or not-so-good friends. God's *elect* model *life more abundantly* every moment of the day, for anyone caring to take notice of Christ working through them, as they *destroy the works of devils* (1Jn 3:8). [Moreover, God's heavenly home is *laden with pure gold* (KJ Rev 21:18-20). It is not a trashy shack with debris strewn alongside the roads as you find throughout Satan's strongholds established and planned by devils.]

The works of *devils* reduce humanity to its lowest form, where evil and poverty are for "*the common good.*" Their Utopia ideologies create stinking-rat-infested-tent-cities where public human excrement replaces human dignity. Even their environmental ideologies—the cause of massive forest fires—destroy millions of acres of valuable timber and wildlife, preventable with common sense that possessive Utopians do not possess.

A fact check! Never will devils live up to their promises for those they control. After all, their mission is to bring **down** the opposition to its lowest level as they lord over their ignorant, self-deprived, poverty-stricken Utopians.

Such downward spirals originated with demonic ideologies about God being unbiased and unconditionally in love with the human race. Those were distractions to manipulate the truth about God to accommodate their corruption.

So, consider what worship should be. First, attending church should be about appropriately worshiping God. It should be about instilling the truth of God's word and obedience to His way as the number one priority. Ask anyone from any of the various agnostic religions about it. Be assured they will say, *"Going to church most certainly is **not** about the Bible, much less instilling God's commands!"* Politically congregating against both and organizing to abandon Christian values—now we are talking about the teachings of agnostics. They are the world's breeding and nesting ground of organizations determined to abolish Christianity and Democracy while being set free from paying taxes disguised as churches! They instill God as a myth, and freedom from God is exhilarating.

Who are they? They are the anti-Christ: Atheists, Communists, Liberals, Leftists, and Socialists. Unfortunately, and to the detriment of God-fearing people, such *dead spirits* have filled the seats in many influential positions.

Hence, dissuading congregations from seeking the truth of God's word and His way is achieved with deception, idol worship, and manipulating the Scriptures. For example, sometimes used is the following to discourage and disgrace anyone in a church daring to reject false mainstream religious beliefs and research the truth about God.

> It is written: *Now as touching things offered unto idols, we know that we all have knowledge. Knowledge puffeth up, but charity edifieth. And if any man think that he knoweth any thing, he knoweth nothing yet as he ought to know.* (KJ 1Co 8:1-2)

Those Scriptures are **demeaning, controlling,** and **misleading when taken out of context.** Therefore, let me remind the *many called* to the Kingdoms of God that the same Paul, who included that statement in a letter to the Corinthians, is the same Paul who abounded with wisdom about God and righteousness. Paul's prolific knowledge enabled him to be chosen by God as a prudent apostle (KJ Ro 1:1). Moreover, he was not a pastor or priest, *devil* or *serpent,* atheist, socialist or communist, but Roman and Jewish. Following the resurrection of Jesus, he carried on with Holy Spirit facts and revelations about Christ worldwide. Furthermore, with the help of scribes such as Tertius (KJ Ro 16:22), Paul is the author of one-fourth of the New Testament. His work includes the Epistles of Romans through Philemon. However, he was also a role model and star witness in Luke's *Book of Acts*.

Now, look at what follows 1Co 8:1-2 for its true meaning authored by the same Paul inspired by the Holy Spirit:

> It is written: *But if any man loves God, the same is known of him.* (KJ 1Co 8:3)

And how does one come to express love to God to have God connect with him (KJ Ge 18:19) instead of puffing up in arrogance or needing a psychiatrist? Choose wisely:

A. Accepting as God's will everything preached and taught about Him in the church, such as *Jesus loves sinners unconditionally; Homosexuals are loved by God and qualify for heaven; Jesus condones lying and stealing; Bless me, Father, for I have sinned.* —OR—

B. Gaining wisdom about God by reading and studying *Genesis through Revelation* on your own, then acting upon the full context of Scripture above all else.

"B" is, by far, the correct answer. By following that lead, you would have a greater chance of knowing the truth behind Scripture. For example, the full context of 1Co 8:1-3 is that Paul corrected the Corinthians concerning animal sacrifice as a form of worship, which Christ abolished through His execution.

Even so, look at a synonym for the word puff, sometimes used to insult anyone questioning false church doctrines.

—Syn. **Puff:** *fill.* [54] —

"Fill" expresses what God expects of His few faithful followers to increase their wisdom and acquire knowledge about Satan's evil world in overcoming it. Overcoming is not to say that everything in the world is terrible, for it is through understanding the full context of Scripture that one distinguishes good from evil and *Kingsmen* from *devils*. Without it, you are like a ship without a rudder.

---

[54] *Puff,* Charlton Laird, <u>Webster's New Roget's A-Z Thesaurus,</u> 3rd ed. (Boston: Houghton Mifflin Harcourt), 2003.

You'll end up on the rocks.

> It is written: *Wise men lay up knowledge: but the mouth of the foolish is near destruction.* (KJ Pr 10:14)

> It is written: *And they that be wise shall shine as the brightness of the firmament; and they that turn many to righteousness as the stars for ever and ever.* (KJ Da 12:3)

On the other hand, remaining ignorant about God and those he hates is **ominous**. It leads to a shameless life of pretentious happiness inspired by *devils, serpents,* and the *worshipers of deception* without heeding warnings in an evil world!

> Def. **ominous:** *1. portending evil or harm; foreboding, threatening; inauspicious; 2. having the significance of an omen: inviting a significant and harmful outcome.*[55]

Hence, the way to draw near to God is evident throughout His Spoken Word. Jesus said,

> It is written: **Man shall not live by bread alone, but by every word that proceedeth out of the mouth of God.** (KJ Dt 8:3, Mt 4:4)

Fact Check: *Every word that proceeded out of the mouth of God* <u>includes</u> THE TEN COMMANDMENTS. God

---

[55] *Ominous,* Webster's Encyclopedic Unabridged Dictionary.

spoke (Ex 20:3-17) **and wrote them twice very early on (KJ Ex 31:18 and 32:15-16 the first time; 34:1, 28 the second time). Never let a day go by without reciting them. Repent and live by them. Make them your constitution!**

Thus, the pathway to associating with God and gaining His approval is through the fullness of the Scriptures. The big question is: Will you be able to acquire all the Scriptures when administered *The Last Rites* or while simmering in *Gehenna* [Catholicism's fictitious denial of Hell]? Contrary to popular belief, the answer to those profound questions is again emphatical:*"NO!"* False religious beliefs, deathbed rituals, and a fictional *Gehenna* do not get anyone into the Kingdom of Heaven. Neither does, *"Lord, you know I'm a sinner!"* Say that at the Pearly Gates, and Jesus will remind you of what He said, *"I never knew you: depart from me ye that work iniquity"* (KJ Mt 7:23).

Created was Hell for **un**repentant sinners! God is not graceful or merciful for wicked people who did **or** did not attend church throughout their lifespan and never were at home with His complete Bible. Being at home with God is being at home in *Genesis through Revelation*. It is **not** *walking in the counsel of the wicked, standing in the way of sinners, or sitting in the seat of mockers* (KJ Ps 1).

A ✝ Ω

In summarizing this chapter, **UNFAILING LOVE** vs. **UNCONDITIONAL LOVE,** the Bible teaches that love is a two-way relationship, especially with God!

> It is written: ***For whoso findeth me findeth life, and shall obtain favour of the L*****ORD*****,*** *but he that sinneth against me wrongeth his own soul: all they that hate me love death.* (KJ Pr 8:35–36)

> It is written: *The Lord is far from the wicked;* ***but he heareth the prayer of the righteous.*** (KJ Pr 15:29)

> It is written: *Come unto me, all ye that labour and are heavy laden, and I will give you rest. Take my yoke upon you, and learn of me; for I am meek {righteous} and lowly {pure} in heart: and ye shall find rest unto your souls. For my yoke is easy, and my burden is light.* (KJ Mt 11:28–30)

Hence, there is a significant difference between **unfailing love** and unconditional love. **Unfailing love reflects integrity.** Unconditional love demonstrates every form of evil, made to look and sound politically correct, formulated for corrupt and perverted minds whose motto is:

> "**Whatever distractions it takes
> to suppress reality and truth to gain power, do it!**"

Serpents and *devils* thrive in Satan's world under that Hell-bound mission. It leads many astray into believing God's love is unconditional while money grows on trees. Falling head over heels over their rhetoric, demonic ideologies, intimidation, and propaganda deserve abandonment and annihilation from God (Eze 9). Both include the works of death angels, crashes, massacres, natural disasters, and suffering beyond imagined, *for the woes of the wicked are many* (NIV Ps 32:10)! The Bible illustrates this repeatedly for all who believe in God's word.

It is written: Mark the perfect man, and behold the upright: for the end of that man is peace.

But the transgressors shall be destroyed together: the end of the wicked shall be cut off.

*But the salvation of **the righteous** is of the* L<small>ORD</small>*: he is their strength in the time of trouble. And the* L<small>ORD</small> *shall help them, and deliver them: he shall deliver them from the wicked, and save them, because they trust in him.*

(KJ Ps 37:37–40)

It is written: . . . Yea, they have chosen their own ways, and their soul delighteth in their abominations. I also will choose their delusions, and will bring their fears upon them; **because when I called, none did answer; when I spake, they did not hear:** *but they did evil before mine eyes, and chose that in which I delighted not.* (KJ Isa 66:3–4)

Therefore, should you open your heart up to the complete Bible, you will likely receive discernment regarding what pleases God and what drives God to wrath.

IX. CHARITY

*I*t is noteworthy that English interpreters and writers of the original King James Bible, authorized English version as of the year 1611, substituted the word charity for *unfailing love* in 1Corinthians 13:4–8.

> It is written: *Charity suffereth long, and is kind; charity envieth not; charity vaunteth not itself, is not puffed up. Doth not behave itself unseemly, seeketh not her own, is not easily provoked, thinketh no evil; Rejoiceth* **not** *in iniquity, but rejoiceth in the truth; Beareth all* {holy and righteous} *things, believeth all* {truthful} *things, hopeth* {that} *all* {disputed} *things* {turn out the undeniable facts}, *endureth all* {challenging} *things.*
>
> *Charity never faileth; but whether there be* {false} *prophecies, they shall fail; whether there be* {lying} *tongues, they shall cease; whether there be knowledge* {of evil}, *it shall* {be made known and then those held responsible for evil shall} *vanish away.*
>
> (KJ 1Co 13:4–8)

There are two factors involved with charities. (1) They are a form of unfailing love, but not all-inclusive **AGAPE**. The word charity denotes giving freely from a good heart and with good intentions: the implied qualifications of charitable giving. (2) God, like a credible and responsible charity, holds organizations accountable that freely receive generous handouts.

It is written: *Withhold not good from them to whom it is due, when it is in the power of thine hand to do it.* (KJ Pr 3:27)

It is written: *He who is kind to the poor lends to the LORD, and He will reward him for what he has done.* (NIV Pr 19:17)

It is written: *Neither is there any creature that is not manifest in his sight: but all things are naked and opened unto the eyes of him with whom we have to do.* (KJ Heb 4:13)

Agape charity is not a form of unconditional love. For example, you may regularly donate to an orphanage because your heart goes out to children. Should the administrators in charge of that orphanage put your charitable donations to legitimate use, your contributions are a pleasing aroma to God. Similarly, most of us have given street people handouts because our hearts went out to them. Nevertheless, God holds all beggars accountable for what they do with what they freely receive. Likewise, all others are responsible for what they do with their earnings.

A † Ω

BEWARE OF NON–PROFIT CHARITIES!

God expects His *elect* to honor Him in all aspects of life, including the financial realm. However, beware of schemes exploiting God's wish to defraud. Should you fall head over heels for beautiful brochures and flattering propaganda mailed out to you by false big-business charities preying on your emotions, they would have accomplished their mission of defrauding you.

For example, I contributed to the *American Bible Society* for several years. Its collectors continually pleaded with me to increase my contributions to their desperate situations in getting Bibles out to the world. However, later, I discovered that this *"non-profit"* organization was Catholic-based: haters of Bible truth. I found that it owned over a billion dollars in assets and indoctrinated the worship of Mary, saints, and *"Bless me, Father, for I have sinned."* Giving to them is giving to the devil.

Moreover, suppose a charitable organization hoarded a billion dollars in assets. In that case, it does not need donations, regardless of who they are and how desperate for money they claim to be. Thus, I stopped donating to their false mission, although they continued to inundate me monthly with false pleas for money and to have me will my estate to them.

By all indications, the prevaricators running that charity *"for-profit"* use Bibles as bait in a critter's trap. Without a doubt, through deception, they collect billions of tax-free dollars to support their demonic cult, far more significant than giving away Bibles that threaten their existence. After all, a billion dollars in assets does not drop out of the sky by doing what these liars overwhelmingly profess!

As in any reputable organization, God expects His loving giving people to hold charitable organizations accountable for using tax-free money. That voids the possibility that charity is unconditional. For example, should you discover your philanthropic donations to build a children's playground in your neighborhood are for drug trafficking, wouldn't you stop giving to that organization? Wouldn't you report their demise to your local law enforcement agency? Of course, you would, unless you had part or all interest in profiting from the children buying the drugs, whose well-being is of absolutely no concern to you.

The Bible writers never intended charity as a form of unconditional giving, unconditional love, or anything else unconditional.

A † Ω

GIVING: AN ENJOYMENT

Giving can take shape in many creative forms as God moves an individual out of a carnal mindset. For example, on November 10, 2016, two days following the presidential election, I decided to give away my extensive Hollywood DVD Collection.

Without hesitation, I quietly packed them away that day and delivered them to Goodwill. I had no second thoughts about abolishing much of Hollywood from my life—from that point forward—having lost total respect for many movie producers and stars I once admired, who revealed their true God-hating natures throughout the election process. It was heart-breaking seeing many in movie productions where good triumphs over evil, exhibiting an opposite personality in real life as cursed liberals: campaigning to have an evil win over good. It was a display of conspiracy against righteousness on a grand scale among wealthy, influential people void of the *Spirit of God* that made giving away their two-faced DVDs rewarding.

A ✝ Ω

Summarizing CHARITY advises that giving freely out of one's heart demands givers to hold receivers accountable. Otherwise, unconditional generosity is saying, *"I don't care what happens to what I freely give, and neither does God:"* along with the thinking of many donors that I will discuss in the next chapter.

Nevertheless, God holds everyone accountable for who and what they support. Hence, boldness in the face of darkness reflects one of God's much-hated elect engaged in talking truth and walking the walk of Christ in hostile territory. God's mission for these blessed but rejected individuals is to *work miracles* (KJ Mt 10:7-8, 1Co 12:28-31), *destroy the works of devils* (KJ 1Jn 3:8), *and inspire others to earn an honest living* (KJ 2Th 3:6-10), rather than taking advantage of generous unsuspecting people.

Additionally, God's will is not to despise those living life more abundantly, who paid the price through honesty, a good work ethic, and financial planning, after which they achieved not only the American dream but also God's promises. God's will is to follow in their steps honorably.

> It is written: {Paul speaking} *Now we command you, brethren, in the name of our Lord Jesus Christ, that ye withdraw yourselves from every brother that walketh disorderly, and not after the tradition which he received of us. For yourselves know how ye ought to follow us: for we behaved **not** ourselves disorderly among you; neither did we eat any man's bread for nought; but wrought with labour and travail night and day, that we might **not** be chargeable to any of you: Not because we have not power, but to make ourselves an ensample unto you to follow us. For even when we were with you, this we commanded you, that if any {who is capable} would not work, neither should he eat.* (KJ 2Th 3:6–10)

Therefore, honorably earning a living is God's expectation for His elect. It is not to allow oneself to become degraded with alcohol, corruption, drugs, gambling, immorality, or God-hating Leftist beliefs and end up as a beggar. Being righteous and maintaining integrity and prosperity is God's will for his people. Doing so brings many blessings, for *it is more blessed to give* {a portion of honorable earnings} *than to receive* {as beggars} (Acts 20:35)!

X. TITHING AND ALMS:
Appreciation vs. Bartering

Def: **tithes:** *the tenth part of agricultural produce or personal income set apart as an offering to God or for works of mercy, or the same amount regarded as an obligation or tax for the support of the church, priesthood, or the like.*[56]

Since the previous chapter clarified the Bible's version of charity and explained that every good cause and legitimate charity holds people accountable, this chapter clears up misunderstandings about *tithing* and *alms*. Mainstream beliefs about *tithing* are as follows:

- *A tithe is the first 10% of one's income that belongs to the church.*
- *Tithing includes service for the church.*
- *The church is the storehouse of God.*
- *God blesses people because they tithe.*
- *God loves a cheerful giver.*

Now, I will present the historical and spiritually coded interpretation of tithing that may come as a total surprise and shock to you. It will take you back to the Old Testament just before God's destruction of the kingdoms of Sodom and Gomorrah, as mentioned in Chapter IV: ABOMINATIONS THAT CAUSE DESOLATION. If you are unfamiliar with the characters in this event, who shaped the future for

---

[56] *Tithes*, Webster's Encyclopedic Unabridged Dictionary.

much of our current age, I hope this will significantly influence you to read an entire Bible repeatedly throughout your lifetime and allow God's righteous principles to govern you. It's a spiritually inspired calling for only God's *elect,* whose names are in the *Lamb's book of life* (KJ Rev 21:22-27).

The Bible's first tithing episode begins in the Book of Genesis, where theft transformed into tithes! It started with King Kedorlaomer and his three allies having robbed the doomed kingdoms of Sodom and Gomorrah.

> It is written: And they {the four kings Kedorlaomer, the king of Elam; Tidal, King of Goiim; Amraphel, King of Shinar; and Arioch, King of Ellasar} took all the goods of Sodom and Gomorrah, and all their victuals, and went their way. **And they took Lot, Abram's brother's son**, who dwelt in Sodom, and his goods, and departed. And there came one that had escaped, and told **Abram the Hebrew**; for he dwelt in the plain of Mamre the Amorite, brother of Eshcol, and brother of Aner: and these were confederate with Abram. And when Abram heard that his brother {nephew} was taken captive, he armed his trained servants, born in his own house, three hundred and eighteen {ancestors of Noah and Shem (KJ 1Ch 1:17-27)}, and pursued them unto Dan. And he divided himself against them, he and his servants, by night, and smote them, and pursued them unto Hobah, which is on the left hand of Damascus. And he brought back

all the goods, and also brought again his brother {nephew} Lot, and his goods, and the women also, and the people (KJ Ge 14:11-16).

Next is where the king of Sodom meets Abram about allowing his people to return home.

> It is written: And the king of Sodom went out to meet him after his return from the slaughter of Chedorlaomer, and of the kings that were with him, at the valley of Shaveh, which is the king's dale. (KJ Ge 14:17)

At about that moment, King Melchizedek came out from Salem: the second name of a township that later became known as *Jerusalem*, but previously known as *Jebus* {Noah—Ham—Canaan—*Jebusites*}. King Melchizedek appeared to honor Abram since God favored and respected Abram over the robbers. Three things of importance:

> 1) King Melchizedek is referred to in the Bible as the *King of Righteousness* (KJ Ge 14:18-20) {*King of Justice* (CB Heb 7:2)}. Also, He was the *King of Salem* {*King of Peace* (CB Heb 7:2)} nine hundred fifty years before Israel's first king, Saul, and 2000 years ahead of Christ.

> 2) King Melchizedek was the territorial ruler and high priest in the order of Jesus Christ, though not Jesus Christ, as the Bible is not into reincarnation. Nevertheless, King Melchizedek stands among the immortalized *Kingsmen without genealogy and the beginning of days or end of life* (KJ Ge 3:22, Heb 7:1-4).

3) *God favored Abram for being a righteous and just man* (KJ Ge 18:17-19). Abram had no hesitation in fearlessly going after and destroying the forces of evil to rescue his nephew Lot—and Lot's family.

What undoubtedly happened next was a siesta in the *King's Valley of Shaveh*. There, *King Melchizedek served bread and wine to Abram for having annihilated forces of evil* {KJ Ge 14:17}. Having the liking of a responsible king, out to destroy forces of evil, King Melchizedek came between Abram and Sodom's King Bera at just the perfect moment {KJ Ge 14:17-18}. His presence was to keep the two apart while reassuring Abram of his right standing with God and allegiance to his king. King Melchizedek knew that his servant, Abram, was exhausted and needed a little time out before making rash decisions and dealings with Sodom's King Bera. King Bera was a repulsive enemy of King Melchizedek and God.

> It is written: And Melchizedek king of Salem brought forth bread and wine: and he was the priest of the most high God. And he blessed him, and said, *Blessed be Abram of the most high God, possessor of heaven and earth: And blessed be the most high God, which hath delivered thine enemies into thy hand.* And he {Abram} gave him {King Melchizedek} tithes of all {plundered from the defeated armies}. (KJ Ge 14:18-20)

Following the siesta, King Melchizedek stepped out of Abram's way to see how Abram would deal with Sodom and Gomorrah's kings, who understandably wanted to restore their kingdoms. While King

Melchizedek brought out bread and wine to Abram—undoubtedly his victorious commander in charge of his fighting forces—Kings Bera and Birsha brought nothing to the bargaining table. All they had was hope for unjustified mercy: typical among doomed, corrupt, fool-hearted, immoral, unrepentant tyrants and their subjects, once they run their course, stand defenseless and are on the verge of slaughter.

Furthermore, none knew God's plan to burn alive Sodom's King Bera and Gomorrah's King Birsha and all people living throughout their kingdoms {KJ Ge 14:2}. That being the case, Abram put to good use their stolen goods. It would have been foolish to destroy everything in what was near at hand (KJ Ge 19:1-29). Hence, Abram's decision to recover the stolen goods and distribute them among his fighting forces of 318 men out from his household and his three allies was what King Melchizedek and God expected of Abram.

> It is written: And the king of Sodom said unto Abram, *Give me the persons, and take the goods to thyself.* {After all, what type of king is a king without subjects?}
>
> But Abram {standing nearby, responded not about the people taken captive, but regarding the greater valued plundered goods} said to the king of Sodom, *I have lift up mine hand unto the* LORD, *the most high God, the possessor of heaven and earth, that I will* **not** *take from a thread even to a shoelatchet, and that I will* **not** *take any thing that is thine, lest*

thou shouldest say, I have made Abram rich: Save only that which the young men have eaten, and the portion of the men which went with me, Aner, Eshcol, and Mamre; let them {King Melchizedek's other generals and fighting forces} *take their portion.* (KJ Ge 14:21-24).

In Abram's victorious mind—where all is fair in a war against the forces of evil, including, *To the victor go the spoils*—Abram told King Bera that he would not take any recovered goods for himself. However, rather than return those goods to Kings Bera and Birsha, Abram obliged the request of King Bera by allowing the captives to return to their homes while becoming creative in his distribution of their stolen and recovered goods:

- first 10% [a tithe] to his beloved king and high priest Melchizedek,
- the remaining 90% was divided equally among his 318 warriors and the forces allied with them, and
- loyal to his oath, Abram took nothing for himself.

Although this was an actual historical event, the episode with the two kings—however righteous King Melchizedek was, compared with how immoral King Bera was—is an allegory by which King Melchizedek serves as the ambassador to God as King Bera serves as an ambassador to Satan. Standing between the two, Abram represents God's people, who sometimes get caught between doing what's right and just in God's sight versus siding with an enemy to condone evil.

First off, God knew all three kings personally. While God favored King Melchizedek, He hated Kings Bera and Birsha. That hatred was due to homosexuality running rampant throughout Sodom and Gomorrah: that which He was out to set ablaze like never seen before. Additionally, the three kings represent pastors of two opposing churches. King Melchizedek represents the righteous clergy for God's Bible truth churches, whereas Kings Bera and Birsha represent *pulpit serpents* for Satan's Bible deception churches.

However, the three kings go beyond that allegory into a second. King Melchizedek was a giver who received even more than he already had. Kings Bera and Birsha gave way to evil and eventually lost all they had.

At the same time, blessed best was Abram with *bread and wine* (KJ Ge 14:18), *life more abundantly* (KJ Jn 10:10), *two wives and eight sons* (KJ Ge 16, 21, 25:1-2), *175 years* (KJ Ge 25:7), and *immortalization* (KJ Ge 11-25). Although tempted, Abram held to his integrity in dealing wisely with Kings Bera and Birsha, precisely as God and his beloved King Melchizedek hoped he would do. Had Abram given ear to Kings Bera and Birsha like Eve with the charming *serpent* and Aaron with Miriam, he would have lost everything in his possession. God and his beloved King Melchizedek would have likely banished Abram from their sights, as God did to Lucifer, Adam and Eve, *serpents*, *giants*, and other first families for insurrection.

Remember also the people that the king of Sodom asked Abram to return. Since all these homosexuals were relieved over being rescued by Abram, remaining true to his word in choosing to do the right thing, he honored that request without hesitation. How can you know that for sure? Good question!

Where recorded in the 14th Chapter of Genesis is the episode, found is the answer in the 19th. Lot and his family are back at their home in Sodom, fighting off an unrepentant mob of rescued gay men in pursuit of God's two magnificent angels. It was where all hell was getting ready to break loose because even when a door of opportunity opens for them to **repent**, it proved that most homoerotics never will. It also confirmed that God's angels are striking in appearance, elegant, brilliant, sacred, all-powerful, and to be feared rather than lusted.

Review the entire episode to untangle any remaining confusion concerning the facts about tithing for God. Melchizedek, an eternal king and high priest of righteousness from Salem 950 years ahead of Israel's first king, Saul, set out to congratulate Abram on his defeat of the forces of evil. There, King Melchizedek offered bread and wine to Abram and his worn-out men for having done their job: annihilated powers of wickedness who were shameless thieves. In showing reverence to his beloved king and high priest, Abram presented King Melchizedek with a *tithe* [a tenth] of all the goods he gathered from the defeated armies. By doing so, Abram's message to King Melchizedek was as follows: *pay tribute to his genuinely righteous king and high priest who ranked higher than himself in the sight of God* (KJ Ge 14:18-20).

Like any great and righteous king looking out for the well-being of his people, King Melchizedek was aware of the conflicts throughout his kingdom. Furthermore, and committed to his promise, Abram was delighted to distribute the recovered goods among his beloved king, his 318 warriors, and his three allies. That displayed how generous, submissive, and unselfish a man Abram was to God's appointed king and those serving under him.

Regarding tithing, the shocking fact is that God blessed righteous Abram before Abram ever hinted at giving King Melchizedek anything. In other words, God does not award blessings solely because of tithes. What results in receiving promises from God is *doing what is right and just per God* (NIV Ge 18:19). Hence, tithing is one's way of paying tribute and honor to God rather than expecting blessings or anything else in return. Tithing is a commandment of God—though not spelled out in the Ten—given per one's means or service (KJ Lev 27:30-34, Dt 14:22-29, 2Ch 31:4-21).

However, do not stop there! What good is tithing where the Commandments of God are offensive and abolished? What good does tithing do for all who donate and believe—as I regrettably used to say—"I gave, and as far as I am concerned, my donations are now in God's hands?" The answer to both questions, based on the preponderance of Bible evidence such as Genesis 18 and 19, is:

It leads to deceivers not being held accountable for what they preach and teach about God. It leads to a growing evil society where only one solution can stop their unconditional immorality, corruption, lust, and sinister ideologies.

Remember, the people of Sodom and Gomorrah were generous, as evidenced by the big-to-do over their stolen goods. However, those goods were all given in vain. They were worthless until Abram confiscated them. Therefore, donations from the people of Sodom and Gomorrah turned out inconsequential rather than their blessing. Their years of sacrifice and Leftist worship could not shield them from the upcoming deadly horrors on the part of God, who was infuriated by their most wicked forms of immorality and repulsive worship.

A ✝ Ω

GOD LOVES A CHEERFUL GIVER

It is written: *Every man according as he purposeth in his heart, so let him give; not grudgingly, or of necessity:* **for God loveth a cheerful giver.** (KJ 2Co 9:7)

Cheerful giving started with **Adam** and continued with his son **Abel**. Unfortunately, it was not so with Eve or Cain, who followed Eve's steps. Hence, God loved Adam and Abel **because** they were cheerful givers; however, He hated Eve and Cain **because** they were callous, defiant, selfish, thankless, and cold-hearted. Eve's selfish ambition cost Adam a perfect immortal life and lordship over

Eden. Cain's selfish ambition led him to murder Abel.

Recall Ananias and Sapphira? They regretted what they pledged and kept back some of what they promised. They lost their lives and salvation because of it. Spiritually, it's best to give to God as your cheerful heart moves you rather than pledge anything that you may come to regret.

A † Ω

Alms

Alms are not to be confused with tithes. Webster defines alms as follows:

> **Alms:** *money, food, or other donations given to the poor or needy; anything given as charity.*[57]

Most clerics define alms slightly differently:

> *Anything given to the church that is beyond one's tithes.*

A † Ω

In summarizing **TITHING AND ALMS:** *Appreciation vs. Bartering,* there are six things of importance whenever it comes to *tithes* and *alms.*

1) Tithes include one's service and investments for exposing and *destroying the forces of evil* (1Jn 3:8).

2) God loves tithers who carefully choose the recipients of their donations since giving to God

---

[57] *Alms,* Ibid.

should occur wherever the *Spirit of God* resides. That place may be out on a battlefield where the favored by God kill off an army of psychopathic thieves, recover all stolen goods, and set free the prisoners of war.

3) God loves the righteous who honor and thank Him with their tithes and alms over all others who pay Him for blessings: that which they are unlikely ever to receive.

4) Abandonment from God is very real to all who forsake His way regardless of their donations; otherwise, God would have influenced Abram to return the stolen goods in exchange for the people!

5) **God blesses all who smite the wicked to uphold righteousness and have justice served (KJ Ecc 3:3).**

6) Regardless of what people choose to become in Satan's world, it does not necessarily make them right with God, where after running their course—whether good or evil—*their deeds will follow them* {either to Heaven or Hell (KJ Rev 14:13)}.

Tithing and giving alms should express appreciation, commitment, and dedication to God. However, living according to God's principles, rather than solely tithing, leads to receiving blessings and miracles from God. (KJ Lev 27:30, Dt 14:22-29, Mal 3:1-18, 2Co 9:6-15). Otherwise, tithing is no more than swapping or making payments to an unwanted obligation, where God owns it all, yet He owes nothing to anyone.

A Reflection of Israel's Tithing Laws

It is written: *A tithe of everything from the land, whether grain from the soil or fruit from the trees, belongs to the LORD; it is holy to the LORD. If a man redeems any of his tithe, he must add a fifth of the value to it. The entire tithe of the herd and flock—every tenth animal that passes under the shepherd's rod—will be holy to the LORD. He must not pick out the good from the bad or make any substitution. If he does make a substitution, both the animal and its substitute become holy and cannot be redeemed. These are the commands the LORD gave Moses on Mount Sinai for the Israelites.* (NIV Lev 27:30-34)

It is written: *Be sure to set aside a tenth of all that your fields produce each year. Eat the tithe of your grain, new wine and oil, and the firstborn of your herds and flocks in the presence of the LORD your God at the place he will choose as a dwelling for his Name, so that you may learn to revere the LORD your God always.* (NIV Dt 14:22-23)

It is written: *At the end of every three years, bring all the tithes of that year's produce and store it in your towns, so that the Levites* {priesthood} *(who have no allotment or inheritance of their own) and the aliens, the fatherless and the widows who live in your towns may come and eat and be satisfied, and so that the LORD your God may bless you in all the work of your hands.* (NIV Dt 14:28-29)

It is written: *He* {King Hezekiah} *ordered the people living in Jerusalem to give the portion* {tithe} *due the priests and Levites so they could devote themselves to the LAW of the LORD.* (NIV 2Ch 31:4)

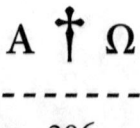

The Significance of Bread & Wine

A ✝ Ω

A   G   A   P   E

SACRED BREAD:
THE PRESENCE OF GOD / NOURISHMENT

© Oleihl

SACRED WINE:
LIFE SOURCE / SACRIFICE
LONGSUFFERING & BLOODSHED:

It is written: And Melchizedek king of Salem brought forth **bread and wine**: and he was the priest of the most high God. And he blessed him, and said, *Blessed be Abram of the most high God, possessor of heaven and earth: And blessed be the most high God, which hath delivered thine enemies into thy hand.* And he {Abram} gave him {Melchizedek} tithes of all. (KJ Ge 14:18-20) [B & W: Pr 9:5-6, Mt 26:26-29, Mk 14:22-25]

A ✝ Ω

XI. PARENTAL LOVE:
The Essence of Agape

© H-Gall

Unified

It is written: *Even a child is known by his doings, whether his work be pure, and whether it be right.*
(KJ Pr 20:11)

Since this chapter highlights children, first get a handle on the significance of children in the eyes of God.

It is written: At that same time {when Jesus and His disciples were questioned about paying a temple tax} came the disciples unto Jesus, saying, *Who is the greatest in the Kingdom of Heaven?*

(KJ Mt 18:1, Lk 9:46)

The first impression of the disciples who asked this is that these fellows must have been up to no good, or they were outright uninformed for not knowing that ***JEHOVAH, art the most high of heaven and over all the earth*** (KJ Dt 10:14, Ezr 7:23, Ps 83:18, 92:8, Isa 33:22). No exceptions! That should be common knowledge among all believers, especially among the twelve disciples who regularly walked with Christ during His three-year ministry.

The truth regarding the question revealed a jealous motive of the two apostles having asked. It played out in Mark 10:35-45, with the sons of Zebedee: James and John. Recognizing that the brothers needed clarification about the Kingdom of Heaven's hierarchy, Jesus did not hesitate to answer their questions. He did so in a style that proved how conditional ***JEHOVAH'S*** love is. He took the opportunity to express the simplicity and pureness of a *few chosen* out of *many called*. His response was as startling as the question.

> It is written: And Jesus called a little child unto him, and set him in the midst of them, And said, *Verily I say unto you, Except ye be converted, and become as little children, ye shall not enter into the kingdom of heaven. Whosoever therefore shall humble himself as this little child, the same is greatest in the kingdom of heaven. And whoso shall receive one such little child in my name receiveth me. But whoso shall offend {deceive} one of these little ones which believe in me, it were*

better for him that a millstone were hanged about his neck, and that he were drowned in the depth of the sea. (KJ Mt 18:2-6)

Replay, who Jesus shockingly said was the greatest in the Kingdom of Heaven.

Whosoever therefore shall humble himself as this little child, the same is greatest in the kingdom of heaven. (KJ Mt 18:4, Lk 9:48)

With Jesus' play on words, the Scripture alone implies that an adult acting like a six-year-old is greater than **ALMIGHTY GOD**. That is mainstream thinking on Matthew 18:4 that led to many abominable teachings. How more direct and clever could Jesus imply that a humble child, or an adult acting like a six-year-old, is above God to a jealous young adult asking the question? Hence, Matthew 18:4 is the type of Scripture often used to claim that devious men and women are above or no less than God. However, it is a snare for prevaricators and their followers set by God: the need for Jesus to have also said what he proclaimed afterward,

But whoso shall offend one of these little ones which believe in me, it were better for him that a millstone were hanged about his neck, and that he were drowned in the depth of the sea. (KJ Mt 18:6)

If that is not an about-face in what He meant to imply, I don't know what is! In other words, what Jesus intended with the full context of His intelligent response was **not** what *serpents* have you believe, such as the following:

Since you are acting as if you are a six-year-old without a clue who the greatest in the Kingdom of Heaven is, go forward in teaching abominations about God. Instill in your followers that they are above or equal to God. Teach that God does not exist. Teach that God's word is outdated and error-filled. Teach that Jesus loves all unconditionally because he bears the burden of all wickedness and turns a deaf ear to crime when hearing, "Bless me, Father, for I have sinned."

Teach congregations to proudly stand in the presence of Jesus by boasting, "Lord, You know I'm a sinner," **without ever teaching repentance.** *Teach evil as good and righteousness as evil. Teach that God is unconditional love. Manipulate the Scriptures in speaking against the truth of God's word as a serpent cleverly did with Eve. Fabricate other lies about God to appease your worshipers of deception. Then, you will have confidence knowing you and them are bound for the Pearly Gates of Heaven at the end of your life!*

Annually, those Leftist ideologies cost the salvation of untold millions, as evidenced by increased wickedness and destruction throughout the country: **the absence of God!** Growing wickedness is especially true in communities where Leftists have taken control through corruption, regardless of their song-and-dance churches on every corner. **Why?** It is because a billion lies never amount to an ounce of truth, much less salvation. Also, not to forget is the deception that condones evil also attracts faithful donors void of the *Spirit of God*. Through much falsehood of what these patrons want to hear, *serpents* keep their houses of entertainment open. Try to introduce these dead spirits to the full context of Bible Scripture and see how fast they turn off, slander, and villainize you.

> **Question:** *How is it possible to know with certainty that the child Jesus chose to stand at His side was holy, pure, and righteous: a model for salvation?*

> It is written: **Even a child is known by his doings, whether his work be pure, and whether it be right.** (KJ Pr 20:11)

The child Jesus chose was pure: the type best not to abuse, corrupt, or mislead.

> It is written: **But whoso shall offend one of these little ones which believe in me** {by teaching them to believe otherwise or abusing them}, ***it were better for him that a millstone were hanged about his neck, and that he were drowned in the depth of the sea.*** (KJ Mt 18:6)

Thus, the unwavering truth regarding the greatest in the Kingdom of Heaven is that *ALMIGHTY GOD* reigns supreme. He has unlimited authority (KJ Dt 10:14, Ezr 7:23, Ps 92:8). **However, becoming righteous through repentance in the likeness of wholesome, pure, innocent children qualifies for His blessings and kingdoms.**

> **Question:** *How many adults in your world do you recognize as having the likeness of a little godly child in being holy, pure, and righteous?*

Should you find yourself void of an answer and repulsed by its possibilities, hopefully, this caused you to experience a change in beliefs, knowing that being *holy, pure,* and *righteous* are requirements for entering the Kingdoms of God. Hence, *are many called but few chosen,* just as Jesus said (KJ Mt 22:14). Here's why:

> It is written: *My people are fools; they do not know me. They are senseless children; they have no understanding. They are skilled in doing evil; they know not how to do good.* (NIV Jer 4:22)

Jesus was very serious about His followers being **holy, pure, and righteous** as qualifiers for God's kingdoms. After all, He was the manifestation of God's word—including Jeremiah 4:22—which separates His sheep from Satan's goats. Hence, He clarified the importance of repentance and righteousness for salvation.

A notable example of one of His *elect* was James Charles Stuart—the infant king—born June 19, 1566, into tragedies and turmoil to Lord Danley and Mary Queen of Scots. [This infant King James Charles Stuart (1566–1625) is often confused with the jolly black Moorish King Charles Stuart II of England (1630–1685)]. Nevertheless, following the murder of his father and 19 years of imprisonment of his mother leading up to her execution [by beheading ordered by her rival, Queen Elizabeth I], infant King James VI of Scotland was put in the hands of a God-fearing, wise, Joseph-type step-father and teacher: sixty-four-year-old George Buchanan. It was through James' passion for *every word of God* being one *poor in spirit*—in addition to his God-fearing teacher of integrity, that

> *James became one of the most learned and intellectually curious men ever to be a king. His legacy and influence crossed the oceans where the first Christian and European settlement in America, **Jamestown**, was named in his honor.* [That set the stage for "God Bless America."] *Though plagued with illness, handicapped legs, and a speech impediment, King James I & VI was committed to producing an authorized English Version of the Bible.* [58]
>
> *In 1566, less than a year old, crowned was he as King James VI of Scotland and served as King for fifty-nine years. In 1603, he was crowned King James I of England, France, and Ireland and served as their King for twenty-two years until his death in 1625. He ordered having the original Hebrew Old Testament and Greek New Testament Bible manuscripts translated into English during his reign.* [59]

These translations, first published in 1611, were to uphold the integrity of the original Bible documents for the benefit of all English-speaking people daring to read, study, believe, and obey it.

A † Ω

---

[58] *King James VI of Scotland and KJ I of England, France and Ireland: Biography of King James I & Jesus is Lord* — Jesus is Lord com/kingbio.htm.

[59] *Origin of the King James Bible,* Ibid.

LOVE FOR CHILDREN:
Conditional vs. Unconditional

According to the Bible, children remain as children until their twentieth birthday: not a day earlier! For example, it was not until age twenty that Israel's boys were considered young adults and became qualified for military service and other adult responsibilities. (KJ Ex 30:14, Nu 1:3 and 26:2)

Furthermore, because of false teachings about God's love, many well-intentioned parents claim they love their children unconditionally. By claiming you love your children unconditionally, you imply that you enjoy them without restrictions by giving them charge over you.

Through unconditional love, children sometimes grow up hating their parents and every truthful aspect concerning God, whose *Spirit* is omnipresent. Hence, unconditional love is the highway to a disaster that yells out,

> *Parents have no reason to love their children because a single cause would make parental love conditional.*

The fact remains that Heaven-bound parents love their children for the same reason God loves them. These are the few who *repent* (KJ Mt 4:17), *obey His commands* (KJ Ex 20:6, Da 9:4, Mt 12:46–50, Jn 14:21 & 23), and *live by every spoken word of His* (KJ Dt 8:3, Mt 4:4).

Hence, Heaven-bound parents love their children primarily **because** they are their children. Since Heaven-bound parents love their children **because** they are their children, their love for their children is conditional. The head preposition—*because*—separates their children from all other children, in the way obedience to God's commandments separates the Heaven-bound of the *many called*. Their compliance expresses their love of, respect for, and faith in God [*the Most High over all the earth* (Ps 97:9)] and steadfast Jesus [the Christ: *Son of the Living God* (Mt 16:16)]. *"Because"* also activates the second monumental condition of God-like parental love: *caring for them*—precisely what *the truth* and *commandments* express to anyone choosing to live by them!

Question: *Is not sincere love about caring for another?*

Anything that requires action in a relationship, such as any form of caring, is a condition of love. For example, when godly parents express love through smiles, hugs, and fulfilling other basic needs of their newborn, their newborn eventually learns to communicate love through body language and speaking in unknown tongues. As newborns come into their native language and forsake unknown tongues, righteous parents typically instill simple expectations to demonstrate a caring love for them. They begin to teach responsibility as God did with Adam. They start their young gardening *to satisfy their desires with good things, having their strength renewed like eagles* (NIV Ps 103:5). Thus, simple expectations for young children would be:

> Brush your teeth, make your bed, hang up your clothes, be good in school, respect your godly teachers, and do your homework. Before sleeping, read a story in your

Children's Bible. Afterward, get on your knees and talk to God about your reading. Then, thank Him for all good things and dedicate your life to Him. When you go out in the morning, serve Him in righteousness in all you do.

Those universal commands—established early on—are for the well-being and protection of very few children destined for the Kingdoms of God. As these select children grow into adolescence, truthful parents instill right from wrong per the Commandments of God. These extraordinary parents issue more responsibilities to test obedience and determine whether their children are developing integrity. Hence, they instill the advice of Jesus to their impressionable children.

> It is written: *Behold, I send you forth as sheep in the midst of wolves: be ye therefore wise as serpents, and harmless as doves.* (KJ Mt 10:16).

That is how God tested Adam, Abel, Noah, Abram, Moses, and Joshua: all touched upon thus far. Hence, in the likeness of God, Heaven-bound parents know that integrity can take their children to new heights and make significant differences in the quality of their lives.

> It is written: *But the noble man makes noble plans, and by noble deeds, he stands.* (NIV Isa 32:8)

Thus, true nobility is being superior in righteousness and integrity. True nobility forsakes one's former sinful self. That is not to say that if you are a liar and a thief, true nobility is becoming better at lying and stealing. Instead, if you are a liar and thief, true nobility ceases all lying and stealing. It earns an honest living. Making a trustworthy living falls under unfailing love since it is the outcome of obedience to Commandments Eight, Nine, and Ten. They are: *(8) **Thou shall not steal;** (9) **Thou shall not lie;** (10) **Thou shall not covet*** (KJ Ex 20:15–17). Hence, bringing up children in unfailing love is merely lifting them in integrity through the Commandments of God.

> It is written: *Wherewithal shall a young man cleanse his way? By taking heed thereto according to thy* {intended} *word.* (KJ Ps 119:9)

For example, when children test their parents through acts of love, which emphatically should say *"NO!"* to many things children desire, godly parents warn their children. They start out teaching the basic commandments: **not** to steal, **not** to lie, **not** to covet people, places, and things of the world, and to honor their family by doing what is right and just. Such acts of love are integrity-based conditions for the well-being and prosperity of all children chosen by God Almighty: *their strength, song, and salvation* (KJ Isa 12:2).

Unfortunately, children often fall short of parental expectations as parents sometimes fall short of God's. When that occurs, a godly parent will not react unconditionally by giving in to demands that could put their children at higher risk or going in the opposite direction by abusing them. Preferably, the condition of showing concern would play out where the parent would weigh things out and respond with appropriate but never abusive discipline. Why is that so important in bringing up God's children? It is because child abuse is a one-way ticket to homosexuality! And homosexuality is an abomination to God *and the broad road to destruction* (KJ Mt 7:13). Also,

> It is written: *And, ye fathers, provoke not your children to wrath: but bring them up in the nurture and admonition of the Lord.* (KJ Eph 6:4)

By bringing up children in the training and instruction of the Lord, a life-long bonding relationship is more likely to develop between children and parents. Why? It is because godly children formulate healthy and positive beliefs such as, "Mom and Dad put restrictions on us because they very much care about us."

That is precisely the parenting skills of God as *Abba* [Father] and Divine Role Model through His spoken word. **The fullness of His word is medical and psychological prescriptions for the well-being of the few who take it to heart 24/7.**

> It is written: *My son, despise not the chastening of the* LORD; *neither be weary of his correction:* **For whom the Lord loveth he correcteth;** *even as a father the son in whom he delighteth.* (KJ Pr 3:11–12, Heb 12:5–6)

For the most part, the LORD **corrects only those He loves.** All others are left to free will at the mercy of the good, bad, and ugly who govern them. *Those He loves abide by His commandments* (Jn 14:15, 15:10)! His commands comprise their constitution and values that regulate, protect, and prosper them. They are not of Satan's world; thus, often hated are they.

So, how does God discipline His children through their parents? To answer the question, consider a youthful, caring father and mother going about teaching their young, playful, and curious son and daughter. Godly parents do not abuse their beautiful and gifted children physically, verbally, or emotionally; however, **early on,** they establish rules to govern their children and lay out appropriate consequences for appropriate and inappropriate behaviors. Proper behavior should result in relevant rewards. This discipline would be in line with God's way of raising children. For example, no place in the Bible will you ever find where Joseph or Mary abused Jesus when he was a child: disciplined, yes—abused, no (Lk 2:41-52). The same caring and kindness were likewise with Jesus concerning His disciples, including Judas Iscariot, His betrayer, whom He—in the end—*identified as a devil and doomed* (KJ Mk 14:21, Jn 6:70-71).

A † Ω
- - - - - - -

SPARE THE ROD VS. NOT SPARE THE ROD

> It is written: *Withhold not correction from the child: for if thou beatest him with the rod, he shall not die. Thou shalt beat him with the rod, and shalt deliver his soul from hell.* (KJ Pr 23:13-14)

Noteworthy is the discovery of *the* hidden mystery behind the infamous *"discipline with the rod."* Although some children require corporal punishment to learn the consequences of doing wrong (KJ Pr 13:24 and 22:15), there are far better ways to discipline highly gifted and sensitive children than beating them.

Touched by God in some unique way are the few with extraordinary angelic talents that glorify God and bring tears to your eyes. They require gentleness from great parents and teachers to guide them in reaching their full potential. Beating them destroys their self-confidence and minimizes the incredible self-motivated persons they could and should become for *His Majesty, Creator of the ends of the earth* (Ge 1-2:9, Isa 40:28).

King Solomon, the author of many proverbs, apparently did not refrain from using the rod with his children, having 700 wives of royal birth and 300 slave girls, referred to in the Bible as concubines (KJ 1Ki 11:1-6). Do you wonder why there have repeatedly been mega problems in the Far East and worldwide? Look to disobedience, polygamy, and child abuse. There are the answers to nightmares, which I will cover in the second message: **A DATE WITH DESTINY:** *Faith in God vs. Faith in the World.*

However wise he became in all things, the multiple beatings Solomon himself may have administered—or that of guardians having charge over his many children—caused horrific hostility and jealousy among them. It created hatred and resentment among their descendants who did evil in the eyes of the LORD as aspiring young adults. It resulted in rebellion and multiple acts of murder.

Insurrection and acts of murder are means of survival for many mistreated children in adult bodies. Having been abused with rods, belts, switches, paddles, and whatever other means out of one's anger, correction, jealousy, madness, and resentment, they are likely to repeat the cycle. Lashing out is their means of survival and having justice served for the horrors they experienced as children.

Being creative can be far better than the rod in bringing up God's children, who may also be your children. After all, godly parents are likely to produce godly children. So consider the following alternative that aligns with Ephesians 6:4: *Provoke not your children to wrath: but bring them up in the nurture and admonition* {advice}*of the Lord.*

Visit a Christian bookstore. There, you will find godly inspirational plaques. They are ideal for building self-esteem in children and adults. For example, engraved on one that I received as a house-warming gift states:

May Faith Light Your Path

(On another, it is written:)

Steven
HIGHEST QUALITY
Thou hast crowned him with glory & honor.
(Ps 8:5)

Those personalized subliminal messages can make significant differences in one's life. They offer hope over death.

For example, these glorious Christian messages can save lives whenever life worsens and challenges seem unbearable. They make excellent rewards that reinforce positive behaviors during one's darkest hours. They represent righteousness in an evil world. They instill God's values in **overcoming** challenges and temptations regardless of how sinful and hopeless Satan's world may have taken an individual (Rev 2 & 3)! They establish the foundation for a godly life with answers that, over a period, will bear fruit abundantly. And like healthy trees, the younger ingrained they are in one's mind, the longer they will produce sumptuous fruit: ***holiness, righteousness, truthfulness, and integrity—treasures in heaven*** (Mt 6:20).

Hence, *Discipline through Esteem* is far more likely to result in children growing in integrity than *Discipline with the Rod*. Life teaches that how disciplined children become will significantly affect their character.

> It is written: {**VERY EARLY ON**} *Train a child in the way he should go, and when he is old he will not turn from it* {whether good or evil}. (KJ Pr 22:6)
>
> ----------------------
>
> It is written: *Fathers, provoke **not** your children to anger, lest they be discouraged.* (KJ Col 3:21)

Where do those Scriptures leave abused children? How would severe beatings impact an adolescent shut out from ordinary life while belittling him continuously? What about going in the opposite direction by giving in to all demands? Answer! In the same way, unwanted dogs struggle to find their way home. Rejected and thrown out like trash along the road by cold-hearted-irresponsible pet owners leaves these intelligent and loving beings scared and uncertain while subject to disease, starvation, and violent death! In plain English, all lead to considerable trouble through **in**appropriate behaviors.

Whenever **in**appropriate behaviors occur, godly parents need a little quality time with their children, should they not be too out of control, to counsel and teach right from wrong. It is an opportunity to bond with one's young and influential children. On the contrary, ignoring **in**appropriate behaviors translates into lifelong regrets. They include—but are not limited to—depression, drugs, hatred, immorality, loneliness, rebellion, and premature death.

Therefore, consider God's ways of handling the challenges of children who often fall victim to Satan's world. **Recognizing that God identifies children by their actions, godly parents would address their children's inappropriate behavior as being who they are!** God did that with Adam and Eve, the *serpent* and Cain, and even Moses (KJ Nu 20:6-13). He boldly confronted their defiance.

For example, review how the LORD dealt with Adam and Eve for defying His command.

> It is written: And they heard the voice of the LORD God walking in the garden in the cool of the day: and Adam and his wife hid themselves from the presence of the LORD God amongst the trees of the garden.
>
> And the LORD God called unto Adam, and said

unto him, *Where art thou?*

And he said, *I heard thy voice in the garden, and I was afraid, because I was naked; and I hid myself.*

And he said, *Who told thee that thou wast naked? Hast thou eaten of the tree, whereof I commanded thee that thou shouldest not eat?*

And the man said {without apologies}, *The woman whom thou gavest to be with me, she gave me of the tree, and I did eat.*

And the LORD God said unto the woman, *What is this that thou hast done?*

And the woman said {without apologies}, *The serpent beguiled me, and I did eat.*

(KJ Ge 3:8–13)

God wasted no time confronting Adam and Eve about their inappropriate and rebellious behavior. Regardless of their passing blame, He did not evade their disobedience or make light of it. Instead, He held both accountable for their actions without procrastination and followed through with His permanent detention phase. [With children, it's best to keep detention reasonable where there is light at the end of the tunnel.]

Thus, it is wise to address behavior as being the child rather than behavior as being apart from the child whenever a child acts out. Address the child as soon as possible with direct and to-the-point questions. Make it clear that according to God, **We are what we do!–AND–Everyone is responsible for their actions** (KJ Rev 20:12–13).

By failing to convey those Bible truths, reality, and the facts of life, an influential, loving child may be well on the way to becoming a devil. To avoid such horror, set aside private time with the child, turn off all distractions, and move on by asking fundamental questions such as:

1) *What did you do that you should not have done?*

2) *What should you have done?*

3) *What will you do next time you are in that same situation?*

4) *When do you plan to live up to doing what you said you should have done?*

5) *How long are you willing to do what you should have done?*

In my second year of teaching, Charles Darby, a psychology professor from Sam Houston University in Huntsville, Texas, came to our junior high campus and introduced us to those five questions. They set our faculty on the path of wiser options for disciplining children. Therefore, I continued using the *"Darby Method"* throughout my remaining twenty-eight years of service in public education. However, I want to extend the *"Darby Method"* into the spiritual realm by adding four profound questions.

6) *Do you know that God recognizes us according to our actions?*

7) *Do you know God does not separate us from what we do?*

8) *Is doing the right thing in the sight of God not an essential part of your life?*

9) *If not, who or what is?*

These thought-provoking questions instill dignity and responsibility, discernment and discretion. Acquired is an understanding of right from wrong when answered sincerely. All leads to foresight, a vital survival skill. Crucial, the answers must come from the child as much as possible, where age is considered a factor.

Finally, there is the all-important punishment or rehabilitation phase. Corporal Punishment is always an alternative to reinforce that consequences are behind every behavior. However, godly parents should be more considerate in certain situations. Much should depend on a child's character, intelligence, maturity, sensitivity, and divine gifts.

Thoughtful parents may have their child summarize the discussion, sign, and date it, and make it into a binding contract. [This we set out doing on specific campuses where I served.] As all agreements have a time associated with them, so should behavioral deals with children. Time together would be an excellent opportunity to teach the significance of commitment and obligation. **It would instill that consequences are behind all actions.** The parent should then save the written contract. When the child becomes an adult and parent, return what he once wrote. That would be God working through a family in unfailing love likely to be forever remembered. It's all so simple and most dignifying.

Following the question and answer session, reinforce right from wrong. The result is not to be abusive to a child of God, as it may be with parents guided by the *spirit of evil*. Instead, it should be creative, like reading a chapter from a Children's Bible and writing two to five pages about it. Consider the life-long embedded values with that behavioral correction rather than repeatedly insulting, yelling, screaming, and beating, often resulting in justifiable and lasting hatred and rebellion on the part of abused children.

Child abuse is an all-around losing situation that has far-reaching consequences. It sometimes causes victims to lash out years later in many ways. And the only answer to their lashing out is to have justice served. But without justice, now we are talking about perfect candidates for *Art of Massacre*.

That is not to mention that abused children—verbal, physical, or otherwise—often live insecure with low self-esteem throughout their lives. Most turn out as introverts between geniuses and heinous *devils*. And in what other direction does abuse point? It points directly to **same-sex attraction** where that child, in an adult body, will go looking for parental love he never received. And that false love is not of God because homosexuality is an abomination that causes desolation!

It is addictive idolatry: a destroyer of *spirits, souls, minds, and bodies* that can multiply from one generation to another until there is only one solution to finally putting a stop to it all (Ge 18 and 19)!

Hence, the best way of persuading children to do the right thing begins with bonding and awarding excellent behavior. It requires great patience, being a good role model, instilling right from wrong, and treating them respectfully. Respectfully treating children involves speaking to them with unshakable conviction, integrity, intelligence, and truth. They know when they are insulted, which is often highly offensive and emotionally abusive.

For example, repeating to a child that he will **not** amount to anything is highly likely to result in low self-esteem and a nobody. Addressing one's son jokingly as a *"Demon"* may produce a devil. On the other hand, repeating to a child that he is unique in God's sight and called out by God to do good is highly likely that he will do what is right and become a child of God. It may motivate the youngster to gain wisdom about God as Jesus did as a child. It may lead to greatness: an inspiration to all as James Charles Stuart became worldwide.

My first childhood esteem and inspiration came primarily from my wonderfully loving grandmother, Volcie Roy Juneau, and my caring first and second-grade teacher, Sister Alawishes. As things turned out, my youthful, very hard-working, dedicated, caring, and loving parents were preoccupied with two very frail infants who came ahead of me. So, initially, I was left to myself much of the time until my grandmother next door intervened. The three of us were born about a year and a half apart to Fred and Bessie—with two others born five and ten years later.

What more can I share besides using discretion when disciplining your children to avoid them returning to hate you? Remember, we were all highly impressionable children at some time or another, learning from adults and from what we saw and heard. Hence, Jesus flawlessly expressed the life-long effects of the learning process.

> It is written: *No man, when he hath lighted a candle, putteth it in a secret place, neither under a bushel, but on a candlestick, that they which come in may see the light. The light of the body is the eye: therefore when thine eye is single, thy whole body also is full of light; but when thine eye is evil, thy body also is full of darkness. Take heed therefore that the light which is in thee* {that you and your children set your eyes and ears upon} *be not darkness* {evil}. *If thy whole body therefore be full of light, having no part dark, the whole shall be full of light, as when the bright shining of a candle doth give thee light.* (KJ Lk 11:33-36, Mt 5:14-16)

And why did Jesus need to come up with those psychology Scriptures? Answer: It is because the human mind—unlike a computer—does not come with a delete button. That points back to the Old Testament, which Jesus drew from repeatedly. So remember Proverb 22:6 when bringing up children!

It is written: {**VERY EARLY ON**} *Train a child in the way he should go, and when he is old he will **not** depart from it* {whether good or evil}. (KJ Pr 22:6)

A ✝ Ω

THE UNIQUE LEARNING STYLES OF CHILDREN

One of the basic psychological needs of a child is parental approval. Parental approval is what builds good character and self-confidence in children. Self-confidence in making the right decisions is the best way of keeping children out of trouble and on the road to success.

Hence, to better understand young children through unfailing love, it is essential to face the reality that not all children are identical. For example, *auditory learners* respond best by being **told** right from wrong. On the other hand, it is best to **show** *visual learners* right from wrong. The remaining others are *kinesthetic*. It is best to have them **act** right from wrong. Hence, it would be far better to **demonstrate** right from wrong with *visual* and *kinesthetic learners* than to **tell** them as with *auditory learners*.

Those approaches to discipline could turn potentially hostile situations into fun-filled experiences. They could engage the entire family, where everyone ends up united and laughing rather than crying, screaming, or thinking about murdering one another. That does happen on occasion. Wouldn't you agree?

Acting and dramatizing right from wrong, where young children and parents become actors on their stage, could have far-reaching and positive consequences. It could result in a life-long, inseparable, and respectable bond between children and their parents, like students bonding with their kindergarten, first-grade, and music teachers.

Having taught and supervised children of various ages and races, I can tell you that children love to have fun like puppy dogs. They need ongoing assurances and responsibility. They will gravitate toward compliments and meaningful rewards. Constant acknowledgment with increased accountability builds their self-esteem, provided they have not come into perversions, been abused, or placed in the hands of a cult, all of which children may yell out through shocking misbehavior at home and in the classroom.

And being an adult does not mean one cannot play and enjoy wholesome and rewarding fun with their children. In other words, at appropriate times, it is okay to give up one's kingship and dedication to work to enjoy the role of kid-ship and instill virtue without jeopardizing integrity.

Those methods of child-caring instill mutual respect because they display trust in one's children, as God was in being alone with Adam, and King Melchizedek was with Abram. It provides a window of opportunity for children to redeem themselves in an embarrassing, lonely, or awkward situation rather than living in guilt over a childhood error for the rest of their lives.

Hence, *Discipline through Esteem* is how to develop integrity in children who could grow into adulthood having the likings of a *Kingsman*: an individual able to represent the Lord according to His principles. It is living honorably through integrity rather than corruption. It is trusting and obeying the Word of God, also known as having *Faith in God*.

A † Ω

In summarizing this chapter, **PARENTAL LOVE:** *The Essence of Agape,* by demonstrating loving care for children, regardless of how minor a correction or reward is, one exercises *unfailing conditional love*. *Unfailing conditional love* also includes being **truthful** about everything early on, which could spare children many disappointments. Having no restrictions on children and lying to them invites trouble.

For example, embedding in children that they are saved by accepting Jesus without any accountability on their part is *The Great Religious Cult Lie*. It points to significant problems. Why? Answer: It condones sinning and defies Jesus' commandments: "<u>**Repent,** *for the Kingdom of Heaven is at hand*</u>" (KJ Mt 4:17), and "<u>*Sin no more, lest a worse thing comes unto thee*</u>" (Jn 5:14). Furthermore, it is what James, the stepbrother **or** cousin of Jesus, and the entire Bible, for that matter, expounds on: **Faith without works is dead** (KJ Jas 2:14-26).

Moreover, the Bible teaches that children are not adults until age 20 (Nu 1:45). Also, throughout the Bible, you will discover that when God saves parents, He will likely keep their children as well. God favors such parents for living according to His principles. They are few among many.

Additionally, no one is immune from temptations, including those God favors. Acting on temptations causes many children and adults dire and horrific consequences regardless of how gratifying they are when acted out. Such outcomes negatively affect family, constituents, and friends and will sever a relationship with God without repentance. It disgraces and imprisons all bearing a conscience: the *many called* by God!

Nevertheless, however excellent or evil children turn out, there comes a day when parents must let go. They must endure the empty nest syndrome by allowing their children to become the adults of their choosing. Hopefully, once they are grown and gone, away from home, and on their own in Satan's world, at some point, they will turn to the Bible and become one of God's.

> It is written: *But as many as received him {Genesis through Revelation}, to them gave he power to become the sons of God, even to them that believe on his name {Jesus Christ: the manifested Word of God}: Which were born, not of blood, nor of the*

will of the flesh, nor of the will of man, but of God.
(KJ Jn 1:12–13)

Children of God honor their parents. Accepting one's imperfect parents comes with a divine blessing. It is the *Fifth Commandment!* There are many ways to honor one's parents beyond the world's recognition. Caring about them has many variables. Just beware that God knows and sees all. And it is God that we should be out to please first throughout life. That is the topic of the first chapter in **AGAPE Part B: ALL KNOWN BY GOD.**

A † Ω

A REFLECTION OF GOD'S WAY

V. Honour thy father and thy mother: that thy days may be long {filled with peace and happiness, prosperity and success, safety and well-being} *upon the land which the* LORD *thy God giveth thee.*
(KJ Ex 20:12, Dt 5:16, Mt 15:3–9, Mk 7:9–10, Eph 6:1–3)

ENGRAVED IN STONE BY GOD FOR HIS ELECT

[Jesus Christ did not abolish this commandment!]
(KJ Mt 5:17–20, Mk 10:19, 1Jn 2:3–11, Rev 14:12)

A † Ω

XII. TRUSTWORTHY FRIENDS:
A Reflection of Agape

WISE AS SERPENTS
HARMLESS AS DOVES
(KJ Mt 10:16)

It is written: {Jesus speaking to his disciples said:} *As the Father hathe loved me* {unfailingly for continuing wholeheartedly in His way}, *continue ye in my love.* ***If ye keep my commandments, ye shall abide in my love; even as I have kept my Father's commandments, and abide in his love.*** *These things have I spoken unto you, that my joy might remain in you, and that your joy might be full.*

This is my commandment, That ye {my elect} love one another, as I have loved you {unfailingly: according to the Ten}. Greater love hath no man than this, that a man lay down his life for his friends. **Ye are my friends, if ye do whatsoever I command you {repent}.** *Henceforth I call you not servants; for the servant knoweth not what his lord doeth: but I have called you friends; for all things that I have heard of my Father I have made known unto you. Ye {12-excluding Iscariot} have not chosen me, but I have chosen you, and ordained you, that ye should go and bring forth fruit, and that your fruit should remain: that <u>whatsoever ye shall ask of the Father in my name, he may give it you</u> {should you wholeheartedly obey His commandments.} These things I command you, that ye love one another {unfailing: according to the commandments}.* (KJ Jn 15:9–17)

Jesus clarified to His apostles that His love was conditional and a two-way relationship. After all, He did refer to them as friends, willing to lay down their lives for Him, as He set out doing for them. Christ did **not** inform them that His love was unconditional. He did **not** tell them that He loved liars, thieves, murderers, and destroyers. Instead, He clearly stated that His joy in them was contingent upon their obedience to the commandments. That He summed up in one word at the start of His ministry: *"Repent."* (KJ Mt 4:17) [Repenting is the cessation of sin.] Then He went on and stated: *"I have told you this so that my joy may be in you* *and that your joy may be complete."* (NIV Jn 15:11)

Living in God's joy [*Zoe and the Sabbath Rest*] is contingent upon obedience to His commandments. And since His *elect* express their love to Him by obeying them, they are loved by Him (KJ Dt and Jn 14:21, 23). They are the *few chosen* to know the mysteries of His kingdom. Denied of that privilege are all others.

> It is written: *Unto you it is given to know the mysteries of the kingdom of God: but to others in parables;* THAT SEEING THEY MIGHT NOT SEE, AND HEARING THEY MIGHT NOT UNDERSTAND. (KJ LK 8:10)

According to Luke 8:10, it is apparent that God reserves His revelations, wisdom, knowledge, blessings, protection, and all other promises to **His** *elect*. **They are the few He trusts and favors, defined by their obedience to His commandments and truth-filled Bible faith.** Thus, earning His trust begins by reading, studying, believing, and obeying *every spoken word of His* (Mt 4:4). Included is the Ten Commandments. These He **twice** wrote on two sides of two stone tablets and handed to Moses to share with the many He calls to His kingdoms (KJ Ex 31:18, 32:15-16, 34:1-3, Dt 10:1-5).

Unfortunately, His teachings had zero positive influence on Judas Iscariot and many others professing *"I got Jesus."* Like Judas, who got Jesus, most do not qualify for the love of God, much less salvation. **EVIDENCE:** *Regardless that he hung out with, embraced, and kissed Jesus* (KJ Mk 14:44-46),

Jesus identified Judas as a devil who would have been better off had his mother aborted him (Mt 26:24).

Jesus sized up Judas the first time He met him. Such is with all professing God as having unconditional love. For example, believing *"Jesus loves you,"* no matter what, the central religious cult lie, will land you in Hell with Judas. So beware! Displayed are ***"Jesus loves you"*** signs by brainwashed *worshipers of deception* to condone evil on the part of all *devils* and *serpents* passing by.

A † Ω

QUALIFICATIONS FOR A FRIENDSHIP WITH GOD

God never looks much at one's outer appearance for friends; instead, He searches the spirit of the inner person, where an eternal friendship may develop. The Bible provides excellent illustrations of what God looks for in people to have them as personal friends. For example, God instructed the prophet [seer] Samuel to appoint one of Jesse's sons as the second King of Israel. The episode speaks volumes about God's selection process of His carefully chosen personal friends and leaders. It also displays how direct He is concerning those He disapproves.

> It is written: And it came to pass, when they were come, {Jesse and his six sons to meet Samuel— God's prophet entrusted to appoint one of the children as Israel's new king (KJ 1Sa 16:1-2)},

that he {Samuel} looked on Eliab {Jesse's tall most handsome firstborn} and said, *Surely the* Lord's *anointed is before him.*

But the {*still small voice* of the} Lord {audible only to him} said unto Samuel, *Look not on his countenance, or on the height of his stature; because I have refused him: for the* Lord *seeth not as man seeth; for man looketh on the outward appearance,* **but the** Lord **looketh on the heart.**

Then Jesse called Abinadab {his second son} and made him pass before Samuel. And he said, *Neither hath the* Lord *chosen this.*

(KJ 1Sa 16:6-8)

Samuel worked his way down to the youngest of the six, only discovering that a search would extend beyond them. Therefore, he asked Jesse whether he had another. Indeed, he did! A seventh was out tending *a few sheep* in the desert (KJ 1Sa 16:9-11). Unlike the other six, this youngest, a strange and awkward rejected outcast to his brothers, proved holy and pure in God's sight. Although still a child, he had all the makings of a *Kingsman*. His name was David! [**Note:** KJ 1Ch 2:13-15 lists the names of the seven—not eight—sons of Jesse, whereby David was the seventh and youngest.]

A † Ω

The Significance of Being Holy

Scripture illustrates the significance of *being holy— pure in heart* (KJ Mt 5:8). Moreover, according to our ways and our doings, God judges us (KJ Eze 36:19, Rev 20:12-13). He assists, guides, and raises these few select individuals to fulfill His call in their lives.

> It is written: *But the path of the just is as the shining light {to the Lord}, that shineth more and more unto the perfect day.* (KJ Pr 4:18)

> It is written: *Since ancient times no one has heard, no ear has perceived, no eye has seen any {true} God besides you, who act on behalf of those who wait for him. You come to the help {and friendship} of those who gladly do right, who remember your ways.* (NIV Isa 64:4-5)

> It is written: *Blessed are the pure in heart, for they shall see God.* (KJ Mt 5:8)

Abolishing the sin in one's life comes with great blessings and responsibility but requires excellent self-control! Throughout the Old and New Testaments, abolishing the evil in one's life is supreme with God. It is **repentance**. By being *repentant, one fulfills Jesus' commands*. Led is he to discover his divine purpose yet hated by the world he leaves behind. Why? **Born again where *holiness* reigns supreme is repulsive in Satan's world.** Yet only then is one's sinful past atoned for through the suffering of Christ. [That voids, "Saved am I just because I say I've got Jesus." (KJ Mt 7:22-23)]

It is written: Therefore, this is what the LORD says {to His select few}: *If you repent, I will restore you that you may serve me; if you utter worthy, not worthless words, you will be my spokesman. Let this people* {of the world with conspiracies, false accusations, hatred, jealously, lies, misunderstandings, and spy cams aimed at you} *turn to you, but you must not turn to them. I will make you a wall to this people, a fortified wall of bronze; they will fight against you but will not overcome you, for I am with you to rescue and save you, declares the* LORD.

I will save you from the hands of the wicked and redeem you from the grasp of the cruel.

(NIV Jer 15:19–21)

Should you come into the wisdom of the complete Bible, you may notice how God meets all the qualifications of a superb friend. *Written in the Lamb's book are the names of these few blessed individuals* (KJ Rev 21:27). Nothing pretentious or unconditional about His straightforward friendship and love for these people (KJ Col 3:12): the *chosen few* for paradise (KJ Mt 20:16). In other words, the love of God evolves out of one's passion for the Bible and living according to its principles: *holiness, righteousness, truthfulness, and integrity while destroying the works of devils.*

A † Ω

FRIENDSHIP: *Conditional*

Now, consider the conditions required for developing friendships based on Biblical principles. The most important aspect of friendship development is to avoid denial. Be truthful about yourself toward others and others toward you. Afterward, move forward with trustworthy friends. Recognize the need to let go of people **not** out for your best interest in serving the Lord, even if it means being alone. That is far better. Reliable friends of integrity are best; however, they are few and far between. It is better to have one or no righteous, trustworthy friends than pretentious friends out to destroy you upon first mentioning your love for the complete Word of God: *Genesis through Revelation!*

A † Ω

RECOGNIZING A TRUSTWORTHY FRIENDSHIP

It is written: *Greater love hath no man than this, that a man lay down his life for his friends. Ye are my friends, if ye do whatsoever I command you. Henceforth I call you not servants; for the servant knoweth not what his lord doeth: but I have called you friends; for all things that I have heard of my Father I have made known unto you.* (Jn 15:13–15)

That takes us to the importance of knowing what to look for in a real friendship. Jesus pointed out these qualifications to those daring to believe true friendship is conditional.

Adhering to God's commandments, a trustworthy friend will always look out for you. An honest friend will sincerely care about your success and well-being! A reliable friend will be someone without pretense who will always prove trustworthy behind your back. A righteous friend will maintain conditional respect through integrity and understands that little two-letter word that will always keep you out of trouble: *"NO!"* A trustworthy friend will give a helping hand without making you feel obligated. A friend you can count on will inspire you to reach the heavens and believe in yourself. A real friend will be proud to associate with you in public. A trustworthy friend will communicate respectfully. A friend with integrity will bring joy and happiness to your life.

Becoming honest, reliable, sincere, and trustworthy is conditional love. Conditional love amplifies, glorifies, and magnifies the wholeness of one's being towards another and vice-versa. Unconditional love causes God to reject you, as were Eve and Cain, *serpents* and *giants*, Egyptians and Philistines, Judas and the Herodian dynasty, and many others serving the *spirit of evil*. Believing that God was unconditionally and madly in love with each of them, they proved to be vainglorious. Forever in Hell, they were destined. **Indeed, *AGAPE* is conditional!**

Hence, developing a friendship with God is up to every individual initiating an association with Him, not vice versa. It starts with knowing what the He expects; otherwise, He will reject you. Knowing what God expects must be discovered. It is the truth about Him. The truth about God is the full context of His word! Developing a passion for it is falling in love with *Genesis through Revelation* and abiding by His principles, enabling Him to connect with you. Once that association is manifested and stabilized, subtle miracles may start happening. That's contingent upon one being *pure in heart* (KJ Mt 5:8). Also,

> It is written: *Hast thou not known? Hast thou not heard, that the everlasting God, the* LORD, *the Creator of the ends of the earth, fainteth not, neither is weary? There is no searching of his understanding.*
>
> *He giveth power to the faint; and to them that have no might he increaseth strength. Even the youths shall faint and be weary, and the young men shall utterly fall:* **But they that wait upon the** LORD {read, study, believe, and obey the fullness of His word} **shall renew their strength; they shall mount up with wings as eagles; they shall run, and not be weary; and they shall walk, and not faint.**
>
> (KJ Isa 40:28-31)

God gives strength to the weary and increases the power of the weak (NIV Isa 40:29) and *meek* (KJ Mt 5:5) to all who take the fullness of His word to heart!

Soul Mates

True friendship grows through daily mutual edification as soul mates discover. For example, When we first moved to Texas, a pleasant elderly couple, formerly from England, lived across the street. One beautiful day, they invited us over for refreshments. Throughout our conversations, when addressing one another, they referred to each other as "*Lovey.*" She was "*Lovey*" to her husband, while he was "*Lovey*" to his wife. Their joy and laughter for one another were tremendously edifying, mutual, and trusting. Hence, they left an impression about a Heaven-bound, conditional soul mate relationship: **Being Lovey to your Lovey!**

There is no more significant a *lovey* relationship above one with God where one walks and talks with Him. The following typifies such an encounter. It occurred immediately upon the completion and dedication of Solomon's massive golden temple, dreamed up by his father, King David.

> It is written: And it came to pass, when Solomon had finished the building of the house of the Lord, and the king's house, and all Solomon's desire which he was pleased to do, **that the Lord appeared to Solomon the second time, as He had appeared unto him at Gibeon.**
>
> And the Lord said unto him, *I have heard thy prayer and thy supplication* {humble sincerity}, *that thou hast made before me. I have hallowed* {made holy} *this house, which thou hast built, to put my name there forever; and mine eyes and mine heart*

shall be there perpetually. And if thou wilt walk before me, as David thy father walked, **in integrity of heart, and in uprightness, to do according to all that I have commanded thee, and wilt keep my statutes and my judgments:** *then I will establish the throne of thy kingdom upon Israel forever, as I promised to David thy father, saying, There shall not fail thee a man upon the throne of Israel.*

But if ye shall at all turn from following me, ye or your children, and will **not** *keep my commandments and my statutes which I have set before you, but go and serve other gods, and worship them, then will I cut off Israel out of the land which I have given them. And this house, which I have hallowed for my name, will I cast out of my sight; and Israel shall be a proverb and a byword among all people. And at this house, which is high {imposing}, everyone that passeth by it shall be astonished, and shall hiss; and they shall say, Why hath the* Lord *done thus unto this land, and to this house? And they shall answer, Because they forsook the* Lord *their God, who brought forth their fathers out of the land of Egypt, and have taken hold upon other gods, and have worshiped them, and served them: therefore hath the* Lord *brought upon them all this evil.*

(KJ 1Ki 9:1–9)

Unfortunately, Solomon did not heed God's advice in all his wisdom despite having two personal encounters with Him (KJ 1Ki 11, Eze). It led to the destruction of the most celebrated and significant temple ever built.

It led to acts of murder among his grandchildren and beyond them. It led to Israel's downfall, where Ishmael's descendants—Muslims—settled in and have dominated ever since. [This very day, there are thirty Islamic Mosques throughout Jerusalem where Solomon's grand temple once stood someplace but is no more.] That takes us to the consequences of betrayal.

A † Ω

Betrayal

> It is written: *Do not give {or tell} dogs what is sacred; do not throw your pearls {dreams, joys, projects, wisdom or writings} to pigs. If you do, they may trample them under their feet, and then turn and tear you to pieces.* (NIV Mt 7:6)

You first came across the King James version of this profound warning from Jesus in Chapter IV: **ABOMINATIONS THAT CAUSE DESOLATION**. However, it is fitting to take this a step further, going from this chapter to the next:

TRUSTWORTHY FRIENDS to PERSECUTION.

Jesus Christ had shocking underlying reasons for having commanded this of his apostles: (1) He hates untrustworthy, evil, two-faced individuals; and (2) not everyone acting like a friend is trustworthy! Oddly, very few will find joy in one's passion and dedication to Bible truth and the commandments, while most others will do their best to dissuade, laugh, mock, run in fear, and falsely accuse. That is because truth sears what they falsely believe about God, as expressed flawlessly in the first psalm.

> It is written: *Blessed is the man that walketh **not** in the counsel of the ungodly, **nor** standeth in the way of sinners, **nor** sitteth in the seat of the scornful {mockers}. But his delight is in the law {Word} of the* L<small>ORD</small>, *and in his law {Word} doth he meditate day and night. And he shall be like a tree planted by the rivers of water, that bringeth forth his fruit in his season; his leaf also shall not wither, and whatsoever he doeth shall prosper.*
>
> *The ungodly {who conspire against God's elect} are **not** so: but are like the chaff which the wind driveth away. Therefore the ungodly shall not stand in the judgment, nor sinners in the congregation of the righteous. For the* L<small>ORD</small> *knoweth the way of the righteous: but the way of the ungodly shall perish.* (KJ Ps 1, 92:7)

The ungodly stay oppressed because their existence relies on deception. For example, many who keep criminals in public office repeatedly illustrate reliance on stinking thinking. Similarly, heathens are kept in darkness because they are not teachable regarding righteousness, something they regard as the vilest of evils. They remain restrained for having allowed *devils* and *serpents* to rule over them and *worshipers of deception* to befriend them.

In summary, **TRUSTWORTHY FRIENDS:** *A Reflection of Agape* is about the condition of trust. Once trust ceases, friendship ends. Furthermore, whenever one betrays another, there are dreadful consequences with which to contend.

Illustrated throughout the Bible are the consequences of betraying God. Likewise, developing a friendship with Him is contingent upon one living per the truth of His Word. Therefore, and of vital importance, God's *elect* must be selective with companions in sharing their joy and accomplishments in God's word. Metaphorically, the following sizes up human nature regarding trustworthy friends:

> *Like birds of a feather, know that eagles have a different mindset than chickens. You will be among many cackling friends with a farmer out to serve you by choosing to be a chicken. On the other hand, if you decide to be an eagle, you will be independent of a farmer but have far fewer friends. So be warned if you are an eagle trying to befriend chickens. It won't ever work! Why? It is because chickens don't trust eagles. Chickens have a great fear of eagles. Therefore, the best friendships have chickens befriend chickens, and eagles befriend eagles.*

Having few or many friends, remember that friends can make or break you. So forever remember that a trustworthy friendship is,

Being Lovey to Your Lovey!

A ✝ Ω

A REFLECTION OF GOD'S WAYS

VI. Thou shalt not murder (NIV Ex 20:13, KJ Mt 19:18); {but} *A time to* {lawfully} *kill* (KJ Ecc 3:3) {to defend against the wicked, serve justice, and uphold righteousness}.

(KJ Ex 20:13, Dt 5:17, Mt 19:18 *{murder}*, Ro 13:9)

VII. Thou shalt not commit adultery (Lev 18:1–30).

(KJ Ex 20:14, Dt 5:18, Mt 19:18, Lk 18:20, Ro 13:9)

VIII. Thou shalt not steal (Lev 19:11–13).

(KJ Ex 20:15, Dt 5:19, Mt 19:18, Lk 18:20, Ro 13:9)

IX. Thou shalt not bear false witness against thy neighbour {or anyone else}.

(KJ Ex 20:16, Dt 5:20, Mt 19:18–19, Lk 18:20, Ro 13:9)

X. Thou shalt not covet thy neighbour's house {or land}. *Thou shalt not covet thy neighbour's wife, nor his manservant, nor his maidservant, nor his ox, nor his ass, nor anything that is thy neighbour's* {or belonging to anyone else}.

(KJ Ex 20:17, Dt 5:21, Mt 19:18–19, Lk 12:15 and 18:20, Ro 13:9)

ENGRAVED IN STONE BY GOD FOR HIS ELECT

[Jesus Christ did not abolish these commandments!]
(KJ Mt 5:17–20, Mk 10:19, 1Jn 2:3–6, Rev 14:12)

A ✝ Ω

XIII. PERSECUTION:
The Effect of Agape

© Romolo Tavani

It is written: Jesus said to his disciples: *Blessed are they which are persecuted for righteousness' sake: for theirs is the Kingdom of Heaven.*

Blessed are ye, when {wicked-devious} *men* {and women} *shall revile you, and persecute you, and shall say all manner of evil against you falsely, for my sake. Rejoice, and be exceeding glad: for great is your reward in heaven: for so persecuted they the prophets which were before you.*

(KJ Mt 5:10–12)

*I*n today's exceedingly evil world, where corruption is both king and queen in many parts, there is tremendous pressure to sell one's soul to evil, such as immorality, lying, stealing, cheating, killing, and destroying. Should you befriend people engaged in such, escaping from them is almost impossible. On the other hand, should you choose to hold to your integrity, persecuted you may be by people who call you friend or neighbor when they may be your worst enemies!

> It is written: ***Indeed, persecution will afflict all who want to lead a godly life in Christ Jesus, while wicked people and impostors will grow ever worse, deceiving others and being themselves deceived.*** (NCV 2Ti 3:12-13)

Thus, we all are given choices in whom we believe and obey, resulting in what we do and become. However, regardless of our preferences, there will always be consequences to deal with, one way or the other.

A † Ω

REASON FOR PERSECUTION

The Bible upholds that God's *elect* may be spared from all disasters and blessed with a good and prosperous life, except for being persecuted. Persecution is a way of life for His *elect*. It is the cross they bear (KJ Lk 14:27). *It is the way of Christ who came to destroy the works of devils* (KJ 1Jn 3:8). Jesus explained the reason for it.

It is written: *If the world hates you, ye know that it hated me before it hated you. If ye were of the* {evil} *world, the* {wicked of the} *world would love* {you as} *his own* {to make you his slave}: *but because ye are not of the world, but I have chosen you out of the world, therefore the world hateth you.* (KJ Jn 15:18-19)

In other words, persecution of God's *elect* occurs because the *Spirit of Christ* and the *Holy Spirit* indwell them. Those precious life-giving *Spirits* are so repulsive to pagans that the simple presence of a *Spirit-filled* individual stirs their hatred and agitates their diseases. Praise God! As Christ and His apostles experienced religious heathens, one can observe the snickering and gagging of adversaries. The following sums up the attitude of these heathens toward God's *elect*.

They are of the devil, a threat to our [corrupt] *establishment. We must frustrate, humiliate, and intimidate them through rejection, slander, or whatever else it takes to drive them out. There will be dire consequences for anyone not with us.*

Why is that so? **Answer:** *Spirit-filled* individuals can sense where things are not right with God. These are places where long-established is evil and righteousness considered repulsive. They are locations void of the *Spirit of God* regardless of churches on every corner. And wherever the *Spirit of God* is absent, it's like a twilight zone scattered in poverty and trash where bullying *devils* exercise control over *worshipers of deception*.

On the contrary, the few possessing the *Spirit of Christ and the Holy Spirit* are as free as the clouds. They cannot be intimidated, humiliated, frustrated, or subject to *devils* or *serpents*. They are eagles that soar, not cackling chickens that *walk in the counsel of the wicked, stand in the way of sinners, or sit in the seat of mockers* (NIV Ps 1). Eagles separate themselves from the communities' prevaricators. Bullied, they can't be. They trap the wicked with the snares the wicked set for them. Integrity is their existence: that which obliterates the lies of the wicked.

Therefore, should you struggle with trying to understand why evil and corrupt people prosper and get away with so much for a period, as you suffer persecution from them while leading a quiet life of repentance to please God in all that you do, consider the following:

1) You are in Satan's world.

2) *Enemies of God* are out to protect and support all other *enemies of God*.

3) The false belief that you can trust a Rattlesnake, and through caring and giving it your very best while singing, *All Is Well*, that the deadly *serpent* will transform into Prince Charming for your safety, well-being, and prosperity.

4) Unable to recognize the pitfalls surrounding you because you are overly trusting and accommodating.

5) Unable to acknowledge Satan's flattering *devils* who are out to destroy you as they conveniently find their way to make you subject to them while belit-

tling you at every opportunity;

6) False belief that running in fear without resisting evil is the best solution to avoid a cataclysm;

7) The mistaken belief that acceptance, grace, forgiveness, mercy, tolerance, and understanding will gain the respect of *devils* out to destroy you;

8) The false impression that God will protect you without taking up arms.

9) The mistaken belief that salvation is for *devils*.

Living in denial of these harsh realities is ominous. Israel's trials and tribulations from the time of Abram in 2100 B.C. were because they failed to heed those warnings. *Repeatedly, it resulted in disaster.*[60]

In John 15:18-19, mentioned earlier, there is a fundamental lesson that Jesus teaches to help soothe loneliness and rejection.

> *Whenever you find yourself hated and rejected, should you be one of His, directed at the righteous Spirit of God within you is that hatred and rejection on the part of heathens believing you are a devil.*

No place was Jesus ever found to be without antagonists hating His presence. Therefore, should you be one of God's *elect*, then His very live *Holy Spirit* resides in you. Although they cannot see Him, His unseen presence convicts prevaricators of their lies

---

[60] Viktor E. Frankl, *Man's Search for Meaning* (New York, NY: Washington Square Press, Division of Simon and Schuster Inc., 1984).

and corruption. He agitates them in secrecy. Hence, be mindful that their cordial pretense and flattery, followed by bullying, back-stabbing, colluding, conspiracy, intimidation, slander, and physical harm, is what the Prophets, as well as Christ, Stephen, and Paul of the New Testament, shamefully experienced. It resulted from sharing their joy in what they knew to be true.

A † Ω

UNDERSTANDING CARNAL MINDS

As far as carnal minds are concerned, believing that unconditional love is the solution to all conflict, beware that turning one's back to God always results in God reciprocating. That predictably results in dire consequences for many who discover that you cannot allow a Rattlesnake to roam freely around you without it wanting to strike you dead.

> It is written: *Do not be deceived: God cannot be mocked. A man reaps what he sows. The one who sows to please his* {as well as the} *sinful nature* {of others}, *from that* {sinful} *nature he will reap destruction; the one who sows to please the* {Holy} *Spirit from the* {Holy} *Spirit he will reap eternal life.* (NIV Gal 6:7-8)

A † Ω

SOLUTIONS TO LONELINESS AND REJECTION

After developing a sincere appreciation and respect for God's complete Word, I could not help but wonder about lonely and depressed people. I considered those torn between right and wrong and without friends who hired out to criminals, joined a cult, fell victim to immorality to fill their voids in life, or committed suicide. Please understand that finding yourself alone and rejected in Satan's world is not undesirable with God. It is a golden opportunity to connect with Him through His Word! At the same time, being depressed and lonely **in a healthy body** is hard evidence that you are **not** in the *Spirit* because if you were in the *Spirit,* fulfilled, you would be with a purpose of pleasing Him in all you do. Therefore, if you are physically healthy yet depressed and lonely, stay in His Word and focus on always pleasing Him **(KJ Mt 11:28-30)**.

Remember Adam? Whenever he was **alone** with the Lord, all was fine and dandy. However, all hell broke loose once brought into fellowship with Eve, his betrayer who flirted with a *serpent* (Ge 3).

Loneliness may be God's call to you as He did with Jesus. Jesus spent much of His time alone in conversation with His Father. Rather than being like Adam, who gave in to Eve, who gave in to a viper, Jesus stood fast against His adversaries by weaponizing the Scriptures against them.

Loneliness and rejection kept me in love with the

entire Bible. Loneliness and repudiation enable me to hear and distinguish the *still small voice* of the *Holy Spirit,* apart from my conscience, tempters, and mind possessing demonic manitous, as discussed in Chapter V: DESTRUCTIVE FORCES OF SATAN.

A † Ω

The Power of God's Commandments

Consider the horrible outcomes for Adam because Eve obeyed a *serpent* and then persuaded Adam to do likewise. Compare it with Jesus in shutting up one.

> It is written: Again, the devil taketh him {Jesus} up into an exceeding high mountain, and sheweth him all the kingdoms of the world, and the glory of them; and saith unto him, *All these things will I give thee, if thou wilt fall down and worship me.*
>
> Then saith Jesus unto him, **Get thee hence, Satan: for it is written, Thou shalt worship the Lord thy God, and him only shalt thou serve.** [This First Commandment—KJ Ex 20:3, Dt 5:7—was not abolished. Instead, it was **weaponized** by Christ to model God's way of *destroying the works of devils* as were the other nine! (KJ 1Jn 3:8)]
>
> Then the devil leaveth him, and, behold, angels came and ministered unto him.
>
> (KJ Mt 4:8–11)

Here, you find Jesus in the desert, forty days and nights alone with God, preparing for His ministry. Before it was over, a deceiver tempted Him with losing faith, committing suicide, and selling His soul to defy God (KJ Mt 4:1–10): temptations to expect should you have a sincere passion for becoming one of God's *elect*.

The Gospel of Mark alluded that the prevaricator, Satan, hounded Jesus throughout those forty days rather than only at the end of the forty days (KJ Mk 1:12–13). The Gospel of Luke alluded that this *devil* of a person somewhat bonded with Jesus throughout the forty days. Then, he tempted Jesus at the end of the forty days (KJ Lk 4:1–13). Nevertheless, all scenarios cover how charming *devils* and *serpents* distract from God's truth, flatter, and manipulate to gain trust. However, after rejecting the manipulator with His talented use of the First Commandment, *the angels of God came and attended Him* (KJ Mt 4:11, Mk 1:13).

By firing the First Commandment at the heart of a flattering liar attempting to destroy Him, Jesus modeled the power behind weaponizing the Word of God against devious people wanting to bully, deceive, humiliate, slander, and ruin you. James also touched on this subject.

> It is written: *Submit yourselves therefore to {the Commandments of} God {as Jesus role-modeled against those out to destroy Him}. Resist the devil, and he will flee from you. Draw nigh to God {Genesis through Revelation}, and he will draw nigh*

to you. Cleanse your hands, ye sinners; and purify your hearts, ye double minded. (KJ Jas 4:7-8)

A ✝ Ω

COMFORT IN STANDING ALONE

It is written: *And ye {chosen few} shall be hated of all men for my name's sake; but he that endureth to the end shall be saved.* (KJ Mt 10:22, Mk 13:13)

Should you find yourself persecuted, consider the rewards of spending time **alone** in the *Spoken Word of God* while attended by angels. There, you may learn how to outsmart *serpents* and *destroy the works of devils* (1Jn 3:8). Moreover, be assured that being *accompanied by* [God's] *angels* (Heb 13:2) is far better than being attended by *serpents* out to deceive you and *devils* wanting to destroy you. In keeping Himself right with God, throughout His brief yet profound ministry, Jesus continued His joy in being **alone** in conversation with God repeatedly. For example,

It is written: But Jesus often withdrew to lonely places and prayed. (NIV Lk 5:16)

That is very different from a Fellowship Church in a Twilight Zone instilling a bald-faced lie on its marquis, which read,

"A man who stands alone is up to evil."

Of course, omitted from its false claim is another lie: *Therefore, join us as Eve joined the serpent and see that our way is above and far better than God's.*

Knowing the full context of God's word, you can learn much about churches by reading their signs. They are almost always void of Scripture or twist its meaning as a *serpent* at that Fellowship Church. Hence, nowhere in the Bible will you find the implication that *anyone alone is up to evil.* That comes from *pulpit serpents* instilling good as evil and evil as good. It is the same level as the lie, *"Jesus loves you"* [to one and all, no matter what].

How about replacing lies on church signs with commandments that attract crowds dying to hear an ounce of God's life-sustaining substance?

THOU SHALT NOT LIE!

THOU SHALT NOT STEAL!

THOU SHALT NOT COVET!

The truth is that a person who stands **alone**, as did the Prophets of Old, Jesus Christ, and His Apostles—on many occasions—is not up to evil but to destroy evil. Thus, time **alone** leads a *chosen few* to repentance, truth, holiness, and confidence through righteousness rather than living corruptly. And at the point of sincere repentance, the Commandments of God become a reality. Hence, saying *"Bye"* to Satan's world of *serpent lies* and *"Hello"* to *Genesis through Revelation* is living in the truth. Therefore, the correct interpretation of Scripture intentionally falsified at the Fellowship Church is as follows:

It is written: *Through* {evil} *desire*(s) *a* {devious wicked} *man, having separated himself* {from the full context of Scripture} *seeketh and intermeddleth with all wisdom.* {Such} *A fool hath no delight in understanding* {the truth}, *but that his heart* {spirit} *may discover itself.* (KJ Pr 18:1-2)

Being **alone** in God's word is what *AGAPE* is all about. It defies prolific pulpit liars by discovering the Bible's consistent facts! It is where you will stumble on the truth, the whole truth, and nothing but the truth, provided you are sincere about wanting the facts.

There, and there alone—however painful it is facing rejection and slander from false friends, evil neighbors, and *worshipers of deception*—is where you discover God wanting to help and strengthen you through every aspect of a life without sin and beyond. While *serpents* and *devils* and their fool-hearted vigilante constituents may be out to dissuade, slander, or destroy you for every success, there you will know that you are walking the walk of Christ, standing steadfast in your integrity with God. The Books of Ester, Job, Proverbs, and Daniel will tell you about it.

A ✝ Ω

PERSECUTED ROLE MODELS

Persecution of God's *elect* started with Cain murdering his brother **Abel** (KJ Ge 4:1-8). It thrived as Ishmael, whose descendants established Islam (Ps 83), mocked **Isaac,** the LORD's *Child of Promise* (KJ Ge 21:8-10), 2,065 years **B**efore **C**hrist). The wife of Potiphar recognized it as she falsely accused **Joseph** of rape and landed him in prison in 1895 B.C. (KJ Ge 39). Regardless that those Israelites served the Egyptians hand and foot for four hundred years, it came to a head in 1446 B.C. as Pharaoh Thutmose III warred against **Moses** and the entire ancient Israelite nation (KJ Ex Chpts. 5-11 & 13-14).

Persecution of God's *elect* prevailed throughout the Old Testament into the New, during which much confusion existed. The following is to bring clarity to significant events during those years.

The year 27 B.C. began the reign of the first Roman Emperor, Caesar Augustus (Lk 2:1), and extended to 14 A.D. **Those years took in the birth of John the Baptist around 7/6 B.C. and the birth of Christ around 6/5 B.C. Augustus' reign also included 1 A.D.: Anno Domini,** *the year of the Lord.* Augustus ruled until 14 A.D. upon his peaceful death at age 75. Without knowledge, not influenced by the birth of Christ, was Caesar Augustus. Tiberius succeeded Augustus as Rome's second emperor.

However, made aware of **Christ's birth** in 6/5 B.C by three wise men who betrayed him, Herod I, King of Judea, who reigned from 37-04 B.C., ordered the slaying of all boys in Bethlehem to two years of age (Mt 2:16).

Then, at the disposal of an adulteress was **John the Baptizer.** Fulfilled as a loner serving the Lord was he. John's mission was to prepare the people for the coming of Christ through baptism and repentance. He would cry in the wilderness over the people's sins and had fiery red eyes (Mt 3:3, Mk 1:3, Lk 3:4, Jn 1:23). Unfortunately, imprisoned for righteousness, was he. Later, beheaded was he at the demand of the Tetrarch, Herod Antipas' adulterated wife, Herodias—also the wife of his half-brother, Phillip the Tetrarch (Mt 14:1-12, Mk 6:17-29).

During his ministry, beginning at age 30 in 26/27 A.D., it was customary for **Jesus** to heal sickly people on Sabbath days. However, He harbored hatred for those offended by His miracles. He referred to them as *"swine"* (Mt 7:6). While on such a mission to *destroy the works of devils* (KJ 1Jn 3:8), falsely accused was He for having worked miracles through the prince of demons: Beelzebub (KJ Mt 12:24, Lk 11:15). [Beelzebub—Lord of the Flies—(Josephus "Ant." Ix. 2, b 1) a fallen angel, demon, or devil: as a prince, he would be second in a hierarchy to Satan].

Regarding the persecuted **Jesus**, the government and religious people of His time hated every aspect of His being. Because of their blindness and hatred for the truth during the reign of Herod Antipas, tetrarch of Galilee, those fanatical, deceitful accusers relating to Beelzebub had Him nailed to a cross in 30 A.D.

Then came **Stephen** around 32 A.D., Galilee still under the reign of the tetrarch Herod Antipas [4 B.C.—39 A.D.], and Tiberius Caesar [14—37 A.D.]. **Stephen** was a well-informed, angel-faced young man, *filled with the Holy Spirit*, boldly proclaiming the truth about the Prophets of Old, Jesus, and God. Moreover, how did those same church people, threatened by every correct word **Stephen** spoke, find pleasure in silencing him? Answer: As he taught the truth about God, caring about their salvation and well-being, the deceived-hateful church crowd stoned him to death (KJ Ac 6:8-15 and Chpt 7). However, persecution for speaking the truth about God did not end with **Stephen**.

Regardless of all the miracles God worked through **Paul** and **Peter**, persecuted were they during the reign of Herod Antipas, who, in 39 A.D., was struck down with flesh-eating worms by an angel (Acts 12:23). Herod Agrippa succeeded Herod Antipas as King of Judea. He ruled from 41—44 A.D. These Biblical episodes occurred during the reign of the Roman Emperor, Tiberius Claudius Caesar [41—54 A.D.] (Acts 18:2, 26).

Following Tiberius was Rome's 5th emperor: Nero Claudius Caesar Augustus Germanicus [54—68 A.D.]. History has it that Nero set Rome on fire in 64 A.D. for two purposes: (1) to rebuild a greater Rome per his design and (2) to falsely blame Christians for the fire to legitimize his annihilation of them by crucifixion, beheading, burning alive, pitting them against gladiators, or had them fed to lions. During the reign of Nero in 64 A.D., speculation has it that crucified was **Peter** per Jesus' prophesy (KJ Jn 21:15-19). Tradition also has it that Peter's counterpart, **Paul**, was beheaded afterward in 67 or 68 A.D. upon his first or second visit with Nero, *the chief enemy of God*.

Hence, throughout the ages, God's *elects* were hated and persecuted (Mt 5:10-12, 22; Jn 15:18). Persecution was at the core of the King James Bible to discredit the teachings and rituals of demonic religions running rampant among the English-speaking people. Once read and understood, that new English Bible, a first of its kind, would hopefully cause *the many called by God* to worship Him in righteousness and obedience over idol worship, beads, and repetitious prayers (KJ Mt 6:1-18). It was central to the Martin Luther Protestant Reformation, discrediting religious cults [1483—1546]. **King James** picked up where **Martin Luther** left off.

Like Jesus in Biblical times—having no beauty or majesty to attract the world to themselves (KJ Isa 53:2)—the presence of a *spirit-filled person of God*, as mentioned, is repulsive to heathens. However, that same hatred forever brings honor and renewed hope to the favored by God. Hence, persecution of the fulfilled lonely *elect* is fourfold:

1) Silence them in whatever way is necessary to prevent the truth from being known.

2) Put fear in their believers to keep them from going against evil regimes and atrocities.

3) Prevent them from *destroying the works of devils* (KJ 1Jn 3:8).

4) Steal their work and heritage and disgrace them.

Hence, anyone chosen by God boldly doing His works will meet resistance. It is a reminder that we are in a satanic world.

JESUS LOVES YOU DEPENDS

Satan's people cringe at any amount of truth regarding any and every righteous thing. Thus, this is why God-haters broadcast *"Jesus loves you"* to one and all. Think about its atrocities. Ponder over its intent. Consider who's behind it!

"Jesus loves you" deceives by condoning evil on the part of *thieves, murderers, and destroyers* (KJ Jn 10:10). It dramatically appeals to all void of the *Spirit of God* and portrays Him as loving to all, which He is not. It condones every evil act while violating the Third and Ninth Commandments. However, it is part of the puzzle for the end of time.

> It is written: *Now the Spirit speaketh expressly, that in the latter times some shall depart from the faith, giving heed to seducing spirits, and doctrines of devils; speaking lies in hypocrisy; having their conscience seared with a hot iron.* (KJ 1Ti 4:1-2)

A † Ω

STANDING FAST WITH GOD

Thus, regardless that persecution comes with serving God on the part of the Kingdom of Satan, wrath comes with serving Satan on the part of the Kingdom of God. The big question is:

Which is your choice?

After everything is said and done, I would prefer to be among the few standing with God, regardless of being persecuted daily. I favor placing my trust in God's way rather than joining the ranks of the many Christ said He never knew and will never come to know.

That should be an eye-opening revelation to all who throw out, **Jesus is Lord,** where **Satan is prince** (KJ Jn 12:31, 14:30, 16:11). Their fake Jesus, void of God's commandments, condones the crimes and immorality they commit: that which the Bible's Jesus would never do. To misguided souls where their stand-alone Jesus is Lord in Satan's world abounding in hatred for the righteous, corruption, and destruction, applauded by *serpents* void of His Word,

> It is written: *Not every one that saith unto me, Lord, Lord,* {I believe whatever, and I got whoever} *shall enter into the kingdom of heaven; but* {only} *he that doeth the will of my Father which is in heaven. Many* {prevaricators} *will say to me in that day, Lord, Lord, have we not prophesied in thy name? And in thy name have cast out devils? And in thy name done many wonderful works? And then will I profess unto them, I never knew you* {psychopathic liars and worthless evildoers}*: depart from me, ye that work iniquity.*
>
> *Therefore whosoever heareth these sayings of mine, and doeth them, I will liken him unto a wise man, which built his house upon a rock. And the rain descended, and the floods came, and the winds blew, and beat upon that house;*

and it fell not: for it was founded upon a rock.

*And every one that heareth these sayings of mine, and doeth them **not**, shall be likened unto a foolish man, which built his house upon the sand. And the rain descended, and the floods came, and the winds blew, and beat upon that house; and it fell: and great was the fall of it.*

(KJ Mt 7:21–27)

Question: *How is it possible to know for sure that it was deceivers who claimed that they prophesied in Jesus' name, drove out demons, and performed miracles?*

Answer: *It is because no one void of the truth or out violating God's commandments has the Gift of Prophecy, the Gift of Driving out Demons, the Gift of Healing, or any other divine gift from God.*

And to drive home their lies, deceivers will reliably have *worshipers of deception* believing that Jesus forbade His followers from prophesying, prohibited them from driving out *demons*, and banned them from performing miracles such as *laying on of hands for divine healing*. The truth is that the *Gifts of Healing, Revelation,* and all other divine gifts are through the *Holy Spirit,* without the world's censorship (KJ Mt 10:8). Simultaneously, manipulation of Matthew 7:21–27 suppresses ill-informed followers of the risen Christ. For example, *serpents* are quick to instill:

"Miracles of God were only through Jesus and His Apostles. Anyone who currently works miracles is *a devil."*

Ironically, the clergy fiercely hated Jesus and His Apostles for their healing ministries!

A † Ω

JESUS:
the way, the truth, and the life

The fact is that Jesus came as *the way* {*the Commandments of God*}, *the truth* {*Genesis through Revelation*}, *and the life* {*Zoe* and *Salvation for repentant souls*} (KJ Jn 10:10 & 14:6). He is the manifestation of righteousness. Hence, only the righteous *elect* whose names are written in His *book of life* receive divine gifts through the *Holy Spirit* (KJ Joel 2:28–29, 1Co 12:28, Rev 3:5, 20:15). Thus, the only option for redemption by Jesus of past sins is,

The Sign of Jonah:
REPENT OR PERISH!

A † Ω

WITH OR AGAINST GOD

Thus, fulfilling *the Way, the Truth, and the Life* (KJ Jn 14:6) in oneself and becoming heaven-bound begins with dedicating oneself to God through *repentance, obeying His commandments, and relying on the full context of Scripture*. Doing so is a matter of choice;

however, all come with persecution. The alternative is destruction by one's sinful desires or following the *enemies of God* among whom the wrath of God and the love of Satan are sure to find their way.

> It is written: *I say to you that many will come from the east and the west, and will take their places at the feast with Abraham, Isaac, and Jacob in the Kingdom of Heaven. But the subjects {impostors} of the kingdom {of the spirit of evil} will be thrown outside, into the darkness, where there will be weeping and gnashing of teeth.* (NIV Mt 8:11–12)

> **Question:** *Do you believe you are one of the few chosen for His kingdoms or will be one of the many thrown outside into darkness* [Hell] *where there will be weeping and gnashing of teeth?*

Should you have the slightest doubt, please keep reading. I am confident that you will find the shocking hidden truth, should you be sincere in wanting to know the qualifying mystery of God required for Heaven.

A † Ω

WHY PERSECUTION?

While walking in the cool of the morning in conversation with **His Majesty, Eli** {*my God* (KJ Mt 27:46)}, as I customarily do, I asked these profound questions:

> *Lord, why didn't you rescue John the Baptizer from*

the hands of the tetrarch, Herod Antipas? Why didn't you save the apostles found right with your Word? Why didn't you rescue Stephen from the hands of Pharisees and Sadducees stoning him?

He answered:

Unless a person is willing to stand down forces of evil and die as those all did for the truth of my Word and commandments as Jesus did, they are not my friends. Thus, called are many, chosen are few. Therefore, one distinguishes himself as a trustworthy friend of mine by being willing to die for me as Jesus died for him. Recall what Jesus said. "Greater love hath no man than this that a man lay down his life for his friends." The friends He referred to were not—as Scripture calls them— the enemies of God and deceivers. Instead, they are the few belonging to the Kingdom of God and the Kingdom of Heaven for dedicating themselves to **the fullness of Christ** *by repenting, obeying the commandments, and believing in Genesis through Revelation. They are poor in spirit (KJ Mt 5:3) and hunger and thirst for righteousness (Mt 5:6).*

About Jesus,

It is written: Although he was a Son, **he learned obedience through his sufferings,** *and when he had been made perfect, he became the source of eternal salvation* **for all who obey him** *{the life}, and he was designated a high priest by God according to the order of Melchizedek.* (NCV Heb 5:8–10)

Hebrews 5:8-10 is not to be confused with Islam's Quran commanding self-sacrifice in murdering *infidels,* referring to the many God calls to be His own. The preferable interpretation is *being willing to stand up for the truth of God's intended Word without fear of thieves, murderers, and destroyers* (KJ Jn 10:10).

For example, strapping bombs around one's waist to commit the *Art of Massacre* over entitlements one is not entitled to are the works of *devils* among whom Jesus was out to destroy. During his ministry, those were descendants of *Shem* (p. 45) / *Abram.* Those descendants included unbelieving Jews, as well as descendants of *Ishmael.* The *Ishmaelites* created Islam 700 years later under the envious *man-of-terror* prophet, *Muhammad the Murderer* (Jn 8:42-44). Others became *serpents* recognized by their false accusations, blatant lies, and shamelessness in wickedness.

> **Question!** What is the solution to achieving victory over the anti-Christ wanting to abolish Christian values, democracy, and the Free Enterprise System?

> **Answer:** Return to God's complete Word, obey His commandments, purge the evil from within yourself, fast, and pray (Dt 28, Jos, Isa, Jer, Eze). Then you may have God as your ally in doing what needs doing through miracles and *death angels.*

INFINITE FORGIVENESS:
A False Ideology

In every church I attended, where expounded upon was forgiveness, *serpents* preach that Christians are always to be forgiving, *no matter what.* However, *no matter what* falls into the category of outright lies on the part of a God-forsaken leftist clergy. It defines *"unconditional!"*

Hence, I sincerely knew that this teaching was demonic. After all, would not Satan be the one having every good, law-abiding citizen commanded to forgive liars, thieves, murderers, and destroyers, *no matter what?* ABSOLUTELY! God's accurate and complete context teaches an opposite lesson from that demonic interpretation.

> It is written: *If your brother {sister, friend, neighbor, colleague or whoever} sins {against you} rebuke him, and {only} if he repents, forgive him. If he sins against you seven times in a day, and seven times comes back to you and says, I repent {for whatever evils he committed}, forgive him.* (NIV Lk 17:3-4)

REFLECT! How many times intentionally persecuted have you been—such as having been lied to, spit upon, hated, rejected, robbed, slandered, and beyond—by bullies who conspired against you, and they returned to apologize for their specific crimes committed to humiliate, intimidate, frustrate, and destroy you? How often? One in a hundred, **or more likely never?** If one in a hundred is the case, then it is only that one that you are to forgive. All ninety-nine others stand **not** to be forgiven by you. Jesus pointed this out.

> It is written: Again Jesus said, *Peace be with you! As the Father has sent me, I am sending you.* And with that he breathe on them and said, *Receive the Holy Spirit. If you forgive anyone's sins, their sins are forgiven; **if you do not forgive them, they are not forgiven**.* (NIV Jn 20:21–23)

Per God and Jesus, believers are to **serve justice** to criminals, **not forgive them** unconditionally, as ingrained in congregations by pious hell-bound *pulpit serpents*.

> It is written: **To do justice and judgment is more acceptable to the L**ORD** than sacrifice.** (KJ Pr 21:3)

> It is written: Thus saith the LORD, **Keep ye judgment, and do justice: for my salvation is near to come, and my righteousness to be revealed.** (KJ Isa 56:1)

God's *elect* must defend themselves in whatever ways are necessary to stop an aggressor. Protecting oneself by standing down the wicked is not a sinful act. However, *serpents* preach that defending oneself against established criminals makes the persecuted person both sinner and villain: that which Jesus and his apostles repeatedly experienced because the justice system was corrupt!

In summarizing this Chapter, **PERSECUTION:** *The Effect of Agape* informs that persecution plays a significant role in standing up for God in *destroying the works of devils* (1Jn 3:8). About them,

> It is written: An oracle is within my heart concerning the sinfulness of the wicked. *There is no fear of God before his eyes. For in his own eyes he flatters himself too much to detect or hate his sin. The words of his mouth are wicked and deceitful; he has ceased to be wise and to do good. Even on his bed he plots evil; he commits himself to a sinful course and does not reject what is wrong.* (NIV Ps 36:1-4)

> It is written: *The desire accomplished is sweet to the soul; but it is abomination to fools to depart from evil.* (KJ Pr 13:19)

Destroying demonic strongholds is God's wish for His people (KJ 1Jn 3:8). Doing so often results in having to stand alone against *devils* in deprived communities. There, they rule by bullying and intimidation to instill fear over the weak-minded, resulting in the abolishment of godly love (KJ 1Jn 4:18). **However, victory over such *strongholds* is achievable, no matter who they are.** But don't expect it to happen overnight because counting on God comes through *longsuffering* (KJ 2Co 6:6). It requires complete faith in His word. Weaponized, it **can** be against the wicked by proclaiming Scriptures such as *The wicked shall* *not go unpunished* (KJ Pr 11:21, Na 1:2-3), *and Evil shall slay the wicked* (KJ Ps 34:21). How refreshing to know both are God's promises we can count on where abolished was *Equal Justice Under The Law*! (Ps 92:7)

Therefore, now is the time to battle for the truth of God's word and obedience to His way. Now is the time to *destroy the works of devils,* even though our voices and legs tremble. Now is the time to join the ranks of God's few true Christians as *Kingsmen.* Now is the time to take back what **demonic strongholds** threw away: INTEGRITY AND THE PROMISED LAND. After all, *the meek* {righteous} *shall inherit the earth* (KJ Mt 5:5), not the corrupt and wicked destined for the *second death—Hell* (KJ Rev 2:11, 20:14, 21:8). **Thus, being righteous is God's will for His few!**

> It is written: *(For the fruit of the Spirit is in all goodness and righteousness and truth;) Proving what is acceptable unto the Lord.*
>
> *And have no fellowship with the unfruitful works of darkness, but rather reprove them. For it is a shame even to speak of those things which are done of them in secret.*
>
> (KJ Eph 5:9-11)

Hence, God's people do not sin whenever they stand against the wicked by telling them where to go: "**Hell!**" That is true prophesying because the unrepentant wicked are doomed to Hell. Likewise, be reminded that God does not backslide whenever He unleashes His wrath to fulfill that prophecy. It is very keen of *serpents* to have God's law-abiding people guilt-ridden over not forgiving *devils* who violated them. How sly having God's people guilt-ridden over defending themselves.

FIRST AND FOREMOST, ABOUT FORGIVENESS:

(1) Granting forgiveness is an option for a violated person.

(2) Refusing to forgive is not a sinful act because forgiveness is not for devils. *It would have been better had they not been born* (Mt 26:24).

(3) Asking for forgiveness must be done by the offender and include reasons for and details of the offense.

(4) An offender may only be forgiven by his non-coerced victim; otherwise, nullified it is.

(5) Righteous, unsuspecting murdered people cannot forgive their killers: *devils*. *Devils* are not forgivable.

(6) God may forgive a murderer if the murderer is one of His elect who sincerely repents and regrets his crime. However, regardless of God's forgiveness, there shall be dire consequences (CB 2Sam 11:1–27 and 12:1–25, Ps 51).

(7) Acting in self-defense by killing an aggressor is not an act of murder because there is *a time to kill* (Ecc 3:3).

It is written: *Blessed are they that mourn* {even

with expletives over the atrocities committed against them by devils}, *for they shall be comforted.* (KJ Mt 5:4)

Should you have experienced unjust persecution, remember that, like Christ, it is through suffering that His elect is made perfect in obedience (Heb 5:8-9), resulting in fulfilled promises!

A † Ω

A Kingsman's Prayer

It is written: *Plead my cause, O LORD, with them that strive with me: fight against them that fight against me. Take hold of shield and buckler, and stand up for mine help. Draw out also the spear, and stop the way against them that persecute me: say unto my soul, I am thy salvation.*

Let them be confounded and put to shame that seek after my soul: let them be turned back and brought to confusion that devise my hurt. Let them be as chaff before the wind: and let the angel of the LORD chase them. Let their way be dark and slippery: and let the angel of the LORD persecute them.

For without cause have they hid for me their net in a pit, which without cause they have digged for my soul. Let destruction come upon him at unawares; and let his net that he hath hid catch himself: into that very destruction let him fall.

And my soul shall be joyful in the LORD: it shall re-

joice in his salvation. All my bones shall say, LORD, who is like unto thee, which deliverest the poor from him that is too strong for him, yea, the poor and the needy from him that spoileth him?

False witnesses did rise up; they laid to my charge things that I knew not. They rewarded me evil for good to the spoiling of my soul. . . . In mine adversity they rejoiced, and gathered themselves together: yea, the abjects gathered themselves together against me, and I knew it not; they did tear me, and ceased not: With hypocritical mockers in feasts, they gnashed upon me with their teeth. Lord, how long wilt thou look on? Rescue my soul from their destructions, my darling {life} from the lions. I will give thee thanks in the great congregation: I will praise thee among much people.

Let not them that are mine enemies wrongfully rejoice over me: neither let them wink with the eye that hate me without a cause. For they speak not peace: but they devise deceitful matters against them that are quiet in the land. Yea, they opened their mouth wide against me, and said, Aha, aha, our eye hath seen it.

This thou has seen, O LORD, keep not silence: O LORD my God, according to thy righteousness; and let them not rejoice over me. . . Let them be ashamed and brought to confusion together that rejoice at mine hurt: let them be clothed with shame and dishonour that magnify themselves against me. . .

(KJ Ps 35 excerpts)

A † Ω

XIV. THE MAGNITUDE OF REPENTANCE

It is written: *Likewise, I say unto you, there is joy in the presence of the angels of God over one sinner that repenteth.* (KJ Lk 15:10)

Repentance is so rare that whenever someone repents, there is joy in the presence of the angels of God. These are not individuals glorified for continuing in sin and repeatedly nailing Jesus to the cross. Instead, through **self-control**, they OVERCOMETH and are canonized as saints by Jesus Christ for having repented (KJ Rev 2:7, 11, 17, 26; 3:5, 12, 21). Also,

It is written: *Little children, let no man deceive you: he that doeth righteousness is righteous, even as he is righteous. He that committeth sin is of the devil; for the devil sinneth from the beginning.* **For this purpose the Son of God was manifested, that he might destroy the works of the devil.**

*Whosoever is born of God doth not {continue to} commit sin; for his {Christ's Holy Spirit} seed remaineth in him: and he cannot sin, because he is born of God {and sinning is repulsive to him}. In this, the children of God are manifest, and the children of the devil: whosoever doeth **not** righteousness is **not** of God, neither he that loveth **not** his {God fearing} brother.*

(KJ 1Jn 3:7-10)

CAUTION: Most living in violation of God's commandments falsely believe they can make it to Heaven with *"Bless me, Father, for I have sinned," "Lord, you know I'm a sinner,"* and *"Jesus loves me."* It will not happen because per Scripture, *he that committeth sin is of the devil,* not God.

Hence, in setting out to make a great future out of a new repentant life apart from religion, I aimed to overcome evil and the evil, regardless that the kind doctor back in Chapter V assured me, *"You are perfectly normal."* I figured it this way: Much of what is reasonable, acceptable, and promotable throughout Satan's world is abnormal, abominable, and condemned by God.

Thus, if God's *elects* become isolated in what they have come to know as His absolute truth, it won't dissuade them from Him in the same way that being alone in the truth about God did not discourage Job [Jobe]. Job was a mighty servant **favored by God** due to repenting earlier in life. Nothing could sway Job away from God. And since **God** was wholly confident in Job's faith, He took up a bet with Satan. It resulted in the disfigurement of Job and the loss of all he had and represented, including his seven sons and three daughters. However, God spared the lives of His wife, brothers, and sisters for some reason. But to add to his misery, four preachers mocked Job throughout his suffering. They were Eliphez, Bildad, Zophar, and Elihus. And daring to remain confident of his righteousness, Job was steadfast against their slander. That angered the four who would come to be the ones disgraced by God. (Book of Job)

Hence, I hope those firsthand experiences will move you to what's number one with God: **obedience and truth**, established by reading, studying, believing, and obeying *every word out of the mouth of God* (Dt 8:3, Mt 4:4). Once you get a grip on the complete Bible with a sincere heart to please Him, your sins will come alive that you considered necessary for your survival! But they are not, which should lead you to repentance. Without doing so, the Bible illustrates that saved you are not, and you most certainly can forget about Heaven! Why? Here's the answer!

Without repentance, there is no obedience to God's way.
Without obedience, there is no trust in or love for God.
Without trust, there is no faith.
And without faith, it is impossible to please God.
(Heb 11:6)

A † Ω

In summarizing this chapter, **THE MAGNITUDE OF REPENTANCE**, beware that *repentance* is a primary condition in attaining the love of God. It is a primary condition for having Christ atone for your past sins. Starting, Jesus commanded, "Repent, for the kingdom of heaven is at hand" (KJ Mt.4:17). Ending, He explained, "Repentance <u>for</u> {**not** and} the forgiveness of sins will be preached in his name to all nations, beginning at Jerusalem" (CB and NIV Life Application Study Bibles—Luke 24:47). **Agape, forgiveness, and salvation require repentance!**

A † Ω

XV. MISLEADING THROUGH SNIPPETS

It is written: *For I testify unto every man that heareth the words of the prophecy of this book, if any man shall add unto these things, God shall add unto him the plagues that are written in this book. And if any man shall take away from the words of the book of this prophecy, God shall take away his part out of the book of life, and out of the holy city, and from the things which are written in this book.*

He which testifieth these things saith, Surely I come quickly. Amen. Even so, come, Lord Jesus.

(KJ Rev 22:18–20)

A *snippet* is to the Bible as a false report is to investors. *Snippets* are very misleading because they rob the truth of God's undeniable, complete, and intended word. Preaching or teaching via snippets is altering or omitting keywords from Scripture to give an entirely false, impotent, irrelevant, and **un**conditional meaning to the Spoken Word of God {**Rhema**}.

The use of snippets is to mislead God's *elect*. Snippet preaching and teachings have cost the salvation of countless congregations falsely made to believe in Scripture stripped of its highly relevant, highly conditional, and intended meaning. That was one of the primary reasons for another profound warning on the part of Jesus:

It is written: *For many are called* {to the Kingdom

of God and Kingdom of Heaven}, *but {only a} few are chosen.* (KJ Mt 22:14)

Manipulating the intended meaning of *God's Spoken Word*, as the *serpent* boldly did with Eve and as Nadab and Abihu altered worship, displays rank arrogance, demonic teaching, and denial of the truth about God. **It violates the third commandment: THOU SHALL NOT MISUSE THE NAME OF THE LORD YOUR GOD (NIV Ex 20:7).** Doing so leads to a breach of all other of God's commands and unleashes abominations that cause desolation.

Comparably, the intent of the US Constitution is altered via snippets by intentionally corrupt lawyers, politicians, and God-hating Supreme Court Justices, making it into a devil's Pandora's Box. It's how trolls rob and twist the truth into fake news to match their demonic ideologies created for *worshipers of deception.*

Therefore, God's *chosen few* learn not to put blind trust in demonic philosophical *serpent* preaching, teaching, and rhetoric coming out of forsaken forms of worship and evil regimes. Instead, they indulge themselves in God's way until mastered as modeled by their master! There, they come to know who is with God's word versus who and where *serpents* and *devils*, disguised as *angels of light*, perform their acts of treason against God, His honest working people, and all others who oppose them. God warns His people through His Word:

> It is written: . . . **There shall be no poor among you;** *for the* L<small>ORD</small> *shall greatly bless thee in the land which the* L<small>ORD</small> *thy God giveth thee for an*

*inheritance to possess it: **only if thou carefully hearken unto the <u>voice</u> of the* Lord *thy God, to observe to do all these commandments which I command thee this day.** For the* Lord *thy God blesseth thee, as he promised thee: and thou shalt lend unto many nations, but thou shalt not borrow; and thou shalt reign over many nations, but they shall not reign over thee.* (KJ Dt 15:4-6)

A ✝ Ω

Jesus is not Lord among the Wicked

It is entertaining to find signs of *"Jesus loves you," "Jesus is Lord,"* and Jesus this and Jesus that throughout Twilight Zone communities where the cartels, corruption, trash, and poverty flourish. It proves their hypocrisy against God, the truth of His word, and a highly religious but fake Jesus.

It is written: And {the truthful} Jesus answered and said unto them, *Take heed that no man deceive you. For many shall come in my name, saying, I am Christ; and shall deceive many.* (KJ Mt 24:4-5)

Rather than instill the Commandments of God in even one of their various forsaken churches, these are communities whose Jesus condones lying, stealing, and coveting. These are communities whose people—*worshipers of deception*—abhor righteousness. These are communities where acceptance into corrupt elitist organizations requires driving out truth seekers.

Truth seekers, like Job, expose the wicked by merely standing fast against them alongside *Jesus Christ by destroying the works of devils* (KJ 1Jn 3:8). God warns against entertaining *thieves, murderers, and destroyers* (KJ Jn 10:10). To such ill-informed persons,

> It is written: . . . *Obey my voice* {not theirs}, *and do them* {justice}, *according to all which I command you:* **so shall ye be my people**, *and* {only then} *I will be your God: That I may perform the oath which I have sworn unto your fathers, to give them a land flowing with milk and honey.* (KJ Jer 11:4–5)

A † Ω

THE GREAT COMMISSION

The resurrected Christ reiterated this concept of obedience to God in The Great Commission. Unfortunately, His Great Commission is highly misleading whenever presented as a snippet. For example,

> It is written: And Jesus came and spake unto them, saying, *All power is given unto me in heaven and in earth. Go ye therefore, and teach all nations, baptizing them in the name of the Father, and of the Son, and of the Holy Ghost.* (KJ Mt 28:18–19)

That is a perfectly misleading snippet giving the false impression that, through baptism, everyone becomes a disciple of Christ and qualifies for Heaven no matter what. That impression is far removed from the truth because the group of words typically omitted from this Scripture is the qualifying **BENCHMARK** for God's kingdoms. Those omitted words are:

Teaching them to observe all things whatsoever I have commanded you. (KJ Mt 28:20)

In other words, with a baptism **void** of repentance by obeying God's commandments, one can forget about ever being a disciple of Christ. So that you may come to fully understand God's intended interpretation of Scripture, from Jesus in this case, is to connect the missing words with the words that comprise the misleading *snippet:* something I touched on in Chapter VII—THE FAVORED BY GOD. Therefore, combine this *serpent's snippet* with the text typically taken out of it to honestly *live by every word out of the mouth of God* (Mt 4:4).

> It is written: Then Jesus came to them and said, *All power is given unto me in heaven and in earth* {among my elect}. *Go ye therefore* {with obedience}, *and teach all nations, baptizing them in the name of the Father, and of the Son, and of the Holy Ghost:* **teaching them to observe all things whatsoever I have commanded you:** *and, lo, I am* {then} *with you alway, even unto the end of the world.* (KJ Mt 28:18-20)

The heart of Mt 28:18-20 is not only baptism. Instead, it requires new converts to repent by living according to God's constitution. However, since His constitution is repulsive to heathens and backsliders, it is not taught or encouraged in most of today's baptismal locations. So, how do congregations come to know it, not to mention being required by God to live by it?

Answer: They do not, and they most certainly have no intention of following it. Basking in sinful pleasures and living in the horrors that they have given way to—as did Eve, Cain, Nadab, Abihu, Ha'-man, and Judas—in expecting this false Jesus and that fake Jesus to atone for their never-ending despicable rebellion and sins unconditionally: ABSOLUTELY!

On the contrary, living per God's commandments and by the truth of His Word becomes the way to prosper throughout life in Satan's world. It demonstrates true faith, love for, and trust in God, Jesus, and the Holy Spirit. Of equal importance is that obedience points to paradise because Jesus was the manifestation of the Commandments (KJ Jn 14:6), and without Him, there is no paradise. That is how it was for our role models who did what was right in the eyes of God. Included were, but are not limited to, the Bible's truthful prophets, Jesus and His Apostles, excluding Judas Iscariot.

Another upside to living according to God's way, even in the face of persecutors, is being Libera: *"Free."* Living free—according to the fullness of God's word—results in *life more abundantly* (KJ Jn 10:10): *joy and happiness, peace and quiet, safety and wellbeing, prosperity and success. Discernment and discretion, wisdom and knowledge, creativity and talent, pureness and perfection* accompany it. It honors *the Sabbath Rest* and wins the ultimate prize: *eternal life in paradise!*

A ✝ Ω

UNCONDITIONAL LOVE AND MERCY: *FALSE*

Other favorite snippets have many believing that God abounds in unconditional love and mercy. However, the Bible teaches an altogether different lesson when thoroughly read. For example:

> It is written: *The LORD is slow to anger and great in power.* (NIV Na 1:3)

That misleading snippet implies that God's grace and mercy are given to all, regardless of how criminally evil they choose to become. That is not at all the case. Allow the Bible to shed the truth concerning the real identity of God. Look at the full context of this Scripture.

> It is written: *The LORD is a jealous and avenging God; the LORD takes vengeance and is filled with wrath. The LORD takes vengeance on his foes and maintains his wrath against his enemies. The LORD is slow to anger and great in power; {but} the LORD will not leave the guilty unpunished.* (NIV Na 1:2-3)

The full context of the Scripture reveals that *the truthful, slow to anger, great in power God is jealous and avenging, has little tolerance for evil people, and, at some point in time, will take His ven-*

geance out on them. This same *slow-to-anger God is wrathful and will not leave the guilty unpunished.*

Hence, *God's jealousy, vengeance, and wrath* are what the *enemies of God* do not want you or anyone else to know about Him. Why? Believing God is unconditionally in love with *liars, thieves, murderers, and destroyers,* there is no need to bear arms. There is no need to rebuke evil. There is no need to interrogate and imprison corrupt politicians! There is no need to execute cold-blooded murderers. There is no need to resist the anti-Christ Communist and Socialist Movements. There is no need to investigate cults under the pretense of tax-free religions destroying Christian values and democracy. There is no need to halt Islamic aggression, **bribery**, blackmail, and teaching the ominous Quran in public schools where Bible teaching was never permitted. There is no need to stand down bullies and all others villainizing God's caretakers.

The more these anti-Christ individuals and groups are tolerated and given into their cold-hearted, demonic, and selfish demands, the eviler Satan's world will become an abomination sure to produce desolation on a massive scale. Ignoring this reality is ominous.

Furthermore, the full context of the Bible sheds an entirely factual version of God. For example, in the Books of Joshua and Ezekiel, God commanded the destruction of every person throughout the nations he hated (KJ Jos Chpt 12 including 13:1-7 and 21:43-45, Eze 9:6). Those demands testify about God as being hateful and vengeful toward heathens with whom He disassociates. It is hard evidence that He sheds no grace, forgiveness, or mercy on them. (KJ 1Sa 15).

What did you just read and hopefully learn that you likely never heard in church or considered?

> It is written: *The LORD is a jealous and avenging God; the LORD takes vengeance and is filled with wrath. The LORD takes vengeance on his foes and maintains his wrath against his enemies.* (NIV Na 1:2)

That is what God-haters [*atheists, leftists, and the anti-Christ*], deceivers [*pulpit serpents*], and destroyers [*devils*] do not want you to know about God. Vengeance and wrath are upon them and the *worshipers of deception* they indoctrinate. Likewise, should this cause a change in your beliefs about God, then awesome! That is God's doing because He is calling you to come out of hypnosis under the spell of liars and thieves. He is calling you to do your eagle thing by flying out of that chicken coup before the farmer you hail serves you in a way you have never imagined.

A ✝ Ω

M A Y:
Not What It's Made Out to Be!

Examine another famous misleading snippet. In the Book of Romans, you will find the perfect bit to support the lie of unconditional love that condones sin. Romans 11:32 is the one. It is not to be confused with Romans 2:7-11, discussed in Chapter VII: THE FAVORED BY GOD.

> It is written: *God has bound all men over to disobedience so that he **may** have mercy on them all.* (NIV Ro 11:32)

How questionable Paul is to condone sinning so that all can congruently request from God: *"Since Jesus loves me, then bless me, Father, for I have sinned!"* OR—how about bragging about it with, *"Jesus, You know I'm a sinner."*

Paul's Romans 11:32, standing alone, condones and promotes every possible evil without holding anyone accountable. Should you advance into Paul's Romans XII, you see Paul correcting himself by preaching that all must take responsibility for their actions rather than believing otherwise. Look how he begins Romans' Chapter XII.

> It is written: *I BESEECH you therefore, brethren by the mercies of God, that ye present your bodies a living sacrifice, holy, acceptable unto God, which is your reasonable service.*
>
> *And be not conformed to this world: but be ye transformed by the renewing of your mind {by reading, studying, believing, and obeying Genesis through Revelation}, that ye may prove what is that good, and acceptable , and perfect*

will of God.

(KJ Rom 12:1-2)

God requires His *elect* to be righteous per His way: that is, offering their bodies as holy living sacrifices. Becoming a suicide bomber, engaging in immorality, draped in body art, smoking, drinking, and other self-destructive abominations is not what Romans 11:32 implies. Instead, *repenting* and being submissive to the fullness of God's intended word is *the Way, the Truth, and the Life* (Jn 14:6). **The Way, the Truth, and the Life** is **not** a stand-alone Jesus.

> It is written: *Know ye not that ye are the temple of God, and that the Spirit of God dwelleth in you? If any man defile the temple of God, him shall God destroy; for the temple of God is holy, which temple ye are.* (1Cor 3:16-17)

> It is written: *Do you not know that your body is a temple of the Holy Spirit, who is in you* (that repent and obey), *whom you have received from God? You are not your own; you were bought at a price* {crucifixion of Christ}. *Therefore honor God with your body.* {Created not were God's *elect* as canvases, beer tanks, smokestacks, or vessels named *SIN*!} (NIV 1Cor 6:19)

Even so, and for the sake of doubters, let's go back to Romans 11:32 and pay careful attention to the most critical word in the Scripture: **may.** Paul wrote that God "**may have mercy**," not He would. There is a significant difference between the two. Wouldn't you agree? For example: How many times have you received written notices in the mail that you *may* have won something, only to discover that they were flat-out lies to entice you to buy worthless objects you would never use?

Thus, if you say to someone, "*I may do this*" or "*I may do that,*" it does **not** mean you will. What it implies is that you will consider doing it. For example, God considered having mercy on the people in Noah's world, but He destroyed all but eight with a great dramatic flood. He pondered leniency on the people of Sodom and Gomorrah but destroyed all but four with molten sulfur. JEHOVAH considered having mercy on Pharaoh's army but killed all in a dramatic ambush by drowning. He considered pardoning Herod Antipas but destroyed him with flesh-eating worms in the presence of all the king's men and all the king's horses that couldn't put him back together again.

There are vital lessons to learn from those ancient but very real annihilations.

1. When provoked to anger, God is not the sinner by any imagination!

2. People without fear of God caused those annihilations. Since they turned their backs on the truth of His word, **especially His commandments**—as we find throughout today's exceedingly evil world and its satanic churches—He annihilated them.

The hidden and spiritually coded interpretation of

Paul's notorious Romans 11:32 is:

> *God has bound all men over to disobedience* {through free will}, *so that he may have mercy on them all* {who read, study, and believe **Every Spoken Word of His**}.

Since God turned all humanity over to free will, He separates His sheep from Satan's goats—the wheat from the chaff, the righteous from the **unrighteous**—*since every person reveals to God who they are by what they do* (Ro 2:6, Rev 22:12-13).

Therefore, as some worlds turn exceedingly wicked—which activates their OMEGA or ANNIHILATION—servants of the *spirit of evil* are snared into exposing themselves shamelessly to horrific acts of corruption and indecency while congruently believing that God loves them unconditionally. It is not so (KJ Ps 92:7, NIV 2Th 2:1-15)!

Those abominations lead to another of Paul's *snippet quotes*. It abolished God's commandments and promoted the lie, *"Jesus loves me unconditionally."*

> It is written: . . . *Happy is he that condemneth not himself in that* {evil} *thing which he alloweth.* (KJ Ro 14:22)

And to what type of absolute arrogance and outright lawlessness would that misleading snippet allude? How about:

> *No matter the immorality, lying, stealing, murdering,*

> *and destroying I commit, if I approve of one or all, I am blessed standing among the community's elite group of organized criminals:* **C**orrupt **I**diots *and* **A**ssociates. *But sheee! Don't tell anybody.*

Or better yet:

> *Since I abolished God's commandments but have Jesus, I am blessed far more!*

Paul's writings opened the floodgates of deception through snippets: precisely their purpose among all Hell-bound *enemies of God*, as do Jesus' parables (Isa 6:9, Mt 13:11, Lk 8:10). However, drawn to the full context of the Bible, God's *elect* discover that Romans 14.22 had to do with food, as in 1Co 8:1-2, discussed back in Chapter VII: THE FAVORED BY GOD. It was about an Old Testament requirement forbidding pork that Jesus abolished.

Romans 14:22 had nothing to do with approving evil conduct or denouncing God's way. Hence, in the sense that the *enemies of God* could not correctly interpret his parables, so were Paul's epistles. In other words, the two aligned perfectly! On the other hand, while keeping things right among God's *elect*, Paul stated the unthinkable:

> It is written: *For the wrath of God is revealed from heaven against all ungodliness and unrighteousness of men, who hold the truth in unrighteousness; because that which may be known of God is manifest in them; for God hath shewed it unto them. For the invisible things of him from*

the creation of the world are clearly seen, being understood by the things that are made, even his eternal power and Godhead; so that they are without excuse: because that, when they knew God, they glorified him not as God, neither were thankful; but became vain in their imaginations, and their foolish heart was darkened.

Professing themselves to be wise, they became fools, and changed the glory of the incorruptible God into an image made like to corruptible man, and to birds, and four-footed beasts, and creeping things.

Wherefore God also gave them up to uncleanness through the lusts of their own hearts, to dishonour their own bodies between themselves: **Who changed the truth of God into a lie,** *and worshiped and served the creature more than the Creator, who is blessed for ever. Amen.*

(KJ Ro 1:18–25)

A † Ω

- - - - - - -

No Condemnation For Those in Christ Jesus <u>Depends</u>

The false opposing views expressed as snippets that echo throughout the walls of *Bible Deception Churches,* apart from repentance, are as follows:

It is written: *There is therefore now no condemnation to them which are in Christ Jesus!* (KJ Ro:

8:1) [**while omitting:** *who walk **not** after the {evil desires of the} flesh, but after the {Holy} Spirit.*

It is written: *For whosoever shall call upon the name of the Lord shall be saved.* (KJ Ro 10:13)

Presented apart from the full context of Paul's epistles, the following is the type of interpretations prevaricators exploited from him:

Jesus, since I call on your name, I know how much you love me. You love me so unconditionally that I realize that it's okay for me to hate righteousness. My dear, sweet Jesus, it's okay for me to ignore your sabbath by plotting evil 24/7, 365 days a year. My sweetly Jesus, since I confess to being a horrible sinner, you make me feel fabulous like a drunken sailor.

Thank you for tolerating my evil to gain my salvation. You're so sweet that I put a tattoo of you over my heart and enormous angel wings on my back to have you close to me, especially when I set out to do evil in your sight. I love you so much, but my love for you will never be as much as your unconditional love is for me, but not my bad. I feel so good to have you forever and look forward to Heaven!

All are lies based on snippet preaching. Undoubtedly, God's *elect* will have heard or witnessed similar analogies and excuses condoning evil on the part of the wicked. It and the wicked belong to Satan! Such misuse of God's word has turned many would-be saints into sly, misled servants of Satan.

Snippet preaching is responsible for driving God-fearing people out of churches. God-fearing people know the truth. They have zero tolerance for the lies and flattery of cobras. They will not follow the stand-alone fabricated Jesus so popular among *worshipers of deception*. They know God through the fullness of His word. Therefore, they go with His *Spirit* above all else.

> It is written: {Jesus speaking} *My {few} sheep hear my voice, and I know them, and they follow me: and I give unto them eternal life; and they shall never perish, neither shall any man pluck them out of my hand. My Father, which gave them me, is greater than all; and no {devious or corrupt} man is able to pluck them out of my Father's hand. I and my Father are one.* (KJ Jn 10:27-30)

God-fearing, *Holy Spirit-filled people* have zero tolerance for false beliefs such as, "As long as I got Jesus but remain a sinner, God will forever love me." Nothing is further from the truth! The truth is that by remaining a sinner, God will forever hate you because sinning is taking joy in repeatedly nailing Jesus to the cross.

"Repent," putting an end to sinning, is what Jesus commanded. Hence, one is better justified through repentance by works than flesh or carnal faith that condones sinning through empty words and a stand-alone Jesus.

It is written: *Ye see then how that <u>by works</u>*

{REPENTANCE} *a man is justified, and not by faith only.* (KJ Eze 36:19, Jas 2:24)

In other words, *confessing Jesus as Lord and believing in your heart that God raised Him from the dead* (Ro 10:9) is a cheap shot and worthless without repenting and living according to God's principles, not to mention heeding His voice! The unrepentant sinners of Sodom and Gomorrah discovered that harsh reality too late when molten sulfur fell from Heaven on them and their children. And, for all journeying the broad road to the *Churches of Bible Deception*, under the leadership of *pulpit serpents*, Sodom and Gomorrah are merely laughable myths.

Nevertheless, Paul corrects himself repeatedly in the **full context** of his epistles. He illustrates what becomes of humanity through snippets on the part of prevaricators condoning every abomination in defiance of God's commands to have their evil way (KJ Ro 1-2). **Hell is their destiny.**

A † Ω

In summarizing this chapter, MISLEADING THROUGH SNIPPETS, the same Paul who wrote Scripture inspired by the *Holy Spirit* was the same Paul who wrote many abridged into misleading snippets. Therefore, I urge you not to put blind trust in the clergy. **You may not want to believe this shocking truth: Joseph, the step-father of Jesus, warned by God's angel Gabriel, certainly did not, nor did Jesus.** Place your trust first in the full context of God's undeniable Word by reading, studying, believing, and obeying it (Jn 8:31-32). Compare it to what you came to think about God. If there is a conflict between what you read, learn, come to believe, and obey with other doctrines, you are at a significant crossroad that will determine your future. So, consider the following from the New Testament in choosing which to follow. Referring to God's *elect*,

> It is written: *Owe no man anything, but to love {respect} one another: for he that loveth {respects} another {unfailingly} hath fulfilled the law. For this, {7}Thou shalt not commit adultery, {6}Thou shalt not kill {murder}, {8}Thou shalt not steal, {9} Thou shalt not bear false witness, {10} Thou shalt not covet; and if there be any other commandment, it is briefly comprehended in this saying; namely, Thou shalt love {respect} thy {righteous} neighbour {per the commandments} as thyself. {Unfailing} Love {Respect} worketh no ill to his {innocent, righteous} neighbour: therefore love {respect} is the fulfilling {obeying} of the law {commandments}.* (KJ Ro 13:8-10)

> It is written: *Keep the commandments of God, and have the testimony of Jesus Christ.* (KJ Rev 12:17)

If that is what your church instills and your values are to those standards, you have a great and infinite blessing coming your way!

A ✝ Ω

[Theme Song]
BATTLE HYMN OF THE REPUBLIC
Lyrics by Julia Ward Howe — Original Version

Mine eyes have seen the glory of the coming of the Lord;
He is trampling out the vintage where The Grapes of Wrath are stored;
He hath loosed the fateful lightning of His terrible swift sword:
> His truth is marching on.
> Glory! Glory hallelujah!
> Glory! Glory, hallelujah!
> Glory! Glory, hallelujah!
> His truth is marching on.

I have seen Him in the watch-fires of a hundred circling camps,
They have builded Him an altar in the evening dews and damps;
I can read His righteous sentence by the dim and flaring lamps-
> His day is marching on.
> Glory! Glory hallelujah!
> Glory! Glory, hallelujah!
> Glory! Glory, hallelujah!
> His day is marching on.

I have read a fiery gospel writ in burnished rows of steel:
As ye deal with my condemners, so with you my grace shall deal;
Let the Hero, born of woman, crush the serpent with His heel,
> Since God is marching on.
> Glory! Glory hallelujah!
> Glory! Glory, hallelujah!
> Glory! Glory, hallelujah!
> Since God is marching on.

[THEME SONG]
BATTLE HYMN OF THE REPUBLIC
Lyrics by Julia Ward Howe — Original Version

He has sounded forth the trumpet that shall never sound retreat;
He is sifting out the hearts of men before His judgment-seat:
O be swift, my soul, to answer Him! Be jubilant, my feet!
    Our God is marching on.
    Glory! Glory hallelujah!
    Glory! Glory, hallelujah!
    Glory! Glory, hallelujah!
    Our God is marching on.

In the beauty of the lilies Christ was born across the sea,
With a glory in His bosom that transfigures you and me.
As he died to make men holy, let us live to make men free,
    While God is marching on.
    Glory! Glory hallelujah!
    Glory! Glory, hallelujah!
    Glory! Glory, hallelujah!
    While God is marching on.

He is coming like the glory of the morning on the wave,
He is Wisdom to the mighty, He is Succor to the brave,
So the world shall be His footstool, and the soul of Time His slave,
    Our God is marching on.
    Glory! Glory hallelujah!
    Glory! Glory, hallelujah!
    Glory! Glory, hallelujah!
    Our God is marching on. [61]

---

[61] The Atlantic Monthly (1865). [Note: World Music omitted the vital Third Stanza in their <u>Hymnal for Worship Celebration</u>. No. 569, KJV, 1986].

MOVING FORWARD

Dear Reader,

Today brings you to the end of **Part A.** **CONGRATULATIONS!** *However, there is much left to cover on this subject regarding God's unfailing love. For example, the truth behind John 3:16, manipulated into God loving the world unconditionally, is followed in* **Part B.** *It will address concerns about resisting not evil and giving in to the demands of the wicked, loving your enemies, overcoming family conflicts, and much more.*

Moreover, I assure you that you will be much enlightened about the fullness of Christ vs. the world's Jesus. Also, you may stand to learn more facts about God, Christ, and the Holy Spirit. Hence, **Part B** *is the continuation of* **the revealed mystery of God regarding Agape.** *While* **Part A** *relies more on the Old Testament than the New,* **Part B** *focuses more on the New than the Old. It details how, indeed,* **God is love** *(KJ 1Jn 4:16)* **only for His elect** *(KJ Mk 13:27),* **whose names are in the Lamb's book of life** *(KJ Rev 21:27).*

To sincerely welcome you to **Part B,** *turn the page. I look forward to having you and yours back in* **Part B** *to continue this remarkable life-changing journey to salvation.*

Sincerely,

Stephen R. Juneau

A † Ω

BEING UPRIGHT WITH GOD:
Commitment to Truth

COURAGE INTO STRENGTH

It is written: *But they that wait upon the {truthful Word of the} LORD {and obey His commands} shall renew their strength; they shall mount up with wings as eagles; they shall run, and not be weary; and they shall walk, and not faint.* (KJ Isa 40:31)

It is written: *If you fully obey the LORD your God and carefully follow all his commands I give you today, the LORD your God will set you high above all the nations on earth.* (NIV Dt 28:1)

[Jesus Christ did not abolish these promises.]

A ☦ Ω

STEPHEN R. JUNEAU

THE ALPHA THROUGH OMEGA PROJECT

I-B
AGAPE:
The Unfailing Love of God
vs.
The Unconditional Love of Satan

TABLE OF CONTENTS
I–B

Introduction

I. All Known by God

II. The Domino Effect of Agape

III. The Chosen: *God's Elect*

IV. Resist not Evil: *The Pathway to Hell*

V. A Truthful Resolve about Jesus

VI. Resist Evil: *The Pathway to Salvation*

VII. Coming to Grips with Family Conflict

VIII. God and Family

IX. An Engagement with God

X. Accepting Responsibility

XI. The Honor of Kings

XII. Answers to Why behind the Great Lies

XIII. Justified Hatred vs. Demonic Hatred

XIV. Paradigm Shifts

XV. The White Horse and Its Rider

XVI. Closing: *The Challenge*

About the Author

[© The Picture People]

Stephen R. Juneau grew up on a small farm in Central Louisiana. He served in public education for thirty combined years between Louisiana and Texas. Additionally, he worked in the restaurant industry, sales, transportation, and the Texas Department of Corrections.

In 1992, Stephen set out to facilitate workshops in education, sales, motivation, and health and created *Freedom Enterprises*. However, overcome by start-up costs and other factors outside his comfort zone, he returned to his profession in public education. Stephen then became far more committed to teaching. However, he continued to be very unsettled about the world by having experienced unusual, dreadful, and regretful circumstances, causing him to rely on God's word.

It all started at age thirty-three, as he set out to read the Bible in its entirety, to learn as much about God and his religion as possible. There, he discovered significant differences between the Bible and Catholicism. That began his long journey for the truth about God and *life more abundantly* (KJ Jn 10:10). Through the years, he attended numerous churches while reading the complete Bible repeatedly. There, he discovered that most other religions and non-denominational churches did not quite match up with the full context of the Bible. Tested in failure, rejection, and sin, it became his passion for sharing what he knew to be Bible truth. That included God's conditions of love and the need for victory over forces of evil, misleading *many called* by God. (KJ Lev 11:44, Mt 4:17, Ro 12:1, 1Pe 1:15–16, Rev 22:14).

Knowing and acting upon the truth matters. The author's purpose, fulfillment, hope, and joy is to instill the requirements for salvation through Bible facts about Our Father in Heaven, Jesus, and the Holy Spirit.

www.ingramcontent.com/pod-product-compliance
Lightning Source LLC
Chambersburg PA
CBHW070531010526
44118CB00012B/1097